Understanding Profound Intellectual and Multiple Disabilities in Adults

This book explores what happens to people with profound intellectual and multiple disabilities (PIMD) when they reach adulthood. It provides an examination of various terms and definitions in use and a critical exploration of current UK policies.

The author brings a wealth of many years' experience as a family carer, independent consultant and trainer to demonstrate the significant changes that a person-centred, specialised therapeutic and incremental approach can make to an individual's life. Advances in medical science mean that, people with PIMD are growing into adulthood. What is this experience like for an adult who needs support in all aspects of their life? How do we include them in planning support when their intellectual disability means they cannot tell us first hand, what they want or need? Too often this group is overlooked or considered as an afterthought in policy and planning. Notions of independence, employment and mainstream inclusion are all problematic policy ideas for this group of people. Within one-size-fits-all service planning this focus means there is less capacity to meet their life-long specialist, complex and individualised needs.

Understanding Profound and Intellectual and Multiple Disabilities in Adults is essential reading for anyone who is involved in the lives of adults with profound intellectual and multiple disabilities, whether as a researcher, student, carer or policy-maker.

Dreenagh Lyle has spent many years trying to understand how best to meet the needs of those with PIMD. As a parent, family therapist, researcher and consultant she has much experience in this. This informs her latest role as visiting lecturer to Learning Disability nursing students.

Routledge Advances in Disability Studies

www.routledge.com/Routledge-Advances-in-Disability-Studies/book-series/
RADS

Intellectual Disability and the Right to a Sexual Life
A Continuation of the Autonomy/Paternalism Debate
Simon Foley

The Changing Disability Policy System
Active Citizenship and Disability in Europe Volume 2
Edited by
Rune Halvorsen, Bjørn Hvinden, Jerome Bickenbach, Delia Ferri and Ana
Marta Guillén Rodriguez

Cultural Disability Studies in Education
Interdisciplinary Navigations of the Normative Divide
David Bolt

Institutional Violence and Disability
Punishing Conditions
Kate Rossiter and Jen Rinaldi

A Sensory Sociology of Autism
Habitual Favourites
Robert Rourke

Understanding Profound Intellectual and Multiple Disabilities in Adults
Dreenagh Lyle

Students with Disabilities and the Transition to Work
A Capabilities Approach
Oliver Mutanga

Understanding Profound Intellectual and Multiple Disabilities in Adults

Dr Dreenagh Lyle

Routledge
Taylor & Francis Group

LONDON AND NEW YORK

First published 2019
by Routledge
2 Park Square, Milton Park, Abingdon, Oxon OX14 4RN

and by Routledge
605 Third Avenue, New York, NY 10017

First issued in paperback 2020

Routledge is an imprint of the Taylor & Francis Group, an informa business

British Library Cataloguing-in-Publication Data
A catalogue record for this book is available from the British Library

Library of Congress Cataloging-in-Publication Data
A catalog record has been requested for this book

ISBN 13: 978-0-367-72726-0 (pbk)
ISBN 13: 978-0-367-02962-3 (hbk)

Typeset in Times New Roman
by Integra Software Services Pvt. Ltd.

Dedicated to my mother Lilian Darrell and my two extraordinary daughters, Wednesday and Odyssey.

In memory of Mr Sydney Antony Miller (1967–2018) for all your kind support and inspiration.

Contents

Preface

The purpose of this book

In the clamour to be heard in a world of competing identities, people with profound intellectual and multiple disabilities (PIMD) are often overlooked. Where is their 'voice'? Who 'speaks up' for them? This is especially true of adults as even identifying these people by a common term, becomes problematic after formal education ceases. The aim of this book is to increase our understanding of a very particular and yet very diverse group of people. It draws together various strands of knowledge that focus on the lives of people who cannot report to us (first-hand with language) due to their intellectual impairment. These people will also usually have a number of additional impairments and health conditions (often life-limiting) which will impact profoundly on their lives and the lives of those who must care for them twenty-four hours a day, seven days a week, three hundred and sixty-five days a year. Most often this care is provided voluntarily by family members; usually their mothers. Formal (paid) care workers are rarely specifically trained or professionally supported. Oftentimes policymakers and commissioners of services have little direct knowledge of these people. Or even if they do, will overlook them in order to promote the group characteristics, which better fit their policy. The *Valuing People* (DH, 2001, 2009) strategy attempts to position all people with intellectual disability (ID) within a distinct definitional category, which this author argues is ultimately at odds with the lived experience of those with PIMD. Notions of independence, employment and mainstream inclusion are all deeply problematic policy ideas for this group. Within one-size-fits-all service planning this focus means there is less capacity to meet their life-long specialist, complex and individualised needs.

This book is written for anyone who is involved in the lives of adults with profound and multiple learning disabilities (PMLD). It is intended as a reader for students who may want to expand their knowledge of 'learning disabilities' (LD) as much as a resource for commissioners, managers, care workers, advocates, practitioners and most importantly, families. The book focuses on the issues associated with 'PIMD' *per se*, rather than looking at the entire spectrum of intellectual impairment. Why a focus primarily on adults with PIMD? Quite simply, the available books tend to focus on children and young people and their education. Oftentimes these young people can access college funding. But this all finishes when they turn twenty-five. What happens then? What do people do? How do they spend their lives? These are people for whom notions of paid employment are rarely an option. The question then is how do we ensure these people can lead a fulfilled life, which is as meaningful to them as is possible? Indeed what is a meaningful life?

The book is intended as a resource, which can be dipped into, depending on what the reader is seeking. It includes much first hand input from family carers and care workers as well as insights I have gleaned over many years as family carer, practitioner, independent consultant and trainer. This includes sitting on my local Learning Disability Partnership Board as High Support Needs champion, working for the Care Quality Commission as an expert by experience and working for the NHS Improving Lives Team (ILT) on Care and Treatment reviews (CTr's) post Winterbourne View.

There is an academic desire, especially since the publication of *Valuing People* for finding ways to include people with ID in research. The discussion has mostly focused on research *with* people. However, there are also researchers who are seeking ways to focus on research *for* people, as they see this as more meaningful for people with PIMD. This book will contribute to that ongoing discussion. For example, in a paper (Samuel and Pritchard, 2001) describe how one specialist learning disability health service attempted to increase its focus on meeting the complex needs of people with profound learning disability (PLD) both with and without additional physical, sensory and medical impairment. They refer to the many different labels being used to describe the same group of people. The authors explain why this is so concerning.

> This confusion in the use of terminology represents a difficulty that must be overcome in the future. If we do not know what we are talking about, how can we possibly understand what the issues are?
>
> (p. 34)

Further, since these terms and definitions vary from one country to another the impact on research can lead to confusion and misrepresentation in the published literature.

Throughout the book I refer to 'profound and multiple learning disabilities' (PMLD) and 'profound intellectual and multiple disabilities' (PIMD). These terms are currently interchangeable, but not always used in data gathering exercises. Sometimes a parent will ask me why we have to use a label at all. We know people with ID who do speak up are very clear about not liking labels. I explain that it is the very fact that people with PIMD cannot speak up, cannot tell us first-hand what they want and feel, that we have to find some formal way to refer to them. Not in our day-to-day interactions but in a way that they can be specifically included in data gathering by the new NHS body, the Learning Disabilities Health Observatory (iHAL) for example, or the Equalities and Human Rights Commission (EHRC). Or any number of local and national agencies that are tasked with providing health and social care services. How can services be adequately commissioned if there is a lack of clarity around numbers and levels of need?

Chapter 1: Terms and definitions

Hence the initial focus of this book is an examination of the various terms and definitions for ID in use in the UK today. The opening chapter examines how those with 'profound intellectual and multiple disabilities' (PIMD) are represented or not as a distinct group within these definitions. It is argued that unclear and shifting terms and definitions in the UK and internationally contribute to the lack of representation (family) carers often describe. Government departments have also acknowledged the dearth of published literature concerning this group (DWP, et al., 2005). Researchers have further described the difficulties with conflating UK and international terms (Leyin, 2010). The overall difficulty lies in how this group of people are represented or not in policy from the outset. This lack of representation or mis-representation abets poor provision and delivery of the lifelong specialist services these people will need.

Chapter 2: Policy frameworks

The second chapter critically examines philosophical underpinnings to policy frameworks underlying service provision for people with ID. The frameworks of normalisation, social role valorisation and O'Brien's Five Service Accomplishments emerged, often in parallel with each other and often complimenting each other. However, the main underlying philosophical thrust of the white paper *Valuing People* (DH, 2001) purported to be the social model of disability. Hence there is a detailed analysis of all iterations of this model and a critique of its fundamental tenet, that people are 'disabled' by a lack of societal structures to accommodate their needs, rather than an individual 'lack' or impairment. This includes examination of the current tension between post-structural proponents of the social model of disability and our ever-expanding knowledge of genetic disorders, which demonstrate a biological basis for ID. The role of environmental factors, including extreme prematurity and foetal alcohol syndrome, are also referred to. The section on self-advocacy seeks to emphatically demonstrate the vast difference between an individual literally 'speaking up' and the concept of making assumptions about what we believe an individual may or may not want. This chapter also cites researchers, writers and practitioners who have all echoed the concerns family carers have constantly relayed to me. Essentially this book is seeking to understand the apparent lack of fit between the current philosophical framework underpinning government policy and the broad ranging and complex needs of individuals with PIMD. It contends that their lack of representation as a distinct group with distinct and particular needs has a negative impact on the lived experience of this population.

Chapter 3: Rights, independence, choice/control and inclusion

The lack of fit discussed in the previous chapter is examined even further here. This chapter analyses the four cornerstones of the VP (DH, 2001) policy, i.e. rights, independence, choice and inclusion, within the context of the lived experience of people with PIMD. This is done by examining a small-scale comparative study carried out in London UK into the impact of *Valuing People* (VP) on the lives of people with PIMD and those who provide their care and support. The investigative study was conducted from three distinct angles in order to better understand the impact of the VP policy on the lives of individuals with PIMD and their informal (unpaid) family carers and formal (paid) care workers. The study sought to understand how family carers make sense of the 'new strategy for learning disabilities for the 21st C.' (DH, 2001). Did they feel that services, attitudes and ideas had changed at all? And if so, was this for the better? It explores family carers and care workers understanding of the principles of rights, independence, choice/control and inclusion. It queries if these ideas are meaningfully embedded in service practice or not by seeking evidence of any theory–practice gap. The study endeavoured to include an individual with PIMD in as meaningful a way as possible. This was achieved by the unique use of filmed excerpts of a young woman with PIMD used to elicit responses in focus group discussions with formal care workers. The study further examines the manner in which people with PIMD are specifically represented in the VP policy or not. Unfortunately for a document purporting to represent the entire experience of ID, the study demonstrated that VP overwhelmingly represents people whose disability sits at the milder end of the ID spectrum. This lack of visibility of people with PIMD echoes a theme of Gaffney's (2012) paper, exploring the manner in which current narratives are 'air brushing long-term disability out of the picture' (p. 22).

Chapter 4: All in the same direction

In much the same way that I situated an individual with PIMD at the heart of the study I discussed in the last chapter, I wanted to do the same here. For this chapter we hone in on one person's life, my daughter Odyssey. The title 'All in The Same Direction' demonstrates the turnaround a truly personalised approach can achieve for someone with PIMD, especially if they are at risk of 'placement breakdown.'. A 'person-centred' approach must first and foremost acknowledge this particular woman's multiplicity of impairments, including the manner in which their gestalt impacts on her day-to-day life. This understanding provides the basis for demonstrating how it is possible to move beyond discussion of 'placement breakdown' through 'challenging behaviour' to issues of comprehension and communication. Our understanding of what we are doing and why is key to a good life. Understanding what is meant by a culture of active support, based on relationships and meaningful activities. Understanding how to develop and encourage trust by using a consistent approach. Understanding the value of professional guidelines and why they are so important. Why have bespoke support guidelines written by professionals if they are filed away and never used? Has anyone ever properly explained their rationale to support staff for example? Understanding the value of therapeutic input, such as physiotherapy, occupational therapy, speech and language therapy, art therapy and music therapy. Understanding the importance of team building and leadership to ensure that everyone is traveling 'in the same direction.' The chapter will outline a number of different domains and describe ways staff and families can work together to support people towards 'a good or better life' (see Walmsley, 2010). Practical guidance is offered in the following particular domains:

Behavioural support needs; where does the 'challenge' lie?

Reflexive practice and why it is necessary for good support;

Therapeutic approaches, including deep tissue massage (DTM), speech and language therapy (SLT) and music therapy;

Medical tests, including AHC, blood pressure/blood tests, scans and dental;

Food and eating, including digestion and elimination;

Shared joy through meaningful activities;

Chapter 5: Raising our sights

Chapter five looks deeper into the lived experience of adults with PIMD. What do people do during the day? Where do they spend their time and who provides their support? How are families supported? The continuing economic climate of austerity means higher and specialised support needs are often ignored in favour of one-size-fits all approaches. When asked, time and again families have the same concerns. They want to see bespoke training for care workers that is tailored to understanding the support needs of people with PIMD specifically. They want residential respite and specialist health services. The late Professor Mansell's report 'Raising Our Sights' (Mansell, 2010) found that families of people with PIMD often had to struggle to gain such services. This is echoed across the UK and almost ten years later families still struggle to obtain appropriate services and competent staff. The only UK accredited training course designed specifically for people who support those with PIMD will be discussed and queries raised regarding the use of in-house generic training. This chapter argues that in the mixed economy of one-size-fits-all planning there is less capacity to meet the lifelong specialist and therapeutic needs of this group. The continuing lack of an agreed universal definition for adults with PIMD has ongoing implications for service design, delivery and provision. Further, by insisting everyone has the potential for employment, it is not then necessary to discuss lifelong dependency and the cradle-to-grave support needs this entails.

Chapter 6: Raising the bar: beyond the 'burden of non productiveness'

Finally chapter six commences with discussion of the various abuse, neglect and premature deaths scandals, which have emerged most recently and have led to many subsequent reviews and initiatives. These include the 'Transforming Care' programme, which resulted primarily from the Winterbourne View abuse scandal. The setting up of the 'Learning Disabilities Health Observatory' (IHAL) resulted from the review of premature deaths, and the 'Learning Disabilities Mortality Review' programme (LeDR) was set up as one of the recommendations of the 'Confidential Inquiry into the Premature deaths of people with Learning Disabilties' (CIPOLD).

The chapter concludes with discussion of the new 'Core and Essential Service Standards' (Doukas et al., 2017) for supporting people with PIMD. These were devised by a group of family carers, practitioners, researchers and providers as an informative and practical resource for health, education and care sectors. The Standards aim to enhance quality and equity of support and service provision for children and adults with PIMD. Whilst they have already been adopted by NHS England and the Royal College of Occupational Therapists the ambition is for them to be adopted nationally. The writers are hopeful that this explicit focus will ensure a national awareness that people with PIMD are entitled to receive good quality services and support wherever they live and from whoever is providing their care.

1 The 'ignored minority' (Samuel and Pritchard, 2001)

Introduction

> But it's not the same. They're not like ours.
>
> (Parent D, 2018)

This was a parent at a local carers' event trying to explain what she saw as the difference between someone with an intellectual disability (ID) and her son who has profound intellectual and multiple disabilities (PIMD). She went on,

> we can't leave them on their own, they can't tell us what they want.
>
> (Parent D, 2018)

Another parent joined in,

> Whenever they have these events for carers I always feel that people don't understand. I mean there's a world of difference between caring for someone at the end of their life and our lifelong cradle-to-grave caring. Yet all we ever hear about is the crisis in care for older people.
>
> (Parent N, 2018)

Family carers of adults with PIMD were interviewed for a study exploring the impact of the *Valuing People* (DH, 2001, 2009) policy on their lives. Over and over again interviewees referred to a lack of choice, lack of available respite, lack of trained staff, lack of management leadership, lack of appropriate and specialist services, lack of planned transitions and lack of public and political awareness. The most prevalent themes to emerge included choice, cost cutting, consultation fatigue and transport (Lyle, 2015). These issues could all be resolved with political will. However there was one overriding concern from all of those who participated in the wider study, including care workers and day centre managers. This was their concern that policymakers, government ministers and even local commissioners did not seem to be aware that people with PIMD even exist. In an attempt to rectify that belief this book will offer a glimpse into the experience of caring for and supporting someone with PIMD.

The book will commence by clarifying some of the terms and definitions in use in UK and abroad, in research and practice settings. The first chapter will summarise why these terms and definitions are important. Not just for understanding the needs of this group of people, but for meeting those needs.

It cannot be acceptable when discussing this group that we are told,

> … there are in fact other groups about whom there is no research at all
> (DWP et al., 2005 Annexe F, p. 31)

and that this lack of information has a direct impact on planning and commissioning of services.

> A key issue for service provision and support is the lack of information about the numbers of people with high support needs. The current lack of information means their needs are not always taken into account when planning or commissioning services.
> (DWP et al., 2005 Annexe F, p. 42)

Further, since these terms and definitions vary from one country to another the impact on research can lead to confusion and misrepresentation in the published literature.

Why terms and definitions are important

> I don't know what any of 'em mean, to be honest. They say he's got "complex needs" now. They used to say he was "mentally handicapped" and before that he was "retarded". I just know he's my brother.
> (WG, 2015)

UK and international terms

The introduction of the UK term 'learning disability' as a replacement for the term 'mental handicap' can be traced to the then Conservative Secretary of State for Health from 1995–1997, Stephen Dorrell. People First, (a user-led self-advocacy organisation for people with ID), had expressed a desire to use the term 'learning difficulties' (Sutcliffe and Simons, 1993). However, the Department of Health was concerned this would lead to confusion since the term was already in use in educational settings, for specific educational learning difficulties such as dyslexia. Currently, the terms 'learning disability' and 'learning difficulties' are interchangeable in adult services. There is further international confusion as Canada and USA use the term 'learning disabilities' to refer to specific educational learning difficulties and have replaced the term 'mental retardation' with 'intellectual disability' (ID).[1] Australia on the other hand uses both terms 'learning disability' and 'learning difficulty' to refer to specific educational learning difficulties and 'intellectual disability' to refer to UK learning disability.[2]

Confused? Many people are. Mencap, the UK campaigning organisation for people with ID, conducted a survey in 2008 in which 1,600 members of the general population and 103 MP's were asked for an example of 'learning disability.' 73% of the public and more worryingly 74% of the MP's gave completely wrong answers. The most common answer was the specific learning difficulty, dyslexia. (Mencap, 2008)

Research issues

This confusion over terminology extends to national and international research. Some of the terms used interchangeably to denote ID include the afore-mentioned learning disability/difficulty, learning impairment, cognitive impairment, mental handicap, mental retardation and global developmental delay. Considering the intellectual heterogeneity of this population it makes sense to look at ID as a continuum (Holland, 2008). However even at the profound end of the continuum there are yet more interchangeable terms. These include, profound motor and learning disability, profound and multiple learning disability/disabilities/difficulties, people with high support needs, people with complex support needs, people with severe learning difficulties, people with severe learning disability, people with severe learning disabilities and/or autistic spectrum disorders and profound intellectual and multiple disabilities. This does not include all the terms employed to describe those additional autism (ASD) effects, which may include (self) injurious and other behavioural support issues (often described as 'challenging behaviour') and general communication impairments, such as elective mutism or delayed and/or immediate echolalia. Additionally the use of terms to denote severity, or profundity of intellectual disability is interchangeable. One researcher may use the term 'severe learning disability,' yet be referring to an individual who is living independently with minimal support, while another researcher may use the term 'self advocating' when referring to someone who needs full 24-hour-a-day support and has a key worker advocating on their behalf.

In a paper discussing classification in the UK and abroad, Leyin (2010) describes the binary system in use in the UK. This simply categorises intellectual impairment as either learning disability or severe learning disability and uses the IQ figure of 50–55 as the indicator of severe learning disability (SLD). This is in contrast to international, four-part classifications, which sub-categorise into mild, moderate, severe and profound. Leyin points out that this has led to a good deal of confusion, especially in the area of research and epidemiological studies. Researchers do not always state which classification they are referring to when they describe SLD. He describes the use of this terminology within *Valuing People* (DH, 2001) as,

> a hybrid system that uses the terminology of the international system but in a way that relates epidemiologically, to the national system.
>
> (Leyin, 2010, p. 37)

He contends this confusion must necessarily impact on service provision, since these estimates are what inform service provision in the first place. The confusion is compounded by the current use of levels of support measures replacing the previous levels of impairment. Davidson (in Leyin, 2010) warns against adopting a purely socio/adaptive measure, since this form of assessment is less reliable, poorly defined and standardised on biased norms. He argues that the intellectual impairment criteria offer greater objectivity and

> the existing thresholds are less likely to be moved as a result of political considerations such as fluctuations in the availability of resources.
>
> (p. 43)

Definitions

If there is confusion over terms it stands to reason the definitions might vary as well. People First Ltd describe themselves as a self-advocacy organisation and voice for people with learning difficulties. Their mission statement that 'they wanted to learn and could' (2011) is problematic in that it doesn't truly or adequately embrace the full experience of ID. It really only applies to those people whom Williams (2006) describes, i.e. those with borderline or mild to moderate levels of ID. Williams in the first of his 'Transforming Social Work Practice' series of books asks, 'Who are people with learning difficulties?' (P1) and 'How then can we define a person with learning difficulties'? (P7) He acknowledges his attempt is to define what is meant by 'A person with learning difficulties' but claims 'learning difficulty can't be defined!' (Williams, 2006, p. 3) He continues thus:

> A person with learning difficulties is someone who has social and personal vulnerabilities associated with impairment of cognitive understanding or of learning practical skills, which has existed since childhood.
>
> (Williams, 2006, p. 7)

Williams rejects this initial definition, by arguing that it is too clinical and also because it attributes the problem to the individual. He proceeds to a definition he believes is more acceptable to social model accounts of disability.

A person with learning difficulties is someone who has been labelled as having difficulties in cognitive understanding, but is someone with rights, including the right to maximum control over decisions that affect them, and who may need help and support to claim those rights. A person with learning difficulties is someone whom society identifies as having an impairment in cognitive functioning, but whose needs and interests are not well catered for by societal structures or by the inter-actions of other people; he or she is a survivor of struggles to overcome this disadvantage and may need help to continue to do so.

(Williams, 2006, p. 7)

This rather convoluted definition would arguably be quite difficult for some-one with ID to comprehend. His argument also illustrates the new focus on social model approaches and seems more concerned with establishing the so-called constructed nature of intellectual disability (ID) by focusing on notions of labeling and societal identification. Whilst both of these claims may well hold resonance with the people referred to as self-advocating, they are not helpful when trying to establish a discussion about the actual nature of ID. And they do little to illustrate the experience of individuals with PIMD.

The nominal figure of 70 for an IQ definition of ID can of course be con-sidered a construction. However, that is a debate regarding borderline or mild ID. (For further discussion of 'construction of normalcy' see Davis, 2006, p. 3.) This book is not concerned with that particular debate. It does however recognise that just as the issues across the extensive range of dis-abilities are often different, so too across the spectrum of ID. To argue that the issues associated with mild to moderate ID are the same for PIMD is disingenuous, especially if those with PIMD are noticeably absent from the research literature. An individual with ID who can use language to commu-nicate can impart their views first hand. They can tell us what they want, what is important in their life, what they might want to achieve or who they want to build relationships with. An individual with PIMD cannot.

This is a very important point and one that will be reiterated throughout this book. We must always make presumptions or assumptions about every-thing to do with their lives. Everything from deciding if someone is thirsty, hungry, bored, tired or in pain to whether or not they would like to listen to music, have a television on, go out to a park, visit a leisure centre in order to go swimming or attend an art, music or movement class.

Of course this list is far from exhaustive and has not broached the notion of choice making. For example is the radio tuned to a station the individual with PIMD likes or is it the preferred music of the person who switches on the radio? Then there are the decisions to do with where someone lives, what their housing arrangements are, whom they live with and who pro-vides their support and care. As most people with PIMD have critical and/ or chronic health issues, these must also be taken into account. What are their therapeutic needs? Who decides what therapies they receive and are those decisions based on need or financial considerations or availability? What about their daily, lived experience? Who decides what they do from day-to-day? Is there a diary of activities or are people dependent on availability of staff and resources? If there is no family involved, there will usually be a number of people making decisions for them in their 'Best Interests' (Mental Capacity Act, 2005). Studies have shown people making the decisions do not always understand the MCA and its implications for people deemed to lack capacity (see for e.g. Williams et al., 2012)

PIMD definition

The PMLD Network[3] describes itself as,

> The online meeting place for people committed to improving the lives of people with profound and multiple learning disabilities.
>
> (Parent N, 2018)

The journal (online and paper) PMLD Link was established to make a difference to the lives of children and adults with profound and multiple learning disabilities (PMLD). It includes the following definition.

> People with PMLD have profound intellectual and multiple disabilities, very severe communication problems, often extreme physical and/or sensory disabilities, and complex health needs. Their needs are frequently overlooked by more general support organisations for people with learning disabilities.
>
> (www.https://our.choiceforum.org/c/pmldnetwork)

These are not always individuals with a profound motor impairment and a learning disability, which is what the term PMLD originally stood for and which may be why there is still some confusion. An individual may have a motor impairment so profound they cannot utilise the muscles necessary to form speech. However, they may have cognitive levels of functioning beyond pre – symbolic and with the right aids and assistance might be able to communicate their 'wishes, views and aspirations' (DH, 2001, p. 21, 46). An example of this is the painter, poet and author Christie Brown, whose autobiography was made into the film, '*My Left Foot*' (Brown, 1990). However, an individual whose cognitive functioning could be described as pre-symbolic will not express herself or himself using language.

Bunning (in Pawlyn and Carnaby, 2009) describes the need for a significant other, who will function as their communication partner. She details research, which has demonstrated how difficult it is to ascribe communication intentionality and how easy it can be to interpret behaviours ambiguously, which the individual with PIMD cannot then refute (Grove et al., 2001). She refers also to Fogel (1993) who describes communication as a continuous processing model reliant on the 'active role of the listener' (Bunning, 2009, p. 48). Bunning further describes the need for attunement to an individual's behaviour in order to recognise subtle changes in mood, body language, facial expressions and vocalisations or even by accepting or rejecting something within a familiar context. Finally, she refers to Nind and Hewitt (1994) who focus on the need to develop a desire for joint attention. This requires

> ... observational acuity and response sensitivity amongst communication partners to any behaviour that has the potential to be signal bearers of meaning.
>
> (Bunning, 2009, p. 57)

The greatest increase in this population, more recently, has been in extremely premature babies who survive, but with very profound and multiple challenges (Lacey and Ouvry, 1998; Carpenter, 2000). The PMLD Network has referred to the lack of recognition of this group including lack of awareness of their specialised support needs (PMLD Network, 2002, p. 4). They further noted the change in demography in their response to *Valuing People Now* (DH, 2009).

Prevalence

Parrot et al. (2008) conducted a local study in Sheffield England, which confirmed these findings (see diagram, Figure 1.1). This small-scale study examined changes in demography and demands for services for people with complex needs and profound and multiple learning disabilities. It also gave some indication of the urgency for acknowledging the predicted future rise in need. It concluded there was a 120% increase in the numbers of children/ young people with ID and a further 70% increase in young people with 'severe/complex needs' (p. 29). Accordingly, demand in Sheffield UK is described in this report as

> outstripping available resources and the gap will continue to grow.
>
> (p. 26)

As the writers pointed out these individuals will require lifelong, high levels of specialised support, for all aspects of their daily lives. This will likely include their personal care and continence needs, breathing and airways management, oral feeding (including dysphagia management) and pressure care associated with supporting individuals' with mobility and transfer needs. They will be more likely to have health issues such as epilepsy (requiring medical management) and may have additional recurrent serious health needs requiring hospital admission. They may also have specific degenerative/terminal conditions (Parrot et al., 2008, pp. 30–31). The

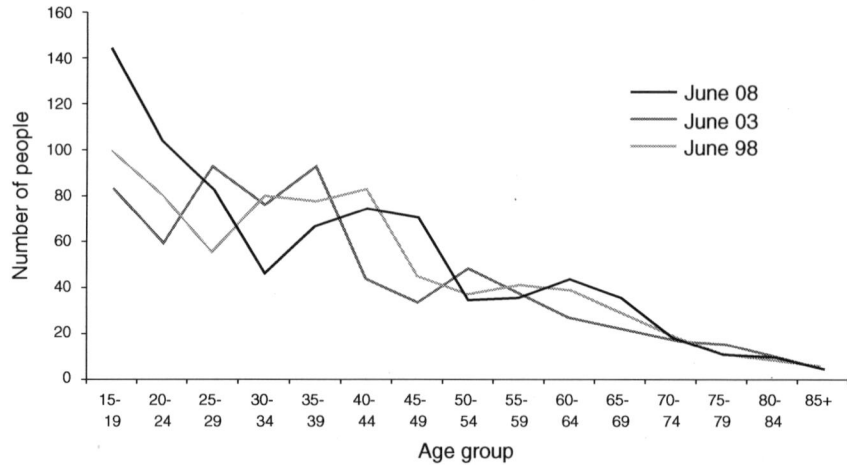

Between 1998 and 2008...

- the overall number of people with severe or complex needs rose by 17% from 682 to 786
- the number of 15 to 19 year olds with severe or complex needs increased by 70% from 85 to 144

Figure 1.1 Numbers of people with a severe/complex learning disability in Sheffield, 1998 to 2008. (Sheffield Case Register June 2008).

study further expanded on the challenge to primary, acute, community based and palliative care services to strengthen their capacity for meeting these complex needs. Finally, the authors pointed out, their study did not include those adults who may have the additional behavioural support needs associated with ASD, although the PMLD Network does acknowledge people with specific conditions such as autism or Down's syndrome, may also have profound and multiple impairments.

The Parrot study fed into the larger Emerson (2009) report 'Estimating Future Numbers of Adults with Profound and Multiple Learning Disabilities in England.' The overall findings suggested

> sustained and accelerating growth in the number of adults with PMLD in England over the time period 2009–2026.

> (p. 7)

and hence the need and demand for health and social care services for adults with PMLD. The annual increase was estimated at 1.4% rising to 3.2% in 2026. The *Valuing People* commitment to improving the national information data resulted in Emerson et al. (2005) and eventually, specifically to Emerson

(2009). Presumably it was recognised, that in the slew of government research informing *Valuing People*, i.e. 130 Projects, completed around 2001, plus another £3 million on 50 studies commencing in 2001 (Emerson et al., 2005, p. 115) people with PIMD had been overlooked.

PIMD overlooked

The ambitious joint report, (its own description) *'Improving the Life Chances of Disabled People'* (DWP et al., 2005) was published by the (now defunct) Prime Minister's Strategy Unit (PMSU). It was prepared with a number of government departments including the Department for Work and Pensions (DWP), Department for Education and Skills (DES), Department of Health (DH) and also by the Office of the Deputy Prime Minister (ODPM). With such a wide-ranging remit (i.e. all disabled people) it is perhaps understandable that people with PIMD were not acknowledged as a distinct group, with particular challenges and barriers to accessing 'the opportunity society' (DWP et al., 2005, p. 7) and 'helping themselves' (DWP et al., 2005, p. 7).

However, considering the study comprised three distinct phases, including an extended scoping exercise, an analytical phase and a policy recommendation phase, it is unclear why PIMD was so overlooked. The F Annexe to the report, *'Improving the Life Chances of Disabled People with the Most Complex Needs'* (PMSU, 2005), includes the results of a literature review of

> specific issues faced by disabled people with the most complex needs.
> (DWP et al., 2005, Annexe F, p. 31)

Here, though, 'complex needs,' include mental health issues combined with drug and alcohol dependency and associated homelessness.

The Summary states,

> there are in fact other groups about whom there is no research at all
> (DWP et al., 2005 Annexe F, p. 31)

and later in Section 1.2.2 entitled 'People with learning disabilities, high support and multiple needs' (DWP et al., 2005 Annexe F, p. 41) states,

> A key issue for service provision and support is the lack of information about the numbers of people with high support needs. The current lack of information means their needs are not always taken into account when planning or commissioning services.
> (DWP et al., 2005 Annexe F, p. 42)

The successor to this report has avoided any mention of people with PIMD at all. Considering the report 'Fulfilling potential. Building a deeper understanding of disability in the UK today' (DWP et al., 2013) outlines its aims to raise awareness, increase public understanding and prompt debate around disability issues, this seems an unfortunate lost opportunity. The section dealing with *'building an understanding'* (DWP et al., 2013, p. 10) for example, refers to secondary health conditions, but merely mentions at the end of the section that

> people with learning disability are less likely to feel confident about managing their conditions themselves.
>
> (DWP et al., 2013, p. 12)

This provides no insight into the complex, varied and multiple health issues associated with people with PIMD. A later section (DWP et al., 2013, pp. 31–55), purports to demonstrate an understanding of the lives of disabled children, yet provides no reference to the Parrot (2008) or Emerson (2009) studies, which have demonstrated a rise in numbers of children with profound and complex disabilities. Indeed there is no acknowledgement whatsoever of children with PIMD. Yet Emerson et al. completed their study estimating future numbers of adults with PIMD in 2009 at least four years previously.

Jo Williams (2008) then CEO of Mencap and Co-Chair of the Learning Disability Coalition responded to the Parrot report thus.

> The Sheffield report has been widely used to demonstrate that social care in England is grossly underfunded.

She continues,

> Parrot's article gives us a vivid description of the overwhelming need for multi-agency co-ordination between primary, secondary and acute health services and social care.
>
> (Williams, 2008, p. 37)

She outlines the need for more accurate information about numbers of people with ID and PIMD, the need for an evaluation of the demographic, social and economic trends affecting demand for services, including their cost and to know what savings can be made from existing funding (Williams, 2008, p. 37). It is unclear why all of this did not happen before the policy of *Valuing People* was devised and published. In an interview with Andrew Holman (2001) Rob Grieg, the author of VP pointed out, the strategy development for VP was achieved completely in eighteen months. Perhaps then it was time constraints that prevented a thorough audit of current and future services including a deeper analysis of the range of needs of this demographic. In the words of Samuel and Pritchard, if we do not know who we are talking about, how can we possibly know what the issues are?

(Samuel and Pritchard, 2001, p. 34)

Tellingly Samuel and Pritchard used the title of their paper to refer to this group of people as 'the ignored minority' (Samuel and Pritchard, 2001, p. 34).

Since *Valuing People* was heralded as

the first government statement about the lives of people with learning disabilities for thirty years

(Grieg, 2005, p. 3)

It is perhaps timely to note what the previous white paper had set out to achieve. '*Better Services for the Mentally Handicapped*' (DHSS et al., 1971) aimed to close hospital places and increase local authority residential places via the model of care in the community. A few years later the Jay Report (1979) recommended provision be geographically local to where people had been born and/or spent their early childhood. However the report was concerned that

certain mentally handicapped people have a temporary or permanent need for specialized skills because of the nature of their handicap.

(Jay Report, 1979, p. 97)

Samuel and Pritchard might also query if we knew in the 1970's that there were certain people with specialist needs, why did we overlook them in such a major piece of policy in 2001?

Cramp (2003) describes himself as a, 'self-advocate and Mencap trustee with a learning disability' (p. 18). He wrote a paper demonstrating that the promises of *Valuing People* (DH, 2001) were likely to be undermined by underfunding and tokenism. He questioned whether the £12 per head/per annum (based on Government figures of £16.7m for approx. 1.5 million people) was likely to bring about radical change. Especially since Mencap suggested at the time £300 million per annum was needed to bring about the changes envisaged by *Valuing People* (Williams, 2008). Cramp (2003) also pointed out that without the services of an advocate, the policy objectives of

increased choice and control over their lives were empty rhetoric for many people.

(Cramp, 2003, p. 20)

And further,

The emerging picture at present seems to be one of very limited progress within a grand vision of change funded by meagre resources.

(Cramp, 2003, p. 21)

And finally,

> The White Paper was an important step from the government, but without more funds and more priority on improving services, there is a danger that Partnership Boards are just talking shops and that Valuing People will have no real impact on the lives of people with a learning disability.
>
> (Cramp, 2003, p. 21)

Considering he is discussing the strategy in terms of delivery for all people with ID, it is clear that those who make up the smallest minority within this population, i.e. those with PIMD are likely to be overlooked or ignored as has been suggested (Samuel and Pritchard, 2001). In a review of the implementation of the VP policy, Cumela (2008) criticised the Department of Health's annual learning disability reports (e.g. DH, 2005) for resembling

> promotional literature rather than performance monitoring.
>
> (Cumela, 2008, p. 178)

The author outlines concerns, particularly in the area of

> person-centred assessments as a means of enhancing choice
>
> (p. 183)

which

> have probably affected only a minority of those eligible, and may have differentially excluded the most disabled.
>
> (Cumela, 2008, p. 183)

The difficulty with being an, 'ignored minority' is made clear in Williams (2006). His textbook written for social work degree students focuses on post VP aims for services for people with ID. There is little discussion of PIMD, apart from a short description of an approach to support called Intensive Interaction (Williams, 2006, p. 38, pp. 120–121). There is some discussion of alternative communication, whereby the author contends that for many people with severe communication difficulties (estimated at 50–90% of all adults with ID) it is more to do with 'our difficulty in understanding' (Williams, 2006, p. 120). This is arguably disingenuous. It is a 'brute fact' (Kristiansen et al., 2010, pp. 47–49) that an individual with severe to profound ID, will be at a very early developmental stage. (This is discussed in length by Garcia and De Haven, 1974; Blunden et al., 2000; Kelly, 2000; Bexley, 2002) The authentic stance would be to acknowledge we ought only ever make presumptions (rather than unfounded assumptions) about an individual's preferences, based on detailed background knowledge and observations and by developing a relationship with said individual over time. We have all encountered people with unclear enunciation. And not only people with ID. It is wholly disingenuous to conflate the two issues. A key contention of this book is that the confusion around terminology is not helped by a perceived unwillingness by some writers to acknowledge levels and multiplicity of impairments, when associated with ID. There are those who describe their position as a post-structural social model stance. These writers deny the biological, by stating that biological assumptions (perceived as negative) are socially constructed (Goodley, 2001; Williams, 2006). A salient counter to this, is raised by the philosopher and parent Eva Kittay who states,

> we might say, in the case of severe developmental disabilities, though the disability itself is not socially constructed, the view that it is a 'problem' rather than an outcome of human physiology is.
>
> (Carlson, 2010, p. 85)

The next chapter will critically examine the frameworks underlying current policy and service provision for people with ID. Social model thinking emerged in parallel with normalisation and O'Brien's Five Service Accomplishments in the form of *Valuing People* (DH, 2001) and later *Valuing People Now* (DH, 2009).

Notes

1 www.federalregister.gov/documents/2013/08/01/2013-18552/change-in-terminology-mental-retardation-to-intellectual-disability
2 www.education.act.gov.au/__data/assets/pdf_file/0020/714332/Learning-Difficulties-Factsheet-1.pdf
3 https://our.choiceforum.org/c/pmldnetwork

Bibliography

Bexley Learning Disability Service. (2002). *Total Communication Strategy and Standards.* London Borough of Bexley, London, UK.

Blunden, R., Corker, J., and Rice, J. (2000). *Let's Meet Let's Talk: Communicating with People with Learning Disabilities: A Handbook for Inspectors.* Oxford Institute of Learning Disabilities, London, UK.

Brown, C. (1990). *My Left Foot.* Vintage Random House, London, UK.

Bunning, K. (2009). 'Making sense of communication.' in Pawlyn, J. and Carnaby, S. (eds) *Profound Intellectual and Multiple Disabilities Nursing Complex Needs.* pp. 46–61. Wiley-Blackwell, Oxford, UK.

Carlson, L. (2010). *The Faces of Intellectual Disability. Philosophical Reflections.* Indiana Free Press, Bloomington, Indiana, USA.

Carpenter, B. (2000). 'Sustaining the family. Meeting the needs of families with children with disabilities.' *British Journal of Special Education*, Volume 27 (3), pp. 135–144. Wiley-Blackwell, UK.

Cramp, S. (2003). 'Valuing people – what's the policy worth?' *CarePlan*, pp. 18–21. (no other details).

Cumela, S. (2008). 'New public management and public services for people with an intellectual disability: a review of the implementation of Valuing People in England.' *Journal of Policy and Practice in Intellectual Disabilities*, Volume 5 (3), pp. 178–186. Wiley-Blackwell, Oxford, UK.

Davis, L. (ed) (2006). *The Disability Studies Reader*. 2nd edition. Routledge, New York, USA and London, UK.

Department of Health. (2001). *Valuing People: A New Strategy for Learning Disability in the 21st Century.* HMSO, London, UK.

Department of Health. (2009). *Valuing People Now.* HMSO, London, UK.

Department of Health and Social Security and the Welsh Office. (1971). *Better Services for the Mentally Handicapped.* Cmnd 4683. HMSO, London, UK.

Department for Work and Pensions. (2013). *Fulfilling Potential. Building a Deeper Understanding of Disability in the UK Today.* HMSO, London, UK.

Department for Work and Pensions, Department of Health, Department for Education and Skills, and the Office of the Deputy Prime Minister. (2005). *Improving the Life Chances of Disabled People.* Prime Minister's Strategy Unit. HMSO, London, UK.

Emerson, E., Malam, S., Davies, E. and Spencer, K. (2005). *Adults With Learning Difficulties in England 2003/04.* HMSO, London, UK.

Emerson, E. (2009). *Estimating Future Numbers of Adults with Profound and Multiple Learning Disabilities in England.* Centre for Disability Research Lancaster University, Leeds, UK.

Fogel, A. (1993). 'Two principles of communication: co-regulation and framing.' in Nadel, J. and Camaioni, L. (eds) *New Perspectives in Communication Development.* pp. 9–22. Routledge, London, UK.

Garcia, E. and De Haven, E. (1974). 'Use of operant techniques in the establishment and generalization of language: a review and analysis.' *American Journal of Mental Deficiency*, Volume 79, pp. 169–178. Albany, New York, USA.

Goodley. (2001). 'Learning difficulties, the social model of disability and impairment: challenging epistemologies.' *Disability & Society*, Volume 16 (2), pp. 207–231. Taylor & Francis, London, UK.

Grieg, R. (2005). 'Valuing people: the story so far.' (online). 22nd March. Available from www.valuingpeople.gov.uk

Grove, N., Bunning, K., and Porter, J. (2001). 'Interpreting the meaning of behaviour by people with intellectual disabilities: theoretical and methodological issues.' in Columbus, F. (ed) *Advances in Psychology Research*. Volume 7. pp. 87–126. Novia Sciences Publishers, New York, USA.

Holland, T. (2008). 'Determining priorities in intellectual disability research.' *Journal of Intellectual Disability Research*, Volume 52 (1), pp. 1–2. Wiley-Blackwell, UK.

Holman, A. (2001). In conversation with Rob Grieg. *British Journal of Learning Disabilities* Volume 29 (4), pp. 119–121. Wiley-Blackwell, Oxford, UK.

Jay Report. (1979). *Jay Report of the Committee of Enquiry into Mental Handicap Nursing Care.* Department of Health and Social Security, HMSO, London, UK.

Kelly, A. (2000). *Working with Adults with a Learning Disability.* Winslow Press, Winslow, UK.

Kristiansen, K., Vehmas, S. and Shakespeare, T. (eds). (2010). *Arguing About Disability: Philosophical Perspectives.* Routledge, London, UK and New York, USA.

Lacey, P. and Ouvry, C. (1998). *People with Profound and Multiple Learning Disabilities a Collaborative Approach to Meeting Complex Needs.* David Fulton, London, UK.

Leyin, A. (2010). 'Learning disability classification: time for re-appraisal?' *Tizard Learning Disability Review,* Volume 15 (2), pp. 33–44. Emerald Publishing Limited, UK.

Lyle, D. (2015). 'Policy to practice: a critical analysis of the "valuing people" strategy.' Available from eprints.mdx.ac.uk

Mencap. (2008). 'Lack of knowledge of learning disability revealed.' (online) Available from www.mencap.org.uk/node/6998

Nind, M. and Hewitt, D. (1994). *Access to Communication.* David Fulton, London, UK.

Parrot, R., Tilley, N., and Wolstenholme, J. (2008). 'Changes in demography and demand for services for people with complex needs and profound and multiple learning disabilities.' *Tizard Learning Disability Review,* Volume 13 (3), pp. 26–34. Emerald Publishing Limited, UK.

Pawlyn, J. and Carnaby, S. (eds) (2009). *Profound Intellectual and Multiple Disabilities Nursing Complex Needs.* Wiley-Blackwell, Oxford, UK.

People First. (2011). (online). Available from www.peoplefirstltd.com

PMLD Network. (2002). 'Valuing people with profound and multiple learning disabilities.' (online). Available from www.pmldnetwork.org/resources/

PMSU. (Prime Minister's Strategy Unit) Department for Work and Pensions, Department of Health, Department for Education and Skills and the Office of the Deputy Prime Minister. (2005). *Improving the Life Chances of Disabled People.* HMSO, London, UK.

Samuel, J. and Pritchard, M. (2001). 'The ignored minority: meeting the health needs of people with profound learning disability.' *Tizard Learning Disability Review,* Volume 6 (2), pp. 34–44. Emerald Publishing Limited, UK.

Sutcliffe, J. and Simons, K. & National Institute of Adult Continuing Education. (1993). *Self Advocacy and Adults with Learning Difficulties: Contexts and Debates.* NIACE, Leicester, UK.

Williams, J. (2008). 'Changes in demography and demand for services for people with complex needs and profound and multiple learning disabilities.' *Tizard Learning Disability Review,* Volume 13 (3), pp. 35–37. Emerald Publishing Limited, UK.

Williams, P. (2006). *Social Work with People with Learning Difficulties.* Exeter Learning Matters, Exeter, UK.

Williams, V., Boyle, G., Jepson, N., Swift, P., Williamson, T., and Heslop, P. (2012). *Making Best Interests Decisions: People and Processes.* Mental Health Foundation, London, UK.

2 Policy frameworks

The right hand of the state does not know what the left is doing.' In other words policymakers have no knowledge about the work of those people who implement their policy. Hence, 'the knowledge of what is going on in society is not shared with decision makers, who in turn do not acknowledge the specific character of socio-professional work

(Bourdieu in Duyvendak, 2006 p. 7)

Introduction

The last chapter was concerned with clarifying what the various terms and definitions in use in the UK and abroad actually mean. And why they are especially important for people with PIMD. Of course no one is advocating using labels to refer to individuals. And of course people are more than the sum of their various impairments. However, if people literally have no voice or whose cognitive development is at a pre-symbolic stage for language development, they simply cannot self-report. How then are these people to be meaningfully included in any aspect of service provision?

In the slew of consultations that fed into the writing of *Valuing People* (DH, 2001) it is unclear how people with PIMD were involved. Much of the current research published is in collaboration with people with ID and little acknowledges the breadth of the ID experience. This leads to the dis-connect Duyvendak (2006) describes. If policymakers assume all people with ID have lower support needs, they will not include provision for those with higher needs. Especially as those needs may be in direct contradiction to the normative roles being promoted, such as employment.

How is a health minister or local authority commissioner or a policy planner meant to recognise and understand their needs? Needs requiring specialist services, for example, are difficult to lobby for if everyone with ID is formally represented by this People First statement.

We do not think in terms of medical labels like autism ... we look at support needs. Some people need a shoulder to cry on every now and

again, some people need help understanding instruction manuals, some
people need a push to get out of a chair.

(People First, 2011)

These words could easily apply to this author but in no way encompass the
lifelong specialised care and support needs of her daughter, Odyssey as will be
seen in chapter four. Certainly the above quote applies to many people with
ID, but not all. Some people, such as those with PIMD, require one-to-one or
two-to one support in every aspect of their daily lives for 24 hours of every day.
Some people need three support workers to assist them out of their wheelchair
or to attend to them when they have an epileptic seizure. Some people have
very complex medical support needs or need to be PEG tube–fed; some have
multiple epileptic seizures daily. Some people have no sight, no hearing and are
physically totally dependent. Some people's lives are so sensorily chaotic that
their only response is to engage in self-injurious behaviour. Yet this all remains
unacknowledged.

Another parent and academic researcher the moral philosopher Professor
Eva Kittay describes her daughter's care needs and does not shy away from
discussion of her dependency. In her book *Love's Labor: Essays on Women,
Equality and Dependency* (Kittay, 1999) she is concerned that a focus on
independence situates her daughter Sesha as somehow 'less than fully
human' (p. 173). She is concerned that a focus on independent living and
inclusion is subsidiary to the real goal for her daughter, which is to live

as full and rich a life as one's capacities permit.

(p. 17)

She continues,

... we must also reconceive development, not only toward independence, but toward whatever capacities are there to be developed. Development for Sesha means the enhancement of her capacities to
experience joy.

(p. 173)

Sadly, in the UK, at an All Parliamentary Group launch, in the Houses of
Parliament, Westminster of the late Professor Jim Mansell's report 'Raising
Our Sights' in 2010, the professor found himself having to point out to
assembled politicians words along the lines of ....

it must be understood, these people are fully human.

It seemed particularly shocking to hear and perhaps is why we have writers
attempting to encapsulate this in their own definitions of 'independent
living.' For example,

Living independently does not mean living alone without support – it is having a place to live that meets the person's needs, with an appropriate level of support, to ensure that the person has choice and control and his or her rights are met.

(Ward and Cooper, 2011 pp. 40–41)

Another parent, of a young person, Parent S in the process of transitioning to adult services recently told me,

We have to hand them over at twenty-five, so they can be independent.

It seems in her mind the concept of 'independence' was reframed as independence from parents.

When *Valuing People* (DH, 2001) was published it was promoted as, 'The first white paper on learning disability for thirty years' (p. 14). It set out a programme of action for improving services by linking the four key principles of rights, independence, choice and inclusion to a new life-long approach for services and opportunities aimed at people with ID and their families. It was anticipated the new approach would lead to positive outcomes in education, housing, health, employment, social service and overall support. As the parent of an adult woman with PIMD, this writer was initially optimistic that the needs of the population of people with ID were visible on the political agenda. However, the initial optimism was clouded by a sense that the strategy had little real substance for her daughter and those like her.

Representation or overlooked?

The white paper included a foreword by the PM at that time, Tony Blair. In it he sets out his vision for the future. He states that he believes people with ID are so affected by discrimination and prejudice that they effectively withdraw from wider society. In order to re-engage, they are to be provided with new opportunities to lead a 'full,' 'active,' 'rewarding' and 'valued' life, in which they might 'play their full part,' hence resulting in a 'brighter, more fulfilled life' (DH, 2001, p. 1). It is worth noting he only refers to the difficulties and anxieties parents of disabled children face in finding

the right care, health services, education and leisure opportunities for their sons and daughters.

(DH, 2001, p. 1)

This could equally apply to the parents of adults with PIMD. Unfortunately, it is not until p. 100 (of a 120-page document) that there is any discussion of *'additional or complex needs'* (DH, 2001, p. 100). The manner in which these needs are itemised suggests the writers may not have been familiar with the range of multiple impairments and complex health, social and psychological support needs an individual with PIMD will have. Indeed, according to Burton and Kagan (2006)

> ... those who have such a profound intellectual impairment that their communication is very limited are absent from the picture. The complex health needs of many (mentioned in VP's section on health) and the need for knowledgeable and skilled specialists is not emphasized here. A kind of inadvertent trick takes place, where the least impaired people are used in the imagery to stand for all the others.
>
> (p. 301)

Carnaby (2001) used the editorial of '*The Tizard Learning Disability Review*,' in an attempt to redress the lack of 'knowledge of what is really going on' (p. 2).

> In other words policy makers have no knowledge about the work of those people who implement their policy.
>
> (Bourdieu, 2006, p. 7)

It is worth noting this was published the same time as *Valuing People* (DH, 2001). He discusses the relative lack of literature, aimed specifically at community services (practice and provision) for those with PIMD. He maintains this is because

> ...they are one of the last groups to leave long-stay hospital.
>
> (Carnaby, 2001, p. 2)

However this overlooks the fact that the majority of adults with PIMD live with their families (Emerson, 2004). Carnaby (2001) describes the challenges including,

> the diverse and increasingly complex needs presented by this population' and 'how the needs are perceived by others.
>
> (Carnaby, 2001, p. 2)

He acknowledges the differing philosophical approaches (medical and social) and argues for WHO style functional assessments, of how PIMD impacts on individual's daily lives. These assessments ought to inform service provision. He further discusses the need for service audits, to review and identify further specific issues. There is a clear outline on definition, as he also agrees clarity is needed. He uses the Lacey (1998) and WHO (1992) definitions.

He goes on to outline the need for,

> a respectful developmental approach, which acknowledges the individual's abilities and disabilities.
>
> (Carnaby, 2001, p. 3)

Notwithstanding the underlying philosophical tensions, he argues for the necessity of medical and social support. Yes, these people will often have a lifelong need for medical interventions, but they

> also need to experience a quality of life built on relationships with others.
>
> (Carnaby, 2001, p. 4)

He uses the editorial and papers cited therein, to drive home his argument, which is for recognition of the extent of need experienced by people with PIMD and an understanding that specialist services might not necessarily,

> meet the criteria for ordinary living approaches.
>
> (Carnaby, 2001, p. 4)

His concerns are echoed by the initial report from the PMLD Network (2002) published in response to VP. This report highlighted

> ... the way it (VP) does not: use consistent terminology, identify that children and adults with PMLD are amongst the most excluded in our society, identify children and adults with PMLD as a priority group, make any specific objective or sub-objective for people with PMLD, identify family carers of children and adults with PMLD as a priority group. (2)

and further argues,

> ... it could be said that *Valuing People* accurately reflects the problems facing children and adults with PMLD – we don't know how to describe them and therefore we don't know how to accumulate the information required to gain an accurate picture of their needs.
>
> (PMLD Network, 2002, p. 2)

Normalisation

Before examining the impact of the *Valuing People* policy (DH, 2001, 2002) on the lives of people with PIMD in particular, it is necessary to briefly summarise the framework for services for people with ID in the UK, at the turn of the 21st century. Whilst an historical account of the subject is beyond the scope of this book, clearly *Valuing People* was not published in a policy vacuum. Race (2002) argues that the concept of normalisation has been influencing services for people with ID for well over thirty years. He cites its influence on the 1979 Jay Committee Report's proposed new model of care, which was to be based on three main principles.

a) Mentally handicapped people have a right to enjoy normal patterns of life within the community.
b) Mentally handicapped people have a right to be treated as individuals.
c) Mentally handicapped people will require additional help from the communities in which they live and from professional services if they are to develop to their maximum potential as individual.

(in Race, 2002, p. 42)

Nirje (1980) first devised the normalisation approach. He was opposed to institutional living and critical of the prevalent medical model of care. His ideas were aligned to the notion of family type small group living. He summed up his approach, based on the demands of the Scandinavian parent *movement thus,*

> making available to the mentally retarded patterns and conditions of everyday life which are as close as possible to the norms and patterns of the mainstream of society.

(Nirje, 1980, p. 19)

These ideas were expanded by Wolfensberger into his 1972 '*Principle of Normalization in Human Services*' and the later 1975 specific application for 'the severely handicapped.'

His definition described,

> utilization of means which are culturally normative as possible in order to establish and/or maintain personal behaviors and characteristics which are as culturally normative as possible.

(Wolfensberger, 1972, p. 28)

His basic principle was later developed into the social role valorisation approach (Wolfensberger, 1983a). This emphasised the manner in which people with ID are socially devalued hence his idea that valuing people could reverse this stigmatisation. His critics however were concerned that this meant imposing societal norms onto people with ID (Ward, 1992; Stainton, 1994). John O'Brien distilled ideas of normalisation into his 'Five Service Accomplishments' (Concannon, 2005, p. 78). These consequences of services comprise notions of community presence, relationships with non-disabled people, service user choice, development of competency and respect. O'Brien ran a number of workshops in the UK with Alan Tyne in the 1980's and Race (2002) notes,

> adherence to and knowledge of O'Brien's "Five Accomplishments", became commonplace as requirements in job descriptions.

(Race, 2002, p. 196)

Race maintains people conflate normalisation, social role valorisation and O'Brien's Five Service accomplishments and further that there are echoes of all approaches in *Valuing People* (Race, 2002, p. 43). Chappell (1997) discusses the climate in the 1980's as one where, '*to criticize it (normalization) was tantamount to heresy*' (p. 47). Yet by the end of that decade the perceived progressive approach to debate, discussion and services for people with ID was losing favour. Writers such as Bayley (1991) were concerned people with ID were being expected to conform to culturally normative roles rather than an acceptance of their own particular characteristics. Chappell also cites Brown and Smith (1989) and Baxter et al. (1990) who highlight the emphasis within the normalisation approaches on the perceived value of these roles which people with ID were expected to aspire to. In this climate Chappell argues that the social model of disability is a better theoretical framework for discussion, but is also concerned that people with ID '*remain as marginal as ever*' within the social model of disability discussions (Chappell, 1997, p. 51; Chappell et al., 2001; Stevens, 2004).

The reason for this could lie with the self-organising nature of the Disability Rights Movement (DRM) in the UK, which was comprised primarily of physically impaired adults. Their basic concerns were with notions of agency and the right to control one's life. From the outset they saw themselves as a separate group to '*the mentally handicapped*' (see Hunt, 1966, p. 13).

Social model

Notwithstanding, the prevailing approach to disability studies in general in the UK is described as the social model. The Office for Disability Issues, (ODI, 2015) encourages its use in policymaking. This radical new way of understanding disability and disablement emerged from the 'Union of Physically Impaired Against Segregation' (UPIAS, 1975) agenda in the 1970s and gradually evolved into Oliver's (1990) Marxist materialist critique. Prior to this the medical model was the prevailing paradigm (Parsons, 1951) Even earlier the eugenics movement were advocating mass sterilisation of people with ID. As Mazumdar (1992) points out widespread debate in the UK at the time led to its opposition. Although the enforced segregation of people in institutions was still actively pursued in order to prevent people with ID reproducing (Mencap 2005). Shakespeare (2006) notes however that campaigners and researchers had considered the social aspect of disability issues for some time previously.

Physically disabled activists in the 1970s questioned why they were deemed incapable of functioning in the community. They started to examine the ways society was organised to segregate and exclude them from mainstream participation (Finkelstein, 2004). New ways were sought to represent disability, which moved the focus away from individual tragedy accounts or medicalised labels to issues of policy and planning (Oliver 1990, Barnes,

1994). This approach describes environments as the locus of disability rather than the impaired individual.

> Disability is not something we possess but something our society possesses.
>
> (Leaman in Swain et al., 2004, p. 14)

Activists maintained it was the organisation of society that needed to change to accommodate the needs of individuals (Oliver, 1990). UPIAS (1975) members were keen to challenge the underlying causes of disability, as defined by them, rather than railing against its symptoms.

From the outset it was agreed to move the focus of their struggle away from individual effects. The shift was towards an examination of the ways society was organised to segregate and exclude disabled people from full mainstream participation. In order to challenge the existing interpretations of disability they declared a fundamental difference between 'impairment' and 'disability.' According to this new interpretation it wasn't impairments that disabled individuals it was societal structures and attitudes. By focusing on societal structures they developed a manifesto framework for fighting this perceived oppression.

> It is the same society which disables people whatever their type, or degree of physical impairment, and therefore there is a single cause within the organization of society that is responsible for the creation of the disability of physically impaired people. Understanding the cause of disability will enable us to understand the situation of those less affected, as well as helping us to prevent getting lost in the details of the degrees of oppression at the expense of focusing on the essence of the problem.
>
> (Finkelstein and Davis, 1975, p. 4)

The overarching concern of the Disability Rights Movement (DRM) in the 1980's was to achieve integration into mainstream employment in order to alleviate the discrimination and poverty disabled people experienced (Abberley, 1987). In a later paper entitled 'The Significance of Work for the Citizenship of Disabled People' Abberley acknowledges the necessity for a

> dual strategy of work facilitation for those who want it and can meaningfully take part in the labour process and the general valorization of non-working lives for those, including impaired people, who are unable to work.
>
> (Abberley, 1999, p. 1)

He argues that a Marxist analysis is useful for understanding the oppression of disabled people in capitalist societies but notes,

it seems of less use in conceptualising a future for those impaired
people unable to work.

(Abberley, 1999, p. 8)

Beresford (2000) emphasises the social model of disability is solely concerned with the socio/cultural and political aspects of a person's lived
experience, rather than individual biological/medical aspects. According to
a social model account, it is the conditions, which restrict an individual's
life opportunities that need to be identified and analysed. These conditions,
it maintains, are bound up in the socio/political sphere rather than within
the personal. For this reason the social model approach has been described
as an outside – in approach, since the notion of disability is situated in society outside of the individual.

There is a fundamental dichotomy here. The claim to represent all disabled people in reality meant only those who were able to represent themselves. This was the manner in which the Disability Rights Movement
gained prominence in the UK. The raison d'être was about an individual's
right to lead an inclusive life, have a job, live independently and so forth.
The primary focus was on the nature and workings of society, rather than
on individual impairments. To this end, the early UPIAS debates were concerned with questioning members' socially inferior status. Was this status
attributable to embodied impairments, they queried, or to the manner in
which society was constructed by people with capabilities, for people with
capabilities? And is this why people with impairments are incapable of functioning (Finkelstein, 2001). As Boxhall notes in Race (2002)

a key aspect of social model theorising is that it has been both authored
and controlled by disabled people themselves.

(p. 217)

Unfortunately, as Chappell (1998) demonstrated people with ID were
noticeably absent from the discussion and debate. The difficulty with devising a model, which was originally focused on the right to work, arises,
when people latterly try to make the model all-inclusive.

UPIAS (Finkelstein and Davis, 1977) makes numerous references to:

our exclusion from the ability to earn an income on a par with our
able-bodied peers.

(Finkelstein and Davis, 1997, p. 1)

to struggle for changes to the organisation of society so that employment and full social participation are made accessible to all people.

(Finkelstein and Davis, 1997, p. 2)

to go forward with the serious struggle for the right to paid, integrated employment.

(Finkelstein and Davis, 1997, p. 5)

integration into ordinary employment. This is the fundamental principle by which schemes for meeting the financial and other needs of disabled people can be judged.

(Finkelstein and Davis, 1997, p. 6)

dependence on the State must increasingly give way to the provision of help so that a living can be earned through employment

(Finkelstein and Davis, 1997, p. 8)

yet the struggle to achieve integration into ordinary employment is the most vital part of the struggle.

(Finkelstein and Davis, 1997, p. 11)

This list is not exhaustive but it illustrates the prominence of this aspect in the very early discussions. Oliver (2004) refers to

... disabled people's agenda that focuses on issues such as employment and social inclusion, independent living and civil rights

(Oliver, 2004, p. 23)

and believes that there is a need for

... adopting a firm target and formulating appropriate plans for the employment of disabled people.

(Oliver, 2004, p. 24)

Bearing in mind this chapter is examining the manner in which those with PIMD are accounted for within service provision frameworks. It is clear a model focused on employment as a panacea may need some refinement.

Social model and embodiment or second-wave social model

Identities of the subject of the social model can therefore be expected to pro-liferate, splinter and collide with increasing frequency as individualizing and totalizing diagnostic and juridical categories offer ever more finely tuned dis-tinctions between and varieties of (for instance) congenital and acquired impairments, physical, sensory, cognitive, language and speech impairments, mental illnesses, chronic illnesses and environmental illnesses, aphasia, dys-phasia, dysplasia and dysarthria, immune deficiency syndromes, attention deficit disorder, attention deficit hyperactivity disorders and autism.

(Tremain, 2006, pp. 193–194)

As she rightly points out an identity-based movement will eventually be challenged for excluding someone or some particular group. This is what has happened with ID and of course PIMD. As Morris (1991) posited,

> there is a tendency within the social model of disability to deny the experience of our own bodies insisting that our physical differences and restrictions are entirely socially created.
>
> (Morris, 1991, p. 35)

> ... to suggest that this is all there is to it, is to deny the personal experience of physical or intellectual restrictions, of illness, of the fear of dying.
>
> (Morris, 1991, p. 35)

Hence second-wave disability activists re-introduced an embodied ontology to disability studies. Feminist researchers with their *'personal is political'* agenda, believed lived experience needed to take account of personal embodied issues and argued for accommodating impairment effects by discussing living with constant pain (see Morris, 1991, 1998) or via the production of non-tragedy positive narratives (Crow, 1996, French, 2004). Thomas (2004) who describes herself as being in the Marxist/materialist camp with the early proponents, later explored the psycho-emotional dimensions of disability, arguing that societal barriers are internally constructed as well as physical. This development could be described as a second wave of the social model. These researchers felt they faced challenges in life, which could not be ameliorated by addressing the social barriers that the early SM proponents identified as constituting disability *per se*. They could demonstrate this through emancipatory and/or participatory research and these issues could be discussed within a framework of independence and inclusion (see also Hasler, 2003; Goodley, 2004).

Whilst some researchers had begun to recognise that those with ID were absent from the whole disability debate (e.g. Shakespeare, 2006), attempting to situate the issues associated with PIMD within a similar participatory framework is problematical. For example, the March 2011 editorial of the *British Journal of Learning Disabilities*, called for,

> papers that are **written** by people with learning disabilities, on their own, or in partnership with other researchers.
>
> (Mitchell, 2011, p. 1) (Bold author's own.)

Surely this further marginalises those individuals with more profound intellectual impairment effects? It is not clear if Mitchell believes individuals with PIMD can effectively write academic research *'in partnership with other researchers'* (Mitchell, 2011, p. 1) or if he is simply using what he believes to be social model friendly language. And yet by simply changing the word 'written' to 'produced,' this would have been inclusive of people with PIMD. This is what families mean when they say they feel PIMD is overlooked.

Post-structural social model and 'brute facts' of genetics

Rapley (2004) argues from a discursive psychological perspective that rather than ID being a tangible, internal, individual thing, it is an interactional product. The identity of ID, he argues, is constructed through moment-by-moment social interactions with others. (Usually care staff or professionals, although oddly he does not mention families.) He further argues, that the range of diagnostic definitions which have been employed since the 1800s, have furnished,

> the appearance ...... of an homogenous disorder, where in practice there is heterogeneity, diversity and uniqueness.
>
> (Rapley, 2004, p. 197)

He refutes the second-wave social model writers who, he argues, need to re-examine their acceptance of the proposition that ID is an essentialised, interiorised and real impairment (Rapley, 2004, p. 201). In essence his argument distils down to a refutation of the original Wechsler (1981) IQ tests. Granted, (in)competence may well be negotiated and constructed locally, as he argues *'for local purposes, by local means'* (Wechsler, 1981, p. 202). However, by focusing on individuals who can self-advocate, Rapley has restricted his own argument. He argues against acknowledging internal mental attributes that may constrain an individual's capacity (Rapley, 2004, p. 202). He argues further that

> ... to theorise ID as such is to confer solidity and permanence on that which is nothing but a habit of speech, a hypothetical construct which homogenizes and totalizes that which it's proclaimers promise to pick apart.
>
> (Rapley, 2004, p. 205)

Goodley is also keen to discuss the constructed nature of ID. He claims

> there is a need to work with and for an understanding of 'learning difficulties' as fundamentally social, cultural, political, historical, discursive and relational phenomenon, rather than sensitively recognizing the existence of an individual's 'naturalised impairment.'
>
> (Goodley, 2001, p. 210)

By focusing entirely on the mild to moderate end of the spectrum, he is denying the existence and validity of PIMD. At least the SM researchers and writers described as second wave, attempted to include the vast range of diverse human experience that is encompassed by all persons including those with ID (e.g. Thomas, 2001, French and Swain, 2004). Rapley concludes his argument by querying if all we have done is reformulate scientifically the moral defective classification of the feebleminded?

It is unclear how these writers can make global claims about ID, such as its socially constructed nature when they only focus their research at the mild end of the ID spectrum. Is this to better fit their theory? Surely opening out the discussion to include the diversity Rapley refers to would be more helpful?

Goodley (2001, 2011) and Goodley and Rapley (2001) have challenged the existing medical definition of ID. Goodley repeats Langness and Levine's (1986) concern and queries why, epistemologically,

> some elements of humanity are open to sociological investigation (MLD), whilst some are left in the realm of static, irreversible, individualised biology (SLD).
>
> (Goodley, 2001, p. 226)

The difficulty with Goodley (including 2011) and the few others who have attempted to include discussion of ID within a SM approach, is that they focus exclusively on individuals who can self advocate and who experience low-level impairment effects, as a result of their (socially constructed?) MID. These are the people Bogdan and Taylor (1982), Langness and Levine (1986) and Dudley-Marling (2004) describe. In fact, Simone Aspis (2004) whom Goodley often quotes was interviewed about her postgraduate work on her MA in Ethics and Law. As a blunt comparison, people with PIMD are,

> experiencing the world using skills that can be conceptualized as functioning at the very early stages of development ....
>
> (Pawlyn and Carnaby, 2009, p. 8)

Many of these people would also fall into the category overlooked by researchers such as Goodley and Rapley. These are people whose ID does in fact have an organic basis.

> .... the presence of an extra chromosome 21 is a brute fact.
>
> (Kristiansen et al., 2010, pp. 47–49)

Vehmas and Makela (in Kristiansen et al., 2010) discuss the way Searle (1995) describes the difference between brute facts of physics and biology, i.e. things, which exist, and mental facts such as feelings or perceptions (Kristiansen, 2010, pp. 46–47). In other words genetic disorders can be described as ontologically objective, since they have an objective organic basis, which is not dependent on representation. Thomas (2007) notes

Bhaskar's term epistemic fallacy might apply when knowledge of things is conflated with the actual existence of things (Thomas, 2007, p. 34).

This may be described as a lack of philosophical fit. On the one hand this handbook attempts to deal with a tangible and real something, i.e. 'PIMD.' However, it is the manner in which this complicated amalgam of definitions has come to be represented or overlooked, which is problematic.

> Discourse constructs the topic. It defines and produces objects of our knowledge. It governs the way a topic can be meaningfully talked about and reasoned about. It also influences how ideas are put into practice and used to regulate the conduct of other.
>
> (Hall, 2001, p. 72)

Therefore, the manner in which language is used (e.g. everyone can self advocate, everyone should work, everyone can make choices) actively constructs a range of expectations and a particular version of reality. This can be unhelpful when dealing with a population whose reality as such needs much clarification.

Dykens et al. (2000) edited '*Genetics and Mental Retardation Syndromes,*' which identifies over seven hundred genetic disorders which,

> … are thought to occur mostly among those with severe and profound mental retardation.
>
> (p. 3)

The authors note these individuals used to account for around 25% of the ID population. However genetic disorders nowadays account for at least 33% and with advances in genetics, more are being discovered every day. As they point out genetic causes occur in 10–50% of people with mild to moderate levels of ID (Rutter et al., 1996). These figures do not include those individuals whose ID is caused by organic rather than genetic issues such as premature and extremely premature birth and/or foetal alcohol syndrome. This 'realm of static, irreversible, individualised biology' (as described by Goodley, 2001) is one we parents certainly recognise. Our children are not 'left there' rather we parents accept their situation. The philosopher Licia Carlson (2010) describes this 'loving ignorance' whereby we 'accept what we cannot know' (p. 204). She refers to Tuana's (2009) essay, 'The Speculum of Ignorance,' which clarifies the value of ignorance as a component of any robust theory of knowledge. Carlson considers the tension between these two positions of ignorance may be where we can best consider the

> challenges and lessons offered by persons with severe intellectual disabilities.
>
> (p. 204)

Personalisation

The discussion so far has focused on attempting to tease out the manner in which acknowledgement of PIMD has been included or not in development of policy frameworks. The New Labour government's adoption of Third Way thinking focused even more on ideas of community, opportunities and responsibilities. These ideas were amalgamated with social model informed thinking in *Valuing People*. As Race (2002) describes, within the context for development of policy for adults

> the emphasis is on support for individuals to build capacity to manage their own lives, to be in control, to gain assets to avoid disadvantage and to strive towards self-sufficiency and greater personal responsibility, thus reducing the role of professionals to care commissioner, coordinator and/or manager, and recognizing that the state will reduce its role as provider.
>
> (pp. 325–326)

Yet Ferguson (2007) notes there is no detailed or precise definition for an approach, which has gained remarkable popularity very swiftly,

> occupying a place at the very heart of emergent British social work, policy, philosophy and even legislation.
>
> (p. 388)

The Social Care Institute for Excellence (SCIE) published their 'Rough Guide' in 2008, which discusses starting with the individual as a person and states that

> ...people can be responsible for themselves and make their own decisions about what they require, but they should also have information and support to enable them to do so.
>
> (p. 3)

Other organisations specifically noted this approach replaced the medical model.

> Person centred planning is a process of life planning for individuals, based around the principles of inclusion and the social model of disability ... Person centred planning replaces more traditional outmoded styles of assessment and planning which are based on a medical model approach to people's needs.
>
> (Circles Network, 2005)

However the glaring question surely is how do we meaningfully involve an individual with PIMD in planning their life? We are told,

It is essential that the person with PIMD is meaningfully involved in the process of developing their person-centred plan.

(DH, 2002)

But how? In the book *Planning for Life Involving Adults with Learning Disabilities in Service Planning* (Concannon, 2005) the rear cover notes state,

> Based on findings from original research and interviews, the author argues that involving people with learning disabilities in service planning is difficult to achieve successfully and is currently, to a large extent, tokenistic.

And this was not a book focusing solely on adults with PIMD. Although not always explicitly stated it is clear that,

> Services need to consider how they embrace the role of the advocate in the development of person-centred plans for people with PIMD.

(Pawlyn, 2009, p. 83)

Finally, acknowledgement that someone other than the individual with PIMD, must speak on their behalf.

Self-advocacy aka speaking up

It is worth noting that *Valuing People* (DH, 2001) did acknowledge a need for advocacy other than 'self-advocacy.' It committed the government to setting up a national citizen advocacy network in every local authority area. Citizen advocacy is a form of independent long-term advocacy that works well for people with PIMD. Unfortunately, a 2012 survey of advocacy organisations revealed only eighteen out of eighty-four who responded provided citizen advocacy. Of those eighteen it was not revealed how many had clients with PIMD (Roberts et al. 2012). It is clear that over fifteen years after publication, the *Valuing People* emphasis on involving all service users in planning their own services remains political rhetoric. In fact it was always less than clear how people with PIMD were to be consulted.

Valuing People was very clear that

> people with severe and profound disabilities, with the right help and support, can make important choices and express preferences about their day-to-day lives.

(DH, 2001, p. 24)

Unfortunately this statement was illustrated by the quote

> people with learning disabilities have been saying for a long time that we can speak up for ourselves.
>
> (DH, 2001, p. 24)

The conflation of reference to people with PIMD and the direct quote to illustrate it is worrying. Was this simply a misguided placing or was it an attempt to convey the idea that people with PIMD can literally speak up and therefore self-advocate? After all, the term 'speaking up' has now become synonymous with self-advocacy groups (see for e.g. Lawton 2009). The paragraph refers explicitly to people with severe and profound disabilities but appears to believe and gives the impression that, with the right help and support they can make decisions about,

> where they live, what work they do and who looks after them.
>
> (p. 24)

It further states,

> we believe that everyone should be able to make choices.
>
> (p. 24)

This statement and the use of the words 'believe' and 'should' are problematic. It is unclear how accepting or rejecting food or indeed only rejecting is actually making an informed choice. (See, Bexley LDS, 2002 for an account of different levels of choice-making ability including notion of informed choice.)

The reason this is so important is linked to front line care. If the overarching service framework is one of 'choice' there needs to be constant training and development of staff. Every effort ought to be made to ensure people have opportunities to make choices. However as will be shown in the next chapter care workers need a clear understanding of levels of choice-making ability. All-encompassing top-down statements are not helpful when working with this population.

The *Valuing People* policy is based on ideas of communication and involvement, yet at least 20% of the ID population, are known not to have intentional communication skills (Concannon, 2005, p. 103). Indeed some writers appear less concerned about individual's communication skills than their own belief that everyone can self-advocate. Armstrong (2002) discusses self-advocacy as

> a policy option through which the citizenship of people with learning difficulties can be asserted.
>
> (Armstrong, 2002, p. 334)

In order to do this, he argues, the starting point must be a rejection of biological assumptions. Here is another writer who uses language, which ostensibly creates the impression that all people with intellectual impairment have the capacity to truly self-advocate. He talks about eliciting perspective when in reality he is discussing very keen observation of an individual with PIMD. He describes the

> … ways in which people with severe and profound intellectual impairments can be listened to, using behavioural and subtle communication cues, in addition to, or instead of, conventional or gestural forms of communication.
>
> (Armstrong, 2002, p. 340)

He then makes assumptions about what he believes the individual may be feeling. It cannot be impressed enough that this is not the same as an individual providing their views first hand. Armstrong may well arrive at a completely different conclusion to somebody else as this is such a subjective endeavour. More recently Darwent (2012) has published an article entitled, 'Quietly Confident,' in the Mencap magazine *Viewpoint*. Whilst the writer initially points out that the subject of the article is a man with PIMD who cannot communicate verbally, she proceeds to describe his new life as a college lecturer and trainer. The use of language such as,

> he set up, he addressed, he advised, he planned, wrote and delivered the course.
>
> (Darwent, 2012, pp. 20–21)

conveys the idea of an involved, proactive, cognisant individual. The article is a good news story, which manages to focus on the notion that employment has turned his life around. The article points out that

> … he was enjoying a social life, he loves going to the pub and eating out, but something was missing.
>
> (Darwent, 2012, p. 20)

It is unclear why his support team could not devise more meaningful, structured or therapeutic activities, rather than make his activities fit the quasi-normative role of so-called employment. ('So called,' as it has been impossible to determine if he is actually paid for his work.) Emails to the author of the article for further elucidation remained unanswered and attempts to contact the social work lecturer (Darwent, 2012, p. 21) failed also.

This writer challenges the *Valuing People* assumption that in order to have value an individual must fulfil society's normative roles. Surely this was what people objected to about the normalisation framework? The question remains how can the individual and specific needs of someone with PIMD be understood in terms of personalised services to be commissioned and delivered? How can they if we all collude in some kind of 'as if' game, whereby people are portrayed as the instigators of their own life opportunities? Surely the starting point must be a respectful acknowledgement of just how such an individual experiences her or his world? And surely a respectful acknowledgment would preclude over ascribing capacity?

Acknowledging difference in service provision

> There is a need to change the approach to practice and policy development. The agenda is not whether people have the same view, but that their *differences* are acknowledged and included in the process.
>
> (Concannon, 2005, p. 171)

Wing (1998) published a paper arguing for an acknowledgement of individuals' differences, as opposed to the way she saw the policy of normalisation, being carried out. She argues as a parent and as a psychiatrist, whose research has enriched our understanding of autism. Her concern was with the way normalisation is often taken to mean that

> disabled people can and should behave as if they have no disabilities and that they should all want to live in the same kind of setting.
>
> (Wing, 1998, p. 24)

She goes on,

> the idealists fail to recognize the enormous differences between people in general, let alone those with special problems.
>
> (Wing, 1998, p. 24)

It could be argued that the underlying personalisation agenda of Valuing People would in fact acknowledge these individual differences, but do they? Carnaby (2001 and 2004) and Wing (1998) are two examples of professionals with an insight into the specific and particular needs of this demographic yet their expertise does not appear to have informed *Valuing People*. Burton and Kagan (2006) have attempted to disentangle or decode the mix of ideologies inherent in the policy. They point out,

> .... there has been no critical analysis of Valuing People that sets it in the broader political – economic context of social policy, while simultaneously focusing on the needs of learning – disabled people and their allies.
>
> (Burton and Kagan, 2006, p. 299)

This writer is attempting to do just this, albeit focusing entirely on individuals with PIMD. For example, the 'problem' of ID is currently framed within a 'social exclusion' discourse. The key to overcoming this 'problem' is seen as 'accessing the community.' This is problematic for those with PIMD. For example when conducting the research for the study discussed in the following chapter a search of the Changing Places (2013) website could find no suitable toilets in the inner London borough and the only one identified in the outer London borough was in a hospital.

Apart from this practicality Firth et al (2010) note,

> what the implementation of such policies often seems to ignore is the meaningfulness of community involvement/inclusion.
>
> (p. 174)

Just how meaningful is the community activity to the individual? Care workers at an outer London borough asked

> why would they want to be dragged around the High street or into Mac Donalds? They need therapeutic interventions and support and that is what we believe is the best thing for them.
>
> (Lyle, 2015, p. 175)

Another worker in an inner London borough, who had been engaged in a discussion about the way their day centre was

> just a base nowadays. The new opportunities are all about accessing the community' added, 'how many times can service users go to the same park? Not being funny I know that place like the back of my hand now. What must K think? "here again."
>
> (Lyle, 2015, p. 176)

Indeed the Inclusion Europe report (Schadler et al., 2008) was entitled 'The Specific Risks of Discrimination' and concluded that

> the more mainstream oriented services become, the less people with severe disabilities are part of target groups.
>
> (p. 54)

They also pointed out that,

> there is a high risk that persons with complex disabilities do not profit from these efforts towards greater empowerment through self-advocacyment through self-advocacy.
>
> (p. 82)

Mansell (2010) points out the soft policy had no hard targets. The vision and aspirations of *Valuing People* were not tied to implementation time-tables or resource allocation; rather, they were about

> enabling people to realize their civil and human rights in all aspects of their lives, therefore as policy it has implications across government.
>
> (Mansell, 2010, p. 12)

One of the few actual targets of VP was the closure of long-stay hospitals. However, the idea of community living for people with the complex support needs inherent in behavioural issues often described as challenging has not been realised. This, he argues, is to do with the growing market in social welfare, which has seen a growth in high cost low value, residential homes away from local areas. He also cites the lack of advocacy, as another reason the policy is not being realised.

Whitehead et al. (2008) published an overview of ID policy in four UK counties. They examined current policy (i.e. *Valuing People*) and its links to the wider policy agenda. Their paper describes how the proposed key out-come of Valuing People, i.e. social inclusion, addressed the issues of hous-ing, employment, general health and education. Unfortunately, years down the line, the gap between rhetoric and reality is still apparent. Of particular concern were the responses by family carers, who voiced their concerns about how achievable the goals were, especially for individuals with complex needs.

Bochel et al. (2008) have broached the issue of representation via advo-cacy. As they point out the government's agenda was inclusion. Making one's voice heard was grounded in the belief that this would produce better politics and therefore better outcomes. The emphasis is on speaking up, but, the authors ask, what about those who literally cannot speak. They must have an advocate or an organisational voice. As was seen the parlous state of advocacy provision is unlikely to improve, which leaves many people with the informal advocacy of their family and/or the pseudo 'advocacy' of a key worker. A key worker cannot provide the same objective approach as an independent non-instructed advocate. However, considering it takes a minimum of two and up to five years to get to know an individual with PIMD and to truly understand their needs it becomes apparent how diffi-cult it is to assign an advocate. Someone with no family involvement can be assigned an Independent Mental Capacity Advocate, but only for issues of safeguarding, long-term accommodation or serious medical issues. This leaves a large gap in the day-to-day lives of individuals. So what of their organisational voice?

Currently, the preferred source is the organisation People First (2011). There is a difficulty with this, as they have a very particular political approach.

Their website states very clearly, with regard to self-advocacy;

everyone can make a choice ... through self-advocacy people's support needs get lower. Once people start to be treated with respect and given responsibilities, they become more independent and find out just how much they can do for themselves.

(People First, 2011)

This statement is troubling for people with PIMD. As will be seen in the next chapter, staff are often exposed to training sessions where big ideas are broached but not necessarily broken down to include the day–to-day support needs of those with PIMD. At some level we can opine that *'everyone can make a choice,'* but we must flesh out that statement to include an understanding of levels of choice making. For e.g. how frustrating must it be for someone to be constantly approached by people asking open-ended questions of you, especially if your cognitive levels are at a very early stage of development? And how frustrating for the care worker? How many times have people said to me, 'Oh (s)he understands everything I say.' Nowadays, I always ask them how they know this. A parent might instinctually feel this but care workers need to have more than a feeling. They need to have an understanding of notions of context, levels of cognition, body language, vocalisations and facial expressions.

A teaching assistant who works with my daughter part-time also works full-time in a Special Needs school. The children have complex health needs including autism, as well as severe to profound and multiple ID. Few of the students use words to communicate. She recently told me how she had remembered my training around contextual issues when supporting one of her students in the hydrotherapy pool. She had thought the boy was responding to certain words, but decided to experiment by using completely different words and sentences, but the same tone of voice. She noted he responded exactly the same to any words, as long as she used the same tone. By recognising the role context plays she is now more alert to the importance of a consistent approach and use of any form of Alternative and Augmentative Communication (AAC).

Sherborne (2001) attempts to broach notions of difference in the context of devising a movement class, by referring to the wide-ranging individual needs of those with PIMD. She notes the particular difficulty for workers when trying to manage a group of people, which will include those who have profound physical impairments and those who

have marked emotional and behavioural difficulties. These people may be destructive and aggressive to others in the group.

(Sherborne, 2001 p. 92)

Indeed. My daughter has been repeating the phrase *'Latifa, leave Odyssey alone'* for well over twenty years now. We have no idea who Latifa is, but some member of staff somewhere was clearly frustrated and lost as to how to support Latifa. I say frustrated, because sometimes we get the further sentence, '*Latifa, go and sit in your BLOODY chair.*' (Her emphasis I should add.)

Sadly it appears that there is a negative connotation associated with the concept of high support needs but it is unclear why. The sense is of someone deciding there are good words such as self-advocacy, independent, inclusive and bad words, such as dependent or specialist, which cannot be tolerated.

Drake (1990) describes Stevenson's notion of 'persuasive definition' (p. 117). This is the manner in which language, which carries an emotive meaning, may be exploited. As an example he points out that the term institution vs. de-institutionalisation conveys emotionally laden connotations of good versus bad, yet evidence exists to demonstrate merely moving into smaller services, will not necessarily reduce bad examples of care (Sinson, 1990). He also discusses the manner in which the term 'community' fulfils the requirements of vagueness necessary for persuasive definition, in having two meanings: a socio-political-geographical area and a friendship network. He points out that

> the danger lies in confusing the two meanings in a glow of nostalgia and fantasy so that geographical location is expected to yield friendship networks.
>
> (Drake, 1990, p. 117)

This notion of persuasive definition is alluded to in Burton and Kagan's (2006) criticism of

> the utopia painted by VP, which sees people making choices about activities in pleasant neighbourhoods, usually suburbs, with plentiful community resources ...... they are likely to have friendships and relationships.
>
> (Burton and Kagan, 2006, p. 308)

They query the assumption that in order to have value disadvantaged groups must aspire to

> fulfill society's idealized norms.
>
> (Burton and Kagan, 2006, p. 306)

As pointed out earlier,

> these assumptions seem to promote an essentially negative conception of differentness.
>
> (Drake, 1990, p. 128)

The shift away from acknowledging individual levels of impairment makes it very difficult to then argue for specialist services. Indeed, the current postmodern ideas of ID being purely a social construction (Goodley 2001; Williams, 2006) receive short shrift from Byrne in Carlsson (2010); where he opines,

> If we abandon the label and the caring institutions which properly go with it, we will have cut off a significant minority of human beings from aid and help which they need.
>
> (p. 90)

Charles Henley (2005) worked for twenty-five years managing various day centres for adults with learning disabilities. He argues that the need for specialist and structured day services, amongst other things, ought to be acknowledged. As he sees it, there ought to be a 'single service solution.'

> ... a single agency with protected financial support, a national policy, standardized specialist training resources, and a competent inspectorate.
>
> (Henley, 2005, p. 164)

His concern about the lack of shared knowledge between diverse departments echoes Bourdieu (2006) again.

For example, in the same year *Valuing People* was heralded as 'A New Strategy' (DH, 2001, p. i), with its inherent visions of 'rights, independence, choice and inclusion' (DH, 2001, p. 3), Stalker (cited in Henley 2005) referred to the conclusions of the Social Services Inspectorate Report (Social Services Inspectorate, 1998) that

> local authorities in England and Wales had identified "sound principles" for their services for people with learning disabilities, namely, promoting independence, respect and community presence.
>
> (p. 165)

Further the report found that

> most day centres were diversifying to offer people a range of activities that included the encouragement of other sections of the community to use the buildings; attendance at further education colleges, use of mainstream community resources, voluntary work, work experience and paid employment.
>
> (p. 165)

Henley (2005) is also critical of the soft target visions and queries how effective

> the fragmentation of responsibility to different agencies concerned with recreation, education, employment, medical, emotional and psychological needs can be.
>
> (p. 174)

In reality he sees this as leading to

> the duplication of bureaucracy and waste of human and financial resources.
>
> (Henley, 2005, p. 174)

This move to an ad hoc mode of delivery cannot be successful, since,

> success depends on a comprehensive overview of needs being consistently and competently maintained and monitored and an efficient process of coordination carried out, within a structured and specialist organization.
>
> (Henley, 2005, p. 175)

He further argues,

> the nature of day service provision should be influenced by those who will be most affected by changing policies.
>
> (Henley, 2005, p. 175)

After all, surely those with real experience of the client group, have a better understanding of their specific needs? As will be seen in the next chapter care workers are rarely included in consultations yet they have such broad knowledge of the people they support. In focus group discussions these seldom heard workers, initially hesitant, were eventually really enjoying the lively debate grappling with difficult abstract concepts engendered.

Beyond social model informed frameworks

Shakespeare (2006) warns against the

> danger of ignoring the problematic reality of biological limitation.
>
> (p. 49)

Chappell et al. (2001) refer specifically to the difficulty the social model has with incorporating notions of intellectual impairment. Carlson (2010) has recently discussed the importance of narrative accounts by the families of people with PIMD, whose voice would otherwise not be heard in this arena. She has echoed the concerns of those who felt the parameters of the social model were too restrictive, in that it only truly represented the voices of a fairly small group of disabled activists. There was no analysis initially of congenital and/or degenerative conditions. There was a very strong opposition to the medical model, to the point where there was almost a denial of any need for medical interventions or restrictions.

Davis (2006) describes how newer researchers in the field of disability studies are now looking beyond notions of collective identity. He points to newer assertions around identity, which look at differences between impairments. The question now being asked is can one model truly represent the entire spectrum of impairments.

Shakespeare (2006) queries how it can be possible to create a barrier-free society for people with ID, or for those who are on the autistic spectrum or who have profound visual impairments? Or for someone who experiences all of these and more. Odyssey has nine significant diagnoses. How can it be possible to accommodate all of her impairments effects within a simplistic rights-based approach? The right to work, the right to own one's own home, the right to marry and have children are all synonymous with ideas about inclusion in a barrier-free society. However, this argument is based on a fairly restrictive view of society. Not everyone believes self-worth and identity only come from paid employment, marriage, children and a mortgage. There is no counterbalance to this and no recognition that for some people,

> those whose needs are profound, multiple or complex, paid employment will be an impossible aspiration
>
> (Johnsson et al., 2010, p. 78)

Whilst this new view of disability can be helpful in certain areas, this approach does nevertheless present some difficulties. There are those in the Disability Rights Movement (DRM) who have questioned the capacity of the model for accommodating the full, lived experience of disabled people. Pinder (1996) argues that separating impairment from disability necessarily misses out the complexity of individuals' lives. It could be argued, that it is this complexity that needs to be grappled with intellectually in attempting a social theoretical approach to understanding the issues involved in supporting people with PIMD. Indeed, Chappell (1998) has referred to this emerging discussion and its particular relevance to people with ID. She queries whether the limitations they experienced could be described as socially or impairment driven. She also suggests it would be helpful if writers were clear about their work, by stating if it was concerned with physical or sensory impairment or disability in general. Surely a scrupulous approach to language would also be helpful when discussing people with ID and PIMD in particular? This came up in discussion at the 2017 PAMIS International Conference in Dundee.[1] Belgian, Dutch and Austrian attendees all described their confusion over the seeming plethora of terms and descriptions in use in the UK for people with PIMD.

Essentially this book is seeking to understand the apparent lack of fit between the current philosophical framework underpinning government policy and the broad ranging and complex needs of individuals with PIMD. It contends that their lack of representation as a distinct group with distinct and particular needs has a negative impact on service delivery and the lived experience of this population.

The next chapter will analyse a small-scale study conducted in two London boroughs. This study incorporated film led focus group discussions with care workers. It sought to understand how embedded the Valuing People drivers of rights, independence, choice and inclusion, actually were in services for people with PIMD.

Note

1 https://pitl.org.uk/about-pamis/.

Bibliography

Abberley, P. (1987). 'The concept of oppression and the development of a social theory of disability.' *Disability, Handicap and Society*, Volume 2 (1), pp. 5–20. Taylor & Francis, London, UK.

Abberley, P. (1999). The Significance of Work for Disabled People. Paper presented at University College, Dublin Eire. www.disabilitystudies.leeds.ac.uk/author/abberley

Armstrong, D. (2002). 'The politics of self-advocacy and people with learning difficulties'. *Policy & Politics*, Volume 30 (3), pp. 333–345. Bristol University Press, Bristol, UK.

Aspis, S. (2004). 'Educating for equality.' *Planet Advocacy*, (online). Volume 10, pp. 18–19. Available from www.acting-up.org.uk/015.pdf

Barnes, C. (1994). *Disabled People in Britain and Discrimination: A Case for Antidiscrimination Legislation*. 2nd edition. Hurst and Co., London, UK.

Baxter, C., Ward, L., Poonia, K., and Nadirshaw, Z. (1990). *Double Discrimination: Issues and Services for People with Learning Difficulties from Black and Ethnic Minority Communities*. King's Fund Commission for Racial Equality, London, UK.

Bayley, M. (1991). 'Normalisation or social role valorization: an adequate philosophy?' in Baldwin, S. and Hattersley, J. (eds) *Mental Handicap: Social Science Perspectives*. pp. 82–106. Tavistock, Routledge, London, UK.

Beresford, P. (2000). 'What have madness and psychiatric system survivors got to do with disability and disability studies?'. *Disability & Society*, Volume 15 (1), pp. 167–172. Taylor & Francis, London, UK.

Bexley Learning Disability Service. (2002). 'Total communication strategy and standards.' London Borough of Bexley, London, UK.

Blunden, R., Corker, J., and Rice, J. (2000). *Let's Meet Let's Talk: Communicating with People with Learning Disabilities; a Handbook for Inspectors*. British Institute of Learning Disabilities, London, UK.

Bochel, C., Bochel, H., Somerville, P. & Worley, C. (2008). 'Marginalised or enabled voices? User participation in policy and practice.' *Social Policy & Society*, Volume 7 (2), pp. 201–210. University of Sheffield, Sheffield, UK.

Bogdan, R. and Taylor, S. (1982). *Inside Out: The Social Meaning of Mental Retardation*. University of Toronto Press, Toronto, Canada.

Bourdieu, P. (1998) 'The Left hand and the Right hand of the State' interview with R.P. Doit and T. Ferenczi. In *Acts of Resistance againsts the new Myths of Our Time*. Polity Press, Cambridge, England.

Bourdieu, P. (1998) in Duyvendak, J., Knijn, T., and Kremer, M. (eds) (2006) *Policy, People and the new Professional: De-professionalisation and Re-professionalisation in Care and Welfare.* Amsterdam University Press, Holland.

Boxhall, K. and Ralph, S. (2011). 'Research ethics committees and the benefits of involving people with profound and multiple learning disabilities in research.' *British Journal of Learning Disabilities,* Volume 39 (3), pp. 173–180. John Wiley and Sons, UK.

Brown, C. (1990). *My Left Foot.* Vintage, London, UK.

Brown, H. and Smith, H. (1989). 'Whose "ordinary life" is it anyway?' *Disability, Handicap and Society,* Volume 4 (2), pp. 105–119. Taylor & Francis, UK.

Bunning, K. (2009). 'Making sense of communication.' in Pawlyn, J. and Carnaby, S. (eds) *Profound Intellectual and Multiple Disabilities Nursing Complex Needs.* pp. 46–61. Wiley-Blackwell, Oxford, UK.

Burton, M. and Kagan, C. (2006). 'Decoding valuing people.' *Disability & Society,* Volume 21 (4), pp. 299–313. Taylor & Francis, London, UK.

Carlson, L. (2010). *The Faces of Intellectual Disability. Philosophical Reflections.* Indiana University Press, USA.

Carnaby, S. (2001). 'Editorial.' *Tizard Learning Disability Review,* Volume 6 (2), pp. 2–5. Emerald Publishing Limited, Bingley, UK.

Carnaby, S. (2004). *People with profound and multiple learning disabilities: A review of research about their lives.* Mencap Golden Lane, UK.

Carpenter, B. (2000). 'Sustaining the family. Meeting the needs of families of children with disabilities.' *British Journal of Special Education,* Volume 27 (3), pp. 135–144. Oxford, Blackwell, UK.

Chappell, A.L. (1997). 'From normalisation to where?' in Barton, L. & Oliver, M. (eds) *Disability Studies: Past Present and Future.* pp. 45–62. The Disability Press, Leeds, UK.

Chappell, A.L. (1998). 'Still out in the cold: people with learning disabilities and the social model of disability.' in Shakespeare, T. (ed) *The Disability Reader: Social Science Perspectives.* pp. 211–220 Cassell, London, UK.

Chappell, A.L., Goodley, D. and Lawthom, R. (2001). Making connections: the relevance of the social model of disability for people with learning difficulties. *British Journal of Learning Disabilities,* Volume 29 (2), pp. 45–50. John Wiley & Sons. Derby, UK.

Circles Network (2005) www.circlesnetwork.org.uk

Concannon, L. (2005). *Planning for Life involving Adults with Learning Disabilities in Service Planning.* Routledge, London, UK and New York, USA.

Cramp, S. (2003). *Valuing People – What's the Policy Worth?* CarePlan pp. 18–21 (no other details).

Crow, L. (1996). 'Including all our lives' in Morris, J. (ed) *Encounters with Strangers: Feminism and Disability.* pp. 1–21. Women's Press, London, UK.

Cumella, S. (2008). 'New public management and public services for people with an intellectual disability: a review of the implementation of valuing people in England.' *Journal of Policy and Practice in Intellectual Disabilities,* Volume 5 (3), pp. 178–186. Wiley-Blackwell, Oxford, UK.

Darwent, J. (2012). 'Quietly Confident.' Viewpoint. (online). May/June. Available from https://www.mencap.org.uk/sites/default/files/documents/ViewpointMayJun12.pdf

Davidson in Leyin, A. (2010). 'Learning disability classification: time for re-appraisal?' *Tizard Learning Disability Review,* Volume 15 (2), pp. 33–44. Emerald Publishing Limited, Bingley, UK.

Davis, L. (ed) (2006). *The Disability Studies Reader (2nd Ed.)*. Routledge, New York, USA and London, UK.

Department of Health. (2001). *Valuing People: A New Strategy for the 21st Century.* HMSO, London, UK.

Department of Health. (2002). *Independent Health Care: National Minimum Standards Regulations.* The Stationery Office, London UK. Available at: www.dh.gov.uk/en/Publicationsandstatistics/Publications/PublicationsPolicyAndGuidance/DH_4085259

Drake, R. (1990). *Understanding Disability Policies.* Macmillan, London, UK.

Dudley-Marling, C. (2004). 'The social construction of learning disabilities.' *Journal of Learning Disabilities,* Volume 37, pp. 482–489. Hammil Institute of Disabilities, Austin TX, USA.

Dykens, E.M., Hodapp, R.M., and Finucane, B.M. (2000). *Genetics and Mental Retardation Syndromes a New look at Behaviour and Interventions.* Brookes Publishing, Baltimore.

Emerson, E. (2004). Cluster housing for adults with intellectual disabilities. *Journal of Intellectual & Developmental Disability,* Volume 29 (3), pp. 187–197. Taylor and Francis, Milton Park, Oxfordshire, UK.

Ferguson, I. (2007). 'Increasing user choice or privatizing risk? The antinomies of personalization'. *British Journal of Social Work,* Volume 37 (3), pp. 387–403. Oxford Academic, Oxford, UK.

Finkelstein, V. (2001). 'A personal journey into disability politics'. (online). Available from http://www.independentliving.org/docs3/finkelstein01a.pdf

Finkelstein, V. (2004). 'Representing disability.' in Swain, J., French, S., Barnes, C., and Thomas, C. (eds) *Disabling Barriers – Enabling Environments.* 2nd edition. pp. 13–20. Sage, London, Thousand Oaks, New Delhi.

Firth, G., Berry, R., and Irvine, C. (2010). *Understanding Intensive Interaction Context and Concepts for professionals and Families.* Jessica Kingsley Publishers, London, UK and Philadelphia, USA.

French, S. and Swain, J. (2004). 'Whose tragedy? Towards a personal non-tragedy view of disability.' in Swain, J., French, S., Barnes, C., and Thomas, C. (eds) *Disabling Barriers – Enabling Environments.* 2nd edition. pp. 34–40. Sage, London, Thousand Oaks, New Delhi.

Goodley, D. (2004). 'Who is disabled? Exploring the scope of the social model of disability.' in Swain, J., French, S., Barnes, C., and Thomas, C. (eds) *Disabling Barriers – Enabling Environments.* 2nd edition. pp. 118–124. Sage, London, Thousand Oaks, New Delhi.

Goodley D.A. 2001. 'Learning Difficulties,' the Social Model of Disability and Impairment: Challenging Epistemologies'. *Disability and Society,* Volume 16 (2), pp. 207–231. Taylor & Francis, London, UK.

Goodley, D. and Rapley, M. (2001). 'How do you understand "learning difficulties"? Towards a social theory of impairment.' *Journal of Mental Retardation,* Volume 39, pp. 229–232. Wiley-Blackwell, Oxford, UK.

Goodley, D. (2011). *Disability Studies: An Interdisciplinary Introduction.* Sage Publishing, Los Angeles, London, New Delhi, Singapore, Washington DC.

Hall, S. (2001). 'Foucault: power, knowledge and discourse' in Wetherall, M., Taylor, S., and Yates, S.J. (eds). *Discourse Theory and Practice: A Reader.* p. 72. Sage Publishing, London, UK.

Hasler, F. (2003). *Philosophy of Independent Living.* Available from www.independen tliving.org/docs6/hasler2003.html

Henley, C. (2001). 'Good intentions-unpredictable consequences.' *Disability & Society,* Volume 16 (7), pp. 933-947. Taylor & Francis, London, UK.

Henley, C. (2005). *Learning Disabilities: The Rise and Potential Demise of Structured Day Services for Adults with Learning Disabilities, 1955–2005.* The Minster Press, Dorset, UK.

Hunt, P. (1966). 'A critical condition.' in Shakespeare, T. (ed) (1998). *The Disability Reader: Social Science Perspectives.* pp. 7–19. Cassell, London, UK and New York, USA.

Jay Committee. (1975). Report of the committee of inquiry into Mental Handicap Nursing and Care, Command 7468. HMSO, London, UK.

Johnsson, K., Walmsley, J. & Wolfe, M. (2010). *People with Intellectual Disabilities Towards A Good Life?* Policy Press, Bristol, UK.

Kittay, E. (1999). *Love's Labour: Essays on Women, Equality and Dependency.* Routledge, New York, USA.

Kristiansen, K., Vehmas, S., and Shakespeare, T. (eds) (2010). *Arguing about Disability Philosophical Perspectives.* Routledge, London, UK and New York, USA.

Lacey, P. (1998). 'Book Review: Creating a responsive environment for people with profound and multiple learning difficulties.' *Child Language Teaching and Therapy,* Volume 14 (1), pp. 112–113. Sage Publishing, Los Angeles, London, New Delhi, Singapore, Washington D.C.

Langness, L. and Levine, H. (eds) (1986). *Culture and Retardation Life Histories of Mildly Mentally Retarded Persons in American Society Culture, Illness and Healing.* Reidel Publishing Company, Dordrecht, Holland.

Lawton, A. (2009). *Personalisation and Learning Disabilities: A Review of Evidence on Advocacy and Its Practice for People with Learning Disabilities and High Support Needs.* Social Care Institute for Excellence, London, UK.

Leaman in Swain, J., French, S., Barnes, C., and Thomas, C. (eds) (2004). *Disabling Barriers – Enabling Environments.* 2nd edition. p. 14. Sage, London, Thousand Oaks, New Delhi.

Lyle, D. (2015). 'Policy to practice: A critical analysis of the valuing people strategy'. PhD Thesis. Available at www.http://eprints.mdx.ac.uk/15731/

Mansell, J. (2008). 'Learning disability policy and practice in the UK.' *Tizard Learning Disability Review,* Volume 13 (3), pp. 12–14. Emerald Publishing Ltd, Bingley, UK.

Mansell, J. (2010). 'Raising our sights: services for adults with profound intellectual and multiple disabilities.' *Tizard Learning Disability Review,* Volume 15 (3), pp. 5–12. Emerald Publishing Limited, Bingley, UK.

Mazumdar, P. (1992). *Eugenics, Human Genetics and Human Failings: The Eugenics Society, its Sources and its Critics in Britain.* Routledge, London, UK.

Mental Capacity Act. (2005). (online) Available from www.legislation.gov.uk/ukpga/ 2005/9/section/32

Mitchell, D. (2011). 'Editorial.' *British Journal of Learning Disabilities,* Volume 39 (1), p. 1. Wiley-Blackwell, Oxford, UK.

Morris, J. (1991). *Pride against Prejudice Transforming Attitudes to Disability.* The Women's Press, London, UK.

Morris, J. (1998). 'Feminism, gender and disability.' Text of a paper presented at a seminar in Sydney, Australia: February 1998). Available from http://citeseerx.ist. psu.edu/viewdoc/download?doi=10.1.1.563.4580&rep=rep1&type=pdf

Nirje, B. (1980). 'The normalization principle.' in Flynn, R. and Nitsch, K. (eds) *Normalization, Social Integration and Community Services.* pp. 17–35. University Park Press, Baltimore.

ODI: Office for Disability Issues. (2015). 'Creating a fairer and more equal society.' (online). Available from https://www.gov.uk/government/publications/2010-to-2015-government-policy-equality/2010-to-2015-government-policy-equality#appendix-9-the-social-model-of-disability

Oliver, M. (1990). *The Politics of Disablement.* MacMillan Publishing, London, UK.

Oliver, M. (2004). 'If I had a hammer: the social model in action' in Swain, J., French, S., Barnes, C., and Thomas, C. (eds) *Disabling Barriers – Enabling Environments.* pp. 7–12. Sage, London, Thousand Oaks, New Delhi.

PAMIS www.pa,mis.org.uk

Parsons, T. (1951). *The Social System.* Free Press, New York, USA.

Pawlyn, J. & Carnaby, S. (eds.) (2009) *Profound Intellectual and Multiple Disabilities Nursing Complex Needs.* Wiley-Blackwell, Oxford, UK.

People First (2011). (online). Availabe from www.peoplefirstltd.com

Pinder, R. (1996). 'Sick-but-fit or fit-but-sick? Ambiguity and identity in the workplace' in Barnes, C. & Mercer, G. (eds.) *Exploring the Divide: Illness and Disability.* pp. 135–156. The Disability Press, Leeds, UK.

PMLD Network. (2002). Valuing people with profound and multiple learning disabilities (PMLD). Available from https://thesendhub.co.uk/valuing-people-with-pmld/

Race, D. (ed) (2002). *Learning Disability – A Social Approach.* Routledge, London, UK and New York, USA.

Rapley, M. (2004). *The Social Construction of Intellectual Disability.* Cambridge University Press, Cambridge, UK.

Roberts, H., Turner, S., Baines, S., Hatton, C. (2012). *Advocacy by and for Adults with Learning Disabilities in England: Findings from Two Surveys and Three Detailed Case Studies.* Improving Health and Lives: Learning Disabilities Observatory. Centre for Learning Disabilities Research, Lancaster, UK.

Rutter, M., Simonoff, E. and Plomin, R. (1996). 'Genetic influences on mild mental retardation: Concepts, findings and research implications'. *Journal of Biosocial Science,* Volume 25, pp. 509–526. Cambridge University Press, Cambridge, UK.

Schadler, J., Rohrmann, A. and Schur, S. (2008). 'The specific risks of discrimination against persons in situations of major dependence or with complex needs.' *Research & Analysis Centre for Planning and Evaluation of Social Services* Volume 2. University of Siegen, Siegen, Germany.

Searle, J. (1995). *The Construction of Social Reality.* The Free Press, New York, USA.

Shakespeare, T. (2006). *Disability Rights and Wrongs.* Routledge, London, UK and New York, USA.

Sherborne, V. (2001). *Developmental Movement for Children Mainstream, Special Needs and Pre-School.* Worth Publishing, London, UK.

Sinson, C. (1990). *Micro-Institutionalisation? Environmental and Managerial Influences in Ten Living Units for People with Mental Handicap.* Joseph Rowntree Foundation, York, UK.

Social Services Inspectorate. (1998). *Quality Standards Assessment and Care Management.* HMSO, London, UK.

Stainton, T. (1994). *Autonomy and Social Policy: Rights, Mental Handicap and Community Care.* Ashgate Publishing, Aldershot, Avebury, UK.

Stevens, A. (2004). 'Closer to home: a critique of British government policy towards accommodating learning disabled people in their own homes.' *Critical Social Policy*, Volume 24 (2), pp. 233–254. Sage, UK.

Thomas, C. (2001). 'The body and society:impairment and disability'. Proceedings of the British Sociological Association Conference : reforumlating bodies. pp. 47–62. Macmillan, London, UK.

Thomas, C. (2004). 'Disability and impairment' in Swain, J., French, S., Barnes, C. and Thomas, C. (eds). *Disabling Barriers – Enabling Environments*. pp. 21–27. Sage Publishing, London, Thousand Oaks, New Delhi.

Thomas, C. (2007). *Sociologies of Disability and Illness Contested Ideas in Disability Studies and Medical Sociology*. Palgrave McMillan, Hampshire, UK and New York, USA.

Tremain, S. (2006). 'On the government of disability: Foucault, power and the subject of impairment.' in Davis, L. (ed) *The Disability Studies Reader*. 2nd edition. pp. 185–196. Routledge, New York, USA and London, UK.

Tuana, M. (2009). 'The speculum of ignorance: The women's health movement and epistemologies of ignorance.' https://doi.org/10.1111/j.1527-2001.2006.tb01110.x

UPIAS. (1975). in Finkelstein, V. and Davis, K. (1997). 'Union of the physically impaired against segregation and the disability alliance discuss fundamental principles of disability.' Being a summary of the discussion held on 22nd November 1975 and containing summaries from each organisation. (online). UPIAS, London, UK. Available from http://disabilitystudiessleeds.ac.uk/files/library/UPIAS-fundamental-principles.pdf

Ward, C. and Cooper, V. (2011). 'Valuing people now and people with complex needs.' *Learning Disability Review*, Volume 16 (2), pp. 39–43. Emerald Publishing Limited, UK.

Ward, L. (1992). 'Foreword.' in Brown, H. and Smith, H. (eds) *Normalisation: A Reader for the Nineties*. p. x. Routledge, London, UK.

Wechsler, D. (1981). *Manual for the Wechsler Adult Intelligence Scale—Revised*. Psychological Corporation, New York, USA.

Whitehead, S., Curtice, L., Beyer, S., Bogues, S. & Mc Conkey, R. (2008). 'Learning disability policy in the UK.' *Tizard Learning Disability Review*, Volume 13 (3), pp. 4–11. Emerald Publishing Ltd, Bingley, UK.

Williams, P. (2006). *Social Work with People with Learning Difficulties*. Learning Matters, Exeter, UK.

Wing, L. (1998). 'Understanding difference.' *Mental Health Care*, Volume 1 (10), pp. 4-8.

Wolfensberger, Wolf P., Nirje, Bengt, Olshansky, Simon, Perske, Robert, and Roos, Philip, (1972) *The Principle of Normalization In Human Services*. Books: Wolfensberger Collection. 1. https://digitalcommons.unmc.edu/wolf_books/1

Wolfensberger, W. (1983). 'Social role valorisation: a proposed new term for the principle of normalization.' *Mental Retardation*, Volume 21, pp. 234–239. Allen Press Inc., USA.

World Health Organisation. (1992). 'International classification of functioning, disability and health.' (online) Available from www.euro.who.int/en/health-topics/noncommunicabledisseases/mental-health/news/news/2010/15/childrens-right-to-family-life/definitionintellectual-disability

3 Disrupting the illusion

> if the constructivist methodologies are preoccupied with the restoration of the meaning of human experience, then critical methodologies are preoccupied with the reduction of illusions in the human experience.
>
> (Schwandt in Denzin and Lincoln, 2003, p. 193)

Introduction

Previous chapters examined the manner in which PIMD *per se* has been marginalised within accounts of disability. This has been ascribed to shifting terms, unclear definitions, the prevailing use of 'social model' approaches and a political unwillingness to acknowledge the notion of lifelong dependency. This chapter critically examines the misrepresentation and the lack of specific representation of people with PIMD within the current policy framework for people with ID in the UK. By adopting a critical realist stance, it is possible to identify and disrupt the 'illusions in the human experience' Schwandt (2003) discusses. If information about people with ID does not include some acknowledgement of those with PIMD, surely we have created an illusion of the ID experience? By locating that experience at the milder end of the spectrum it becomes easier to overlook more complex need. *'Valuing People: A New Strategy for Learning Disabilities in the 21st Century'* was published as a white paper by the Department of Health in 2001. The updated refresher document, *'Valuing People Now: a new three-year strategy for learning disabilities. Making it happen for everyone'* was subsequently published in 2009,

> to make the vision a reality.
>
> (DH, 2009, p. 7)

The illusion of the ID experience is here created by the Good News stories and the First Person narrative accounts, which are used extensively throughout the strategy. The illusion that, everyone can make choices about where they live, what work they do and who looks after them.

(DH, 2001, p. 24)

The emphasis is on increased autonomy and self-determination, which will ensure the right,

> to be as independent as they wish to be.

(p. 14)

The use of the word 'wish' is problematic for a discussion of people with PIMD, who are lifelong 'dependent' on care and support in all aspects of their lives. The writers of *Valuing People* are of course promoting a social model of disability approach to the idea of 'independence' here. The idea that being in control of making decisions about one's life is more important than is measuring one's ability to undertake self-care, for example (Reindal, 1999). Unfortunately, in her paper discussing this notion, Reindal refers to 'learning disabled,' with no acknowledgement of those people described thus.

> Children and adults with profound learning disability have extremely delayed intellectual and social functioning with little or no apparent understanding of verbal language and little or no apparent symbolic interaction with objects. They possess little or no ability to care for themselves. There is nearly always an associated medical factor such as neurological problems, physical dysfunction or pervasive developmental delay. In highly structured environments, with constant support and supervision and an individualised relationship with a carer, people with profound disabilities have the chance to engage with their world and to achieve optimum potential (which might mean even progress out of this classification as development proceeds). However, without structure and appropriate one-one support, such progress is unlikely.

(Samuel and Pritchard, 2001)

Whilst some writers and researchers are uncomfortable with discussing the idea of 'PIMD' in clinical terms, as some 'thing,' something discrete, I believe there is value to this. I often refer to the following quote, discussing the confusion over terminology for this group.

> If we do not know who we are talking about, how can we possibly know what the issues are?

(Samuel and Pritchard, 2001)

At the very least, it seems important to have some idea of the numbers. How else are people's needs be considered when services are commissioned? And how is it possible to provide person-centred support if we do not know the person? I believe we need to re-visit our understandings of 'dependency' (see for e.g. Kittay, 1999; Nussbaum, 2006) and find ways to respectfully acknowledge those people with PIMD who cannot 'speak up' for themselves and who often literally have no voice. This chapter listens to the people who know those with PIMD the best. Their families and care workers. These are the people who spend the most time with them, day-to-day. These are the people who have relationships with them, who attune to them over many years. These are the people who formally or informally make daily decisions on their behalf in their best interests. These are the people who can help readers to gain a deeper insight into the lived experience of this population.

As *Valuing People* (VP) has been in place for a number of years I was keen to explore the on-the-ground understandings of this policy and its impact. To do this I conducted a small-scale study in two London boroughs with family carers and formal care workers. This included interviews with families and film-led focus group discussions with care workers. I wanted to understand how embedded the *Valuing People* drivers of rights, independence, choice and inclusion, were in services for people with PIMD. To explore this, I decided to use film of a woman with PIMD to illustrate those drivers. First, I needed to thoroughly examine the original white paper via an initial critical discourse analysis (CDA). This examination of language, text and images revealed an overwhelming representation of the target population as self-advocating (Lyle, 2015, p. 112). There is scant reference to people with PIMD. Oddly there is a graph on p. 15 of the original document describing the prevalence of ID in the UK. It states,

'In the case of severe and profound learning disabilities ...' yet the graph only represents 'severe' and 'mild-to-moderate' learning disability (DH, 2001, p. 15).

There is a footnote explaining what these two definitions mean. Why exclude a definition for PIMD? Perhaps the authors really do believe people with PIMD simply need,

> significant help with daily living
>
> (DH, 2001, p. 15)

which is their own definition for 'severe learning disability.'

At a more fundamental level we will see from the discussions with care workers in this chapter how shifting the focus to all-encompassing statements, such as 'everyone can make choices,' is not helpful to their practice. The authors of the policy claim over ten thousand people responded to the initial consultation. The 137-page document is illustrated with many stories and direct quotes. It is hard to believe no one was representing people with PIMD. Where is their voice in the document? Who speaks for them? Unfortunately, the document clearly states in the preface,

> all the quotes are from people with learning disabilities
>
> (DH, 2001 p. 10)

There is a footnote explaining that

> family carers helped us to develop the new strategy
>
> (DH, 2001 p. 10)

yet there are no direct quotes from any family carers anywhere in the document. Not even in the chapter 'Supporting Carers' (pp. 53–57). The term is mentioned three times opposed to thirty-seven times in the refresh document *Valuing People Now* (DH, 2009) published eight years later. This suggests family carers were involved much more in the later consultation, but does not explain their absence from the original.

Schneider and Ingram (2003) discuss the manner in which policymakers employ a strategy of constituting group characteristics, which better fit the application of a particular policy. The reason being any differences or inherent paradoxes might well jeopardise the validity of the model (pp. 99–100). As they further point out this is also the reason for many policy failures. This strategy is still evident in *Valuing People Now* (VPN), which states, unequivocally that,

> All people with learning disabilities can speak up and be heard about what they want from their lives, the big decisions and the everyday choices
>
> (DH, 2009, p. 97)

Why could this not have simply said 'most' people? By implying there must be some who cannot 'speak up' it then becomes an inclusive statement.

Instead, across the entire document there seems confusion over what PIMD actually is and a reticence to acknowledge the specific needs and financial implications of those needs for this group of people. The document purports to be written from a social model of disability stance, which focuses on the removal of barriers. Surely the biggest barrier one could face would be one of invisibility?

Family carers

Interviews were conducted with family carers in order to explore the seeming mismatch between the formal policy discourse and the understandings of those who care for adults with PIMD. Interview questions were derived from analysis of the objectives in the original VP document. Fifteen family carers of adults with PIMD were interviewed in two areas of London. I was determined to include only families caring for someone with PIMD, so had to be scrupulous and of course sensitive when recruiting. People were often confused by the newish term High Support Needs (HSN). I would ask them how their son or daughter expressed themselves. If they replied along the lines of 'she speaks for herself' or if it transpired that they could travel on public transport alone, I would explain that I did not want to confuse the issue by having family speak for those who could speak up for themselves, albeit with support. For this reason, I had to disallow three family carers in the inner London (IL) borough and two in the outer London (OL) borough, despite their belief that their adult sons and daughters had High Support Needs. Equally one of the Day Centre managers told me they believed all people with an intellectual disability could be perceived as having complex needs. I tend to agree but many do not. I will return to this in the final chapter.

Concerns

The family carers I interviewed ranged from those who were very well informed to those who were resigned and overwhelmed by years of constant caring. The former actively lobbied by sitting on various Boards and subgroups concerned with ID and PIMD. The latter had actively withdrawn from participation. These families presented an almost siege-like mentality. One was even refusing any services or help. 'Tired of fighting' was an expression used by most of the families. This fatigue included the constant consultations they responded to with no discernible results, with families querying what they had achieved. Those carers in both boroughs who were active on their Learning Disability Partnership Boards (LDPB) believed they had achieved little. They reported that all decisions were taken at a higher level, where carers did not have a voice or a vote. A number of carers in the inner London borough described their constant input to the local Partnership Board as '*a waste of time.*' They questioned the role of the Board, believing it to be merely '*a talking shop,*' since no strategic decisions were made there. For this reason, they felt their influence was minimal.

Carers in both boroughs felt their views remained unheeded. Their responses were framed in replies suggesting their concerns were falling on deaf ears. There was a definite feeling that their constant lobbying was ineffectual.

They reported a reduction in services alongside a general feeling that existing services were not improving. Families believed this could be attributed to the use of generic agency workers. These workers were unskilled, especially when working with those people whose behavioural support needs are described as 'challenging.'

Carers in the outer London borough reported meetings with commissioners, who sat and listened, but did not make notes or keep any written record. These carers were trying to discuss their dismay at the move to the use of informalised, outsourced services and the extensive use of agency workers, but felt no one was paying heed to their concerns. A number of these carers reported a 'take it or leave it' attitude from their local authority (LA) when any service was queried.

Carers in the inner London borough expressed a concern with constantly changing personnel at senior commissioning levels. Each time someone new came into post they felt they had to start lobbying all over again to apprise the new personnel of the specific needs of those with PIMD. This concern was further borne out in the focus group discussions with care workers in the inner London borough.

An aspect of choice outlined by *Valuing People*, was choice of support. Even though staff at one of the inner London day centres (IL2) insisted all their service users had a choice of supporter, families in the same inner London borough reported lack of choice of service, support worker and transport escort. In the outer London borough families also reported lack of choice of provider and support worker. These findings alone demonstrate a significant lack of fit between VP's aims and the families' reported experience.

All families described their caring responsibilities in terms of 'battling' or 'fighting' for services.

There were a number of areas of disconnect with the critical discourse analysis (CDA) of *Valuing People* (VP). One of the families interviewed, explained that they had queried the exclusion of people with PIMD from the policy. Their LA had advised them that all of the objectives, promoting delivery of VP aims applied to all people with ID and this included those with PIMD. This seems a disingenuous explanation. As was demonstrated by the CDA (see Lyle, 2015 pp. 102–123) the various objectives were associated with the overall aim of mainstreaming services. There was no specific objective associated with the delivery of specialist services (p. 105). However, most of the families interviewed discussed their need for and the local lack of these specialist services. For example, families in both boroughs cited the historical lack of funding, recruiting and retaining of specialist physiotherapists. Families gave graphic examples of the physical problems that resulted from this glaring need. These included long-term loss of body-shape, severe spasticity, pressure sores and chronic respiratory illness.

In the outer London borough, the families who were lucky enough to have even one day's attendance allocated at the specialist Day Centre, could then access the specialist physiotherapy service, including their hydrotherapy pool. Unfortunately, the centre, which the manager explained had been purpose built for twenty-four people, was now oversubscribed with more than one hundred clients. This means that those new-to-adult services are being placed in the generic alternative. This is a much less formal, community-based service without the specialist therapeutic input available at the oversubscribed centre. Families felt they were being pressured to accept more informal and therefore unsuitable services. They were concerned their sons and daughters' needs were being overlooked and disregarded.

Valuing People's objective that mainstream health services ought to be available to all has not been realised for many with PIMD. Indeed, it cannot, since mainstream services do not cater to or offer more specialist services. A number of families confirmed this in interview. Families were also concerned that staff had no specific training in autistic spectrum disorder (ASD) issues. Their concerns were confirmed in the later focus group discussions with workers at one of the inner London Day Centres. (IL2)

Families in both boroughs reported a reduction in services and this was borne out in discussion at all three Day Centres. No one accessed a centre five days a week, as they used to. The average nowadays, being one to three days a week. Families interviewed in the outer London borough were mostly receiving the newer more informal services, provided by local care agencies. They reported less one-to-one provision in their care packages. These reductions inevitably meant some people were spending more time at home, thus increasing the caring responsibilities for already burnt-out families.

Families overall believed services were getting worse rather than improving.

There was a concern that agency workers and transport escorts were not trained to support people with intellectual disability (ID) let alone those with the more complex issues associated with PIMD. Even allowing plenty of time was impossible, as agency care workers were always rushing to their next appointment.

Considering most of the families interviewed provide between 40 and 167 hours of unpaid care, per seven-day week, it is not surprising that respite is so important to them. Unfortunately, the families reported that the vague wording of 'breaks' in *Valuing People* (DH, 2001 p. 19, 30, 48, 57) means local authorities can fulfil their requirement by simply renaming services. Hence attendance at a Day Centre may be described as a break for the carer rather than a service for the adult. In the inner London borough carer's meetings and coffee mornings are even described as 'carer's breaks' (even when carers have had to attend with their son or daughter due to having no support in place.) This borough also has an historical problem with local residential respite, which had been unavailable for well over fifteen years. The primary form of respite on offer in both boroughs was a home sitting service, whereby someone would come and sit with the individual, whilst carers went out for a couple of hours.

This again was evidenced in the CDA. One of the good news stories (DH, 2001 p. 55) clearly promoted this new style of respite, as being an improvement on residential respite. This type of informal service might well be appropriate for those with lower levels of need, looking for an alternative and flexible service. However, as families pointed out the idea of the individual having respite care provided in their home, presupposed the family carer(s) were well enough and had somewhere, or could afford to go somewhere for their own break. Further, a number of families described the positive side of residential respite for their son or daughter, as being one of opportunities for experiences outside the home. All fifteen families in both boroughs described their need for residential respite and all families either reported difficulties in accessing this, or a concern with the ad hoc nature of breaks provision. As they pointed out, it can take years for people with PIMD to build a relationship with supporters. They questioned how this was possible, if they were simply offered a few days break when and if there was a suitable opening.

VP discusses and promotes Carers Assessments, but family carers who had received one, described the benefits as negligible. Those interviewed in the outer London borough confirmed the assessments were only now being introduced, over fifteen years since publication of the Carers Recognition Act.

VP went to great lengths to describe,

> 'the lifelong commitment' carers make
>
> (DH, 2001, p. 53).

They are described as

> 'a crucial resource' due to the 'vital contribution they make,' which includes 'providing most of the support'
>
> (DH, 2001, p. 53)

and yet one very relevant piece of information was excluded and needs to be firmly reiterated – family carers of adults with PIMD do so **voluntarily.**

The statutory responsibility for those adults who lack the capacity to care for themselves lies with the state, not the family (see for e.g. Clements, 2012, pp. 37–38). Families in both boroughs believed they received less help because their LA's assumed they could depend on them to keep providing care. It must never be assumed that carers can or will provide care. Carers choose whether or not they will provide care and the level of support they are prepared to offer. The amount of caring they can and are willing to provide must be negotiated and regularly reviewed. Unfortunately, this was not the case for any of the families interviewed in either borough.

Families with younger children were 'bewildered by the lack of preparedness' for their transition to adult services. This was certainly borne out in the wider research document, 'From the Pond to the Sea.'[1] VP's focus for the transition years was on the delivery of education, training and employment and family carers believed this was evidence of the low priority people with PIMD had within the overall policy. They also felt it demonstrated their views, in consultation, were not heeded.

Another area of disconnect between VP's aims and family carers' experiences, was the approach known as personalisation (see Glasby, 2001, pp. 36–42). Person-centred approaches and the use of individual budgets (IB) were a key aim of this initiative, which was touted as the route to

> enabling individuals to have more control over their lives.
>
> (DH, 2001, p. 44)

Unfortunately, the LA's focus has been primarily on the use of IB's. Most families had been offered this option to manage their daughter or son's care. Only one family had embarked on this route, via a local provider. They recognised it was more work for them, but they were conflicted as to whether the outcome was positive for their daughter or not. Families overall felt they were being pressured into taking this option and were adamant they did not want to. IB's are seen as a way of empowering service users by drawing up their own support plans and recruiting and managing their own personal support workers. However, it is not surprising so few of the families interviewed have taken up this option. Whilst it may well be viable for someone with capacity, in the case of an individual with PIMD, the work yet again, falls to the family. And, of course, is unpaid. The family becomes the unpaid social worker and staff manager as well as default 'bank' care worker. It is no surprise that local authorities are enthusiastic about an approach that is clearly a cheaper option when taking this into consideration. (NB: see next chapter for my own account of ten years 'managing my daughter's budget,' which actually means recruiting, inducting, managing and developing a team of six workers for no pay and providing the care myself when they are not available). The examples quoted in VP tend to gloss over this family involvement, by simply stating,

> existing networks support the person receiving the direct payment'
>
> (DH, 2001, p. 48)

VP's examples also illustrated the shift to informalised services families interviewed had expressed concerns about. The first example discusses how,

> a man, living with his parents, receives a direct payment to employ a support worker from an agency for short breaks. Breaks can be a few hours in the evening and weekend or longer.
>
> (DH, 2001, p. 48)

It is unclear if there is anything else in this man's life, such as attendance at a Day Centre or access to continuing education or training for employment. Therefore, it suggests his family provides the bulk of his care and support. It also states that he employs a support worker, but this could mean his parents do the formal side of employing and managing the staff. Clements (2011) has noted,

> the disabled or older person (or perhaps more commonly his or her family carer) takes control.
>
> (Clements, 2011, p. 2)

The second example in VP states that this particular man,

> wanted to move on from the day service'
>
> (DH, 2001, p. 48)

However, the direct payments only help in accessing leisure facilities in the evening. So, what is he doing the rest of the time and who is providing the support? Is it solely his mother? Both these examples were provided by Hampshire Social Services to illustrate their new flexible direct payments scheme. It is unclear if the men provided the statements or if they had been a part of the consultation. Therefore, it must be assumed that this is further evidence of no people with PIMD being included in these illustrative narratives.

Another example is Susan. VP outlines the process by which her circle of support enabled her to live independently,

> with a rota of support workers'
>
> (DH, 2001, p. 50)

Is this a good news story about a woman with PIMD? Demonstrating she was unhappy with her existing care arrangement, by

> actions, facial expressions, verbal responses and moods
>
> (DH, 2001, p. 50)

conveys to the reader the profound nature of her ID. It is therefore confusing to read that,

> her expressions and views guide how the money is spent, so she is in control of the money.
>
> (DH, 2001, p. 50)

This may well make sense to people working closely with her. However, stretching the language to accommodate a discussion of her within this framework feels deeply problematic. To present her story in this manner, to a policymaker or commissioner, or to someone who is not acquainted with her, is highly disingenuous. It lays claims to capacity she clearly does not have. How can this be described as a person-centred approach? Surely it is denial not acknowledgment? Is she really in control or are the financial decisions, ultimately made by her circle of support, based on their combined assumptions about her?

Finally, David's story is an example of an individual becoming known to services, after the death of his mother. He inherited the lease on the bungalow, so rather than being moved somewhere else, the LA was able to provide the personalised care package and his life was not further disrupted. Of course, the inclusion of a reference to his siblings living nearby and providing

> emotional and practical support.
>
> (DH, 2001, p. 70)

hints that the arrangement would not be possible without them. The fact that he is also receiving

> some intensive support ...... to improve his cooking and domestic skills.
>
> (DH, 2001, p. 70)

demonstrates the man is unlikely to have PIMD.

It was also reported by all Day Centre managers that they had stopped running carers groups due to a lack of interest. This may reflect the older profile of some family carers and the fulltime employment status of others. Or there could be a myriad of other reasons. The Princes Royal Trust published a guide for consulting with carers (Keeley and Clarke, 1999) in which they discuss 'harder to reach' carers (p. 26) in a physical, rural context. Carers in cities may also be 'hard to reach,' due to their aforementioned consultation fatigue.

Family carers, some of whom had been caring for up to fifty years, felt no one was listening or responding.

> One of those commissioners came to one of our meetings and we all told him about our experiences. He sat and listened, but he didn't write anything down. So what was the point?
>
> (Lyle, 2015, ND:O)

They also queried what power they had, if any.

> They said they're going to re-organise the Partnership Boards so we can have more influence. I'm not really sure what that means. We can say all we like but is that really influence?
>
> (NN:O)

As noted, families were concerned about constantly changing senior posts in their Adult Care Services department. As they saw it, people would come into post for a relatively short time, set certain strategies in motion, but not oversee them to completion. The carers felt each new person arrived in post with their own agenda. This meant they would start off on some strategy or project with no reference to what had previously taken place.

> It's always about what they're going to do. It's all what M is going to do somewhere in the future. All these new people. Every meeting there is some new senior person. They all come down and talk about what they are going to do. As soon as I hear that now, I just switch off. Oh he's another 'going to' man.
>
> (GH:I)

Many of the carers interviewed had attended their local Learning Disability Partnership Boards regularly. These boards were the mechanism for rolling out the *Valuing People* agenda. With the onset of the 'austerity agenda,' first with the Coalition government (2010–2015) and then further rolled out by the later Conservative government (2015–current), some local authorities have disbanded these Boards. The inner London borough have done this, the outer London borough has retained its Board. The inner London borough claims the newer assembly model they have introduced empowers people but could not explain how. There is no perceptible mechanism for attendees to influence any decision making which affects them. Nor is there any formal link to the Health & Wellbeing Board for example. It is unclear if this is the re-organisation referred to by a parent in the study. Tellingly families interviewed were not asked any specific questions about cost or cost cutting, but they all brought it up.

I think it's, well you've seen it here, they don't want to acknowledge our lot, cos they're too much in terms of cost. You saw it on that last form. They used a picture of people with PMLD and said that was why they hadn't made bigger savings, cos this lot were expensive to support. They don't fit the bill. All that getting a job and into the community malarkey, that don't work for our lot.

(WD:I)

Rob Grieg (author of *Valuing People*) was adamant it wasn't about saving money. However, if you point out to LA's as he did, that there is a potential to save money, then they will adopt the strategy to save money.

(NX:I)

By insisting on everyone moving to the community, there is a massive saving straight away. No need for day centre staff or transport. Library seems to be the answer for everything. They say we are going to have a Carers Centre in the library that the bases Jim Mansell talked about, are going to be in the library. Of course, the library isn't built yet.

(EP:I)

There may have been some well meaning people feeding information into to the department, in the consultation phase, but the overarching plan was always about cost cutting. Say getting a life, or whatever it is they say. For most people with a learning disability that means moving into the community, away from the day centre or into supported living, away from residential. Both are cheaper options.

(DX:I)

I'd say Valuing People is an ineffective policy, an excuse for cutting services. See all them the pen pushers, the budget men. They don't want to spend the money. They spend it all on these new name, ah 'modernisation,' but it was all just to cut services. That's what it looks like to me.

(TD:I)

Care workers

After contacting three Day Centres across London, it was agreed with the managers that I would hold film led focus group discussions with the staff in their usual training slot. This meant I was able to include all thirty-four care workers and not compromise staff cover in any way. As previously noted I had devised a set of questions, after analysing the Valuing People documents. These were based on the stated Objectives therein. These objectives were described as two-tier and based on better outcomes for people and better systems for delivering said outcomes. The eleven objectives were based on the key principles of rights, independence, choice and inclusion. The questions were intended as prompts to draw out the workers' understandings and experiences of the policy and of more general attitudes and beliefs about the nature of PIMD.

Film elicited focus groups

I have long believed there is much use to be made of film with regard to consultations, for raising awareness and enabling inclusive participation by people with PIMD. I used the techniques of photo elicitation with filmed excerpts. In this way the images shown are used to stimulate discussion (e.g.). Images, which have significance for the interviewees, are shown to the group with the aim of,

> exploring participants beliefs, attitudes and meanings.
>
> (Prosser, 1998, p. 124)

Further, the film provided a platform for the care workers to demonstrate their observational and analytical skills. In a sense the object of the film became a palette for their projections and reflections. The film itself is not analysed, it is the manner in which the participants respond to it. In particular the meanings they attribute to the actions of the individual. It was anticipated the viewing of the film would generate responses and insights that interviews could not.

Pink (in Seale et al., 2004) discusses the use of video as a prompt or topic for discussion in focus groups and describes the manner in which the elicitation creates a space for personal interpretations. Lapenta (in Margolis and Pauwels, 2011) notes it can also be seen as collaboration between the researcher and participants as the meaning of images is explored in conversation. Harper (1998) describes the use of an image introduced in an interview setting as one, which elicits a deeper response and different information. This is because older parts of the brain are engaged to process visual images and entirely different parts to process visual rather than textual information. A viewing of the film, which comprises short clips, filmed in real time on a number of different occasions, prefaced all the focus group discussions. I believe this is an excellent way to include people with PIMD in consultations, either at policymaking level or locally, by including film of individuals in the ongoing training and development of their support team.

Being part of a group discussion can be most valuable, especially when a group might include various stakeholders with differing agendas.

> ... discussing collectively their sphere of life and probing into it as they meet one another's disagreements, will do more to life the veils covering the sphere of life than any other device I know of.
>
> (Blumer, 2010, p. 41)

I used film clips of my daughter, although, these were filmed by her care worker for added objectivity. The worker filmed short moments she believed demonstrated the core principles of *Valuing People*. The film was played with no information given beforehand about its content. The first excerpt shows Odyssey inside our flat, demonstrating certain skills that could be associated with 'independence.' These skills have taken four years to develop and have involved constant 1:1 support and constant staff development. Her care plan is entitled TIME and the film clearly demonstrates why. As an example, walking with the aid of her indoor cane, approximately six feet, from the living room to the toilet, with audio and vocal prompting, takes almost two minutes. Carrying a plate and later a cup and following audio and vocal cues, covering a distance of ten feet, takes some three minutes. Neither task is actually completed.

The reason for including these clips was to prompt discussion about notions of agency, training issues and additional support issues. These are all highlighted in *Valuing People* (DH, 2001, p. 7, 14, 23, 44 and 90 and *Valuing People Now* (DH, 2009, p. 9, 10 and 116). It was anticipated workers would respond with thoughts on pockets of independent action or potential for independence islets, in spite of Odyssey's over riding state of dependence. In fact, the workers focused their discussion on the health and safety issues they perceived, the degree of prompting the individual needed and the time it took her to (almost) complete the task. Similarly, a clip showing her attempts to follow auditory and vocal cues to complete a task (flicking a switch on the kettle) had the same response. The day centre workers all focused their concerns on health and safety issues. Considering this occurred at all three sites, it suggests a reluctance to explore 'creative risk taking.' The clip used to portray 'choice' was included in order to demonstrate her lack of capacity to respond to a verbal offer. Odyssey has extremely limited functional language. She possibly understands four to ten words. Although everyone appeared to be listening and concentrating on the film, only one person out of thirty-four over three sites observed,

> this individual doesn't understand words.
>
> (Lyle, 2015, p. 163)

She noted that Odyssey's support worker had asked if she wanted to 'take the lid off' the container she was holding. In response Odyssey had handed the worker her cane. This clip was referred back to a number of times throughout the discussion, especially when trying to hone in on the care workers' understanding of capacity to make levels of choices. For example, accept or reject, either/or, multiple choice of object, open-ended choice and right up the scale to choosing who to vote for.

A longer clip, just over ten minutes, shows Odyssey 'accessing the community.' This notion is a key concept of the *Valuing People* strategy. This particular outdoor sequence was included with the knowledge the outings can be a stressful experience for Odyssey, at times. She is filmed negotiating a walkway with support and later seated in the public area of a local arts organisation. I anticipated this would open out the discussion with regard to accessing the community. I assumed people would discuss the benefits and the barriers people face and whether people thought intellectual and neurological barriers could be overcome. Instead most of the responses were focused on Odyssey's face tapping. This particular clip was filmed at close range, which did make the tapping obvious. Most people with PIMD engage in some kind of sensory-based self-stimulatory behaviour, which can perseverate and indeed escalate into self-injurious behaviour. When this occurs with Odyssey there are various methods we adopt to provide alternative stimulation.

Unfortunately, the workers appeared to understand all self-injurious behaviour as a choice.

> Oh you mean like R. He always bangs his head on the wall. I used to worry about it, but then they told me it was stimulating him. So now I know its his choice.
>
> (SM:IL2)

When I agreed he was getting some sensory feedback, but was not sure how anyone could have meant it was okay for him to do it, I was told,

> See, we don't know it, but for some of our service users, they feel things differently to you or I.
>
> (SM:IL1)

Concerns

Mostly the workers had little knowledge of the Valuing People policy, which was not unexpected. Care work is seen as relatively unskilled work in the UK. Qualifications such as the (now defunct) NVQ level 2, as described in *Valuing People* (DH, 2001, p. 98) do not cover ID or PIMD specifically. In fact, as of 2018 the availability of PIMD specific training is fairly scant. The newer (although now also defunct) Learning Disability Award Frameworks (LDAF) were described by a senior very experienced worker at the outer London (OL) day centre as 'mind numbingly boring.'

Terminology was seen as ever-changing. Workers at both inner London (IL) centres had even stopped mid-sentence to change the word 'disability' to 'difficulties.' Oddly they still used 'disability' when referring to physical impairment. They had been told the old terminology was 'no longer appropriate' but could give no further explanation.

All the care workers at all three sites expressed concerns about how safe it was for my daughter to be carrying a plate or a cup. But they also all stated they would not have the time for her to carry out the tasks she was filmed attempting. The OL centre pointed out she needed constant one-to-one support, which they could not provide.

The idea of offering choice is certainly embedded, but most workers understandings of levels of choice-making were no more than superficial. For example, staff at the IL1 centre offered open-ended options, 'what do you want to do' to someone who did not have verbal language skills or capacity to respond. The staff at the IL2 centre described how they measured changes in body temperature to ascertain if somebody wanted to go out or not. These workers had very muddled ideas about the concept of choice. Their overall understandings of the four concepts of rights, independence, choice and inclusion were negligible.

There was however a very lively discussion at the IL1 centre around ideas of choice.

> We offer them choice but their development doesn't enable them to make clear-cut choices. Like do they really understand we are offering them a choice?
>
> (Lyle, 2015, p. 170)

A longer exchange centred on a woman who had been referred to the Behaviour Support Team. They had suggested offering her more choice in her day. The staff had been offering open-ended choices, but believed the change in her behaviour was due to

> 'the 1:1 not the specifics of choice' (p. 172), meaning the additional directed support she was receiving, rather than the actual choices she was offered.

The workers at IL2 were keen to stress they

> put the service user at the centre of the service,

yet could not accommodate supporting an individual to carry her plate from the table to the kitchen hatch.

> We don't have the time for that.
>
> (Lyle, 2015, p. 172)

Considering this task took less than five minutes in the film, there was clearly something else at work here. This will be discussed in more length in the next chapter. I believe the issue of 'time' is key to a truly person-centred service, as is an understanding of the difference between doing something 'to' someone or doing it 'with' them.

Just as family carers in both London boroughs had raised concerns about the lack of preparedness for transition to adult services, so did the care workers. They described the manner in which new clients arrived.

> Transition is still diabolical. They come with nothing there is no follow on. It's not like six weeks before they start, no there's no gradual getting used to it. No coming with all their paperwork. Parents are lost as they are just told that there is no service.
>
> (p. 195)

The care workers also perceived a lack of preparation for the implications of the new policy. They felt they had to deal with on the ground reactions. One worker opined wryly,

> It's a pity they didn't tell the community we were coming.
>
> (Lyle, 2015 p. 179)

Overview of valuing people

By understanding how people with PIMD are situated within current policy or not, it is possible to examine how that policy then impacts on their lives. It is also necessary to understand this policy was introduced during a particular economic and political climate. Following Margaret Thatcher's neo-liberal reappraisal of the Welfare State (see Hall, in Rutherford and Davison, 2012), on election Tony Blair introduced his 'New contract for welfare. New ambitions for our country' (DSS, 1998a). His new contract set out a third age for welfare policy in the UK. Blair described the first age as defined by the Elizabethan Poor Law (Concannon, 2005, p. 5). This was concerned with alleviating destitution amongst the deserving poor. The second age focused on alleviating poverty via insurance-based, cash benefit systems. His new third age was to be defined by welfare reformation: the basis of which would be a contract between the citizen and the state. This contract would involve the promotion of opportunities and empowerment, rather than dependency on state benefits. The rhetoric of Third Way policy was primarily concerned with moving from the old idea of a passive recipient of welfare benefits to the active citizenship of paid employment. Seizing the newly available opportunities for education and training would enable individuals to attain the goal of paid employment. This centrality of work to the new welfare policy leaves one in no doubt. The citizen has rights, to be conferred by the state and in recognition the active citizen must take individual responsibility and participate in the labour market (Powell, 1999). In this new welfare state the citizen has a moral responsibility to work. As the government paper *Valuing Employment Now* states (DH, 2009)

> ...... all people with learning disabilities **can and should** work.
>
> (DH, 2009, p. 2)

Valuing People was nested within this wider overarching strategy of welfare reform. Ruth Lister argues that by replacing the term social security, which ensured security through social means with means tested financial support for people of working age New Labour adopted the American style of social assistance. Changing the name of the Department of Social Security to the Department for Work and Pensions confirmed this ideological shift. Unfortunately, by focusing on employment as the route to well-being, those who cannot are overlooked and somehow aligned with the enduring discourse of the feckless and workshy poor underclass. The Conservative chancellor George Osbourne promoted this discourse when his party took power. He hardened the softer third way approach to one of 'austerity,' but the essential concern was still that citizens had a responsibility to work. He gave interviews, where he asked,

> Where is the fairness, we ask, for the shift-worker, leaving home in the dark hours of the early morning, who looks up at the closed blinds of their next door neighbour sleeping off a life on benefits?
>
> (Osbourne, 2012)

I worked for the Care Quality Commission for a number of years and will discuss this more in chapters five and six. Here though, I wanted to highlight how distressing Mr Osbourne's pronouncements were to one particular woman I met. This woman is in her late fifties. She has spent most of her life in long-stay institutions and now lives in a residential home with a number of other people in a suburb of London. She has mental health diagnoses and an intellectual impairment. I was able to hold a conversation with her. She has a manner of stringing lots of words together, which may or may not be descriptions of hallucinations, dreams, items she had heard on the television or abuse shouted at her in the street. I was trying to piece them all together during our interview. To hear this vulnerable woman quietly stream off a litany of negative experiences and interactions, quite clearly based on Mr Osbourne's speech[2] was heart breaking.

> I'm not sleeping all day. My curtains weren't closed at 11.00. I'm not sleeping on benefits.
>
> (Resident P)

Had locals yelled this at her in the street? Had she heard the speech on television? The manager of the home had told me there had been problems with locals not being particularly welcoming of their new neighbours. She was now frightened to leave the house on her own, even though previously she had been attending at least two local groups that met in a café and at a drop-in centre.

No one is arguing against the idea that people with ID ought to be supported into paid employment where appropriate. Families (myself included) simply query how this idea can extend to all of those with PIMD? Over many years of researching paid employment of people with PIMD I have found one individual who has been involved in occasional co-productive projects.

A recent article in PMLD Link magazine, referred to the NHS,

> …. successfully employing people with all levels of learning disability.
>
> (Slowie and Hebron, 2016)

I eagerly attempted to follow this up, but yet again, enquiries were fruitless. I struggle with the notion of 'employment,' as a concept, if the individual does not have cognisance of the concept and especially if they are not paid. I struggle even more with articles paying lip service to ideas of inclusion framed within an employment discourse. A specialist physiotherapist writing for PMLD Link journal describes the motivation for her team's work thus.

> The driver for all our work with this client group is that we value them for being themselves, not for what they can do, not for what we wish they could do, not for what society thinks they should do.
>
> (Cook, 2016)

I know a number of people with PIMD who love being taken to new and different places all the time. They enjoy the stimulation of new sounds and sights and interacting with new faces. Why can we not simply acknowledge this? Why must we impose our normative assumptions on to ideas of shared activities and rename this 'employment'? No one could argue that the parents interviewed for this study, were not ambitious for their daughters and sons. However, the family carers had a keen grasp of the day-to-day practicalities they struggled with.

Not being funny, but what opportunities are they talking about? The day centre a couple of days a week and that's it. And you know he didn't even go there most of last year, well over nine months, cos they hadn't got his wheelchair sorted. Nothing happens unless you lose your rag. It's all bullshit.

(Lyle, 2015, UF:I)

He used to go to that day centre five days a week and now it's only one. The rest of the week it's supposed to be this new community life. But he does nothing. He goes nowhere. They just don't take him out. They tell me nothing. I've had him home for the last two months because of all this business with social services.

(GH:I)

What care plan? He does nothing. He doesn't go out. He sits in his wheelchair or they put him in another chair. He sits there all day in front of the television

(BL:O)

You know we had one (trainer) the other day. I know she had no idea about our service users. I sat there as she waffled on about getting into work. It was just so inappropriate. I was thinking, you know what, this probably cost a lot of money. We just had our budget cut and I was thinking the money spent on her could have provided some really lovely outings for our service users.

(Day Centre care worker, OL)

Whilst the numbers of people with PIMD are relatively low, estimated at 78 per 250,000 (Emerson, 2009) this factor seems to work against them when it comes to service planning. All fifteen families interviewed believed their concerns about lack of specialist services and support remained unheeded.

Could it be that a policy based on self-empowerment and independence does not adequately accommodate issues associated with lifelong dependency and a lack of mental capacity to self-advocate?

The new vision: rights, independence, choice and inclusion

People with learning disabilities have been saying for a long time we can speak up for ourselves

(DH, 2001, p. 24)

All this can be done by believing people with learning disabilities can move on and be independent

(DH, 2001, p. 24)

These are the quotes used to illustrate the four key principles of *Valuing People*. The policy writers could have included a small section discussing the implications of the new vision for people with PIMD. The fact they did not suggests an unwillingness to acknowledge the difficulties the framework poses for those who are wholly and lifelong dependent. Indeed, *Valuing People Now* (DH, 2009) specifically argues that to assume people cannot live independently and achieve full employment,

> sets a ceiling on what progress can be made by individuals and by society
>
> (p. 32)

The next paragraph does include a more conditional statement,

> For some people such as those with profound and multiple learning disabilities paid employment poses particular challenges, **although it remains an aspiration**.
>
> (p. 32, Author's bold)

One might reasonably ask, whose aspiration? Are we really meant to believe people with profound levels of intellectual impairment harbour aspirations to employment?

> They say they are preparing my son for the world of work. He's never going to work. I know that. They know that. With all the best will I the world, it's just not going to happen.
>
> (TD:I)

My own daughter, Odyssey has been consistently assessed as having a developmental age of approximately 18–20 months. These assessments have been conducted at various stages of her life, in different countries and by various educational and clinical psychologists. Having spent the last 40 or so years in her mercurial yet delightful company I have no reason to doubt these assessments. Of course, I do not treat her 'like a child.' She is far from infantilised. I only bring it up in relation to the idea that she may harbour an aspiration to employment. The dictionary tells us 'aspiration' is the 'strong desire to achieve an end, an ambition.' My daughter is over forty years old now. I think the strongest desire I have seen her express, is a desire to avoid. (The next chapter recounts her inspiring journey, detailing her progression from 'withdrawal' to 'initiating' contact and her 'use your hands' retreat from tactile defensiveness.) Unfortunately, the use of language, which over ascribes capacity to our sons and daughters, leads families to question if policy writers have ever met someone with PIMD.

> Do you really think that lot who wrote *Valuing People* have ever met someone like my J? Maybe they think Learning Disability is just like,

yeah Downs. And maybe they are people who can be independent, but not ours. That's never gonna happen.

UF:I)

Another family carer summed up her feelings,

Same old same old as far as I can tell. Just all these new buzzwords, innit? Well H ain't never gonna be independent, she can't make choices, she don't have control of her body or you know her bladder, her bowels, never mind her life and as far as I'm concerned she has the same rights as you and me.

(SF:I)

Rights

The key principle of legal and civil rights is addressed on p. 23 of the original *Valuing People* (2001) document. The section discusses the right to

a decent education, to grow up to vote, to marry and have a family, to express opinions, with help and support to do so where necessary.

(DH, 2001, p. 230)

Unfortunately, none of this has particular relevance for a person with PIMD. With all the support in the world, my daughter will never learn to read, write or spell. But within the context of her intellectual capacity she can learn. Rather than 'decent education,' what about 'lifelong learning opportunities'? This would be far more meaningful and appropriate for learners who may not be ready to engage in learning until they have traversed the tumultuous journey to adulthood. Why do we have a cut-off point of twenty-five years? What do policymakers and commissioners assume people do for the rest of their lives?

And just how does an individual with PIMD choose which political party to support, or engage in a sexual relationship and have children? Or indeed form opinions? Parents interviewed bluntly asked me, how many two-year-olds I know who have a job, live independently, vote and are married with children. Framed like this the statement does appear ludicrous and far from inclusive.

Valuing People Now (DH, 2009) emphasises a human rights-based approach (p. 8) and notes that

people with learning disabilities and their families have the same human rights as everybody else.

(p. 16)

This was in response to the report '*A Life Like Any Other?*' (JCHR, 2008, p. 8) The main concern raised by the Joint Committee on Human

ceased. With the newer Health and Well-being Boards Nind and Sheehy's (2005) article is a timely discussion. 'Emotional well-being for all: mental health and people with profound and multiple learning disabilities,' describes the factors, which particularly affect people with PIMD

> .... an historical failure to acknowledge their human status; deficit-based services, a lack of voice and communication barriers. Whilst these factors are of importance to all people with learning disabilities, evidence is presented that those with profound and multiple learning disabilities are the most likely to experience challenges to their mental health and the least likely to receive appropriate support. A strategy for developing our understanding and good practice in the area is suggested. This prioritises areas for future work and suggests that a collaborative approach is most likely to yield positive outcomes for these individuals.
>
> (p. 34)

Independence

The principle of independence is illustrated by the quote,

> All this can be done by believing people with learning disabilities can move on and be independent.
>
> (DH, 2001 24)

'Move on' from where is the first question? It's hard not to surmise the use of language appears to be designed to fit the policy storyline. After all, by simply inserting the word 'many,' this statement would have been inclusive. The use of the all-encompassing description 'people,' means those with enduring high support needs are excluded. Insisting that everyone is equal and has the same hopes, dreams, wishes and aspirations denies their intellectual diversity. Was this an oversight or deliberate? Oversight confirms what families tell us that they feel PIMD is overlooked. Deliberate in wish fulfilling manner is not helpful. Surely it smacks of the triumph over tragedy model that the social model proponents were eager to see an end of? Why must people have talents?

And again, the use of statements such as,

> .... *The starting presumption should be a state of independence*
>
> (DH, 2001, p. 23)

are deeply problematic for people with PIMD. Focus group discussions with care workers in London day centres (Lyle, 2015) suggested such ideas were being incorporated into their practice but with a negative impact for some. For example, when I tried to veer the subject towards ideas of rights for service users, one worker stated,

> you have the right to privacy, so we shut the door when he goes to the toilet
>
> (SM:I)

I remembered a number of family carers had raised concerns about personal care and asked how that was managed.

> Well we encourage the SU to be independent so they do it themselves.
>
> (SM:I)

I asked about those who cannot manage and was told,

> We change their nappy for them.
>
> (SM:I)

I then asked very specifically, as I knew families with sons and daughters who could be taken to the toilet, but who could not manage their own personal care.

> I'm still trying to focus on the personal care for someone who can use a toilet but cannot wipe themselves.
>
> (SM:I)

The worker replied,

> No no they can do it. They can do it by themselves.
>
> (SM:I)

This directly contradicts families interviewed. These workers were not being uncaring, but they clearly believed

> the starting presumption should be a state of independence.
>
> (SM:I)

Unfortunately, it appears they are confusing 'presumption' with 'assumption.' This impacted on their communication with some families.

> One of the workers told me I am too overprotective. She said M would be married by now if I hadn't tied him to my apron strings. She said they had just been to training in independence.
>
> (GH:I)

The 'independence' discourse tends to portray all people with ID as being less impaired. In fact, *Valuing People*'s representation of people with ID does not tally with its own figures (p. 17). Most LA's nowadays only provide services to people describes as having a substantial or critical need. As *Valuing People* clearly states,

> many people with learning disabilities need additional support and services throughout their lives.
>
> (DH, 2001 p. 18)

Yes, as a day centre manager pointed out 'All people with LD have complex support needs.' Complex support needs are not necessarily the same as complex health needs. However, people with PIMD do not simply need 'more life opportunities,' although that is certainly a concern parents have raised. The reality is, these people need highly specialised input, for their health care, for structured and consistent support and for lifelong meaningful and learning activities. Pawlyn and Carnaby (2009) describe this as

> meeting complex needs through complex means.
>
> (p. 348)

By ignoring this complexity, the approach becomes less formalised and more reliant on informal (i.e unpaid) support from family, friends and volunteers. Vague ideas directed towards 'training for employment' or voluntary work, do not best serve people with PIMD.

Choice

The paragraph in *Valuing People* discussing 'choice,' explicitly states;

> this includes people with severe and profound disabilities, who, with the right help and support, can make important choices and express preferences about their day-to-day lives
>
> (DH, 2001, p. 24)

One family interviewed was deeply concerned at the way this concept was interpreted by health practitioners.

> He wouldn't let them do the blood tests and they said it was his choice.
> Then later he wouldn't take the medication and they said the same thing about it being his choice. So I asked them, when do they or where is the point that they take over? If my son won't swallow his medication and he needs it for his health, when are they obliged to do something? They couldn't answer me
>
> (NN:O)

A number of families were concerned at the way staff constantly offered open ended options to those who were non-verbal, and therefore could not respond anyway. Four of the five parents interviewed in the outer London borough had a family member with PIMD, which included autism, a physical/sensory impairment and additional health issue, most commonly epilepsy. These people are frequently referred to simply as having 'a severe learning disability.' Surely this vague description must make it difficult for those care workers who support them?

> what you have to understand is they have this, the severe learning disability, they can't speak and they have this autism as well. It's really frustrating and confusing for them if you keep firing questions. I've seen the workers sometimes and they're all 'how are you today,' 'what do you want to do now,' 'where shall we go.' On and on. No wonder he lashes out. He just wants them to shut up.
>
> (NN:O)

This particular family felt their son had fallen through the net. There are two specialist day centres in the borough, but they are now extremely oversubscribed. Those who do not have a place, especially those young people coming through transition, now have to attend the third centre. The parents are concerned at the informality and 'holding centre' style.

> It's not all mild there you know. There are some like mine, with the autism and all the behaviours and such. Then there are others with very severe and complex health needs. Services seem to think if they go there they are more able, but many have just fallen through the net.
>
> (NN:O)

Families overall and the care workers (particularly at the outer London day Centre) adopted a more realist stance. This is the view that something (in this case PIMD) exists independently of being perceived.

The families made statements such as

> you can't change biology or whatever it is
>
> (SB:I, p. 128)

or

> ... H ain't never gonna be independent, she can't make choices, she don't have control of her body, or you know her bladder, never mind her life.
>
> (SF:I, p. 137)

This stance chimes with the ideas of Vehmas and Makela (2010) and Kittay (in Carlsson, 2010), which were discussed earlier. Families described expressions of choice being made through body language and behaviour, but importantly they felt staff often ignored or misunderstood these cues. They referred to minute pockets of autonomy and as demonstrated in the film elicitation, believed these meaningful, albeit contextually dependent choices were overshadowed by bigger less meaningful ideas. These views and concerns were at odds with VP's contention that everyone can make choices. As will be seen, it appears staff at the inner London Day Centres are under instruction to offer 'choice,' with no real insight into what this means for people with PIMD. When pressed these workers could give no examples of individuals with PIMD actually making choices. Considering an individual's front-line care is dependent on workers having a thorough understanding of these concepts, this lack of insight is worrying. As family carers pointed out;

> My daughter's behaviour is how she demonstrates choice, but they won't accept this. They're always reacting as if the choice she makes is wrong. 'where are you going, sit down, come here, don't do that,' on and on.
>
> (SB:O)

Or the parent who was concerned because,

> They keep telling me my daughter is happy, because she does this grin, like a rictus grin when she's having a panic attack. She's not happy, she's very, very anxious.
>
> (GH:I)

Most people with PIMD will have difficulties making the most basic-level choices. These are described as 'accept or reject.' It seems there is a lack of fit between what family carers understand and what care workers are being taught. For example, care workers at an inner London day centre for people with PIMD told me they were about to undertake training in a software programme

> that will help those with more severe needs to access communication skills.
>
> (p. 188 CW:I)

It was not possible to draw them further, as they had not commenced the training. But the wording seemed to have come from a training pamphlet.

I wanted to understand just how you 'access communication skills' if you are at a pre-symbolic level for language. I was able to discuss this later at the outer London Centre. The programme being described was eye-tracking software, which was being trialled by their local speech and language therapy team. As they explained,

> this also depends on the person. You know they have to be at a certain level where they know what they want to say... So yes, someone with

a very profound physical disability will be able to use it as a tool for communication. We are only at trial stage here and we only use pictures. So yes, we can see if a service user is following the picture by tracking their eye gaze movements. But it's not a way of interpreting body language. We cannot say,

   Oh look he moved his leg slightly, that means he wants a drink type of thing.

(SM:O p188)

There needs to be much clarity around an individual's care and support. This is why there is such a need for constant training and development of staff. Of course, every effort ought to be made to ensure people have the opportunity to make choices, however small but it needs to be recognised that simplistic top-down, all-encompassing statements are not necessarily helpful when working with more profoundly impaired individuals. They are clearly not helpful for front-line staff. The section discussing the concept of choice in *Valuing People* includes the statement

   for too many these are unattainable goals.

(DH, 2001, p. 24)

   Yes, this is absolutely right. For many people with PIMD, these are unattainable goals and it ill behoves us not to acknowledge this!
   Surely it is better to 'adopt a stance of honest acknowledgement,' which recognises 'a need for planned dependence' (Pawlyn and Carnaby, 2009, p. 348). Rather than the over ascribing of capacity that, for example Bartlett and Bunning (1997) refer to in their discussion of the importance of communication partnerships.
   As has been noted families were concerned that the idea of choice was meaningless in connection to services.

   We don't get no choice. What choice? You take what you're give, innnit?

(UF:I)

   The choice they are insisting we take is this supported housing. I am fighting it. How can they say my daughter will be alright?

(SB:O)

One of the three families, whose adult child was now living in residential care, tried to complain to their local adult services department about a recent decline in standards in his care home and was told,

   if you don't like it there are plenty of other people on the waiting list.

(BL:O)

Another parent recounted a worrying meeting where it was claimed her son had expressed a desire to move out of the family home.

> On my son's report it said, he wants to go to a home. I asked them, how did he tell you that? He doesn't speak. He doesn't have language. We demanded to see it in writing, that he ever said that. You might feel he benefits from moving. Fine then say that. But don't say that my son said it. Then one lady said, 'I don't think that he could have said that.' Because one person was supporting me, they all shut up. Before they were all shouting at me all the time that I don't trust.
>
> (TW:O)

This family are British/Asian and have expressed a strong desire to continue caring for their family member at home. They described what they felt was bullying by those present at the meeting. Whilst there may have been a genuine concern to prepare for the future, tact seems to have been sadly lacking. But more importantly, were the social workers using this 'as if' language? In other words, describing what they imagined this person might want, AS IF he were saying it himself. Individual assumptions would surely need to be framed within a Best Interests discussion and this would have to be fully explained to the family.

When care workers discussed ideas of 'choice' in the focus groups, they demonstrated a wide range of comprehension with regard to the people they supported. Two of the centres responses could be described as considered (IL:1) and pragmatic (OL). The workers at these centres were thoughtful and open to deeper discussion of the concept of choice. The workers at IL2 however, were very focused on the idea of offering choice as an end in itself. They claimed to offer choice around food, drink, workers and outings via verbal queries, picture exchange systems (PECS) and Objects of Reference (OR). They were keen to impress on me that this was a feature of their service.

> From the time of the placement the key worker will work with the service user to see their choice is represented in the plan. All their choices are listed in the plan.
>
> (IL:2)

When pressed for examples they responded thus,

> Well you know a lot of them want B to feed them. They express that choice because they won't let no other worker feed them.
>
> (IL:2)

Another worker added,

> Like take meal times. If this was an institution they would have set meal times. They have no choice, they have to eat then. But if someone

doesn't want to eat right now, or like D who likes to eat his meal on the couch, we let him, that's his choice.

(IL:2)

During this exchange I asked if withdrawing to the couch and refusing his lunch was actually a choice.

'It's still a choice innit? You have a choice, yes or no' (IL:2).

What about those people who cannot communicate 'yes' or 'no' I asked?

We just meet the service users' needs, when they make their choice, we make sure we offer them their choice.

(I:2)

These workers appear to understand choice as 'accepting' or 'rejecting' based on known preferences. This is the most basic level of choice-making and the one the majority of their service users would employ. Unfortunately, the workers did not have an understanding of the different levels of choice-making nor the concept of making an informed choice. Someone who is at such an early developmental stage they can only accept or reject, is unlikely to understand the next level of an either/or choice and highly unlikely to understand an open-ended question. The workers at the other inner London day centre recognised this, but still offered.

We offer them choice, but their development doesn't enable them to make clear cut choices. Like, do they really understand we are offering them a choice.

(IL:1)

I mean we offer them bowling or swimming, do they really know what we mean?

(IL:1)

The answers at both these centres suggested managerial directives compelling staff to 'offer choice.' As the discussion progressed it appeared a local Behaviour Support team (BST) had also recommended this for one particular woman without explaining what choice is and what the varying levels of choice-making and informed choice actually are. I will be expanding on this in chapter six. I will especially focus on the dynamics of communication between care workers, managers and healthcare professionals. Too often support guidelines are devised but not embedded in the service delivery. As a family expert by experience accompanying CQC inspectors on visits to residential care homes and on Care and Treatment reviews I frequently came across unused guidelines. They were neatly filed away in 'plans' locked away in offices.

Cos over the years her behaviour has got worse an worse, so the behaviour team suggested this choice.

(IL:1)

The workers described the ways they tried to incorporate ideas of choice into this woman's routine. Unfortunately, the open choices were likely to be meaningless to her.

Hers are complete choice, like what do you want to do today?

(IL:1)

It transpired the behavioural support team had also recommended 1:1 support. All the workers agreed this was more likely to have helped her.
'I think it's the 1:1 which is changing her behaviour not the specifics of choice' (IL:1). This group of workers decided after discussion that 'preference' was a better word than choice, when they discussed meals.

He prefers the consistency of mashed not liquidized food.

(IL:1)

She prefers water, but speech and language say she must have juice with thickener.

(IL:1)

The care workers at the outer London day centre were quite clear.

Even though we interpret it is still an assumption. We presume what we think they are communicating. We don't know for sure.

(OL)

Another worker expanded,

Someone may appear to be making a choice, but that's not always the case. Sometimes people will note that someone doesn't like a particular food or drink, but that may only have been for that day. It's not forever. Sometimes it's hard to know, this is why we have the feedback sheets.

(OL)

This was the only centre using feedback sheets throughout the day in a variety of settings. The workers referred to the use of them throughout our discussion.

There are many, many charts and forms for each client. Their individual programme is monitored as are all interventions. As this client group cannot self-report, the staff are developed along Intensive Interaction lines in order to develop an acute attunement to their client responses.

(OL)

INCLUSION: 'It's a pity they didn't tell the community we were coming.'

Henley (2005) points out, there have been many and various policies over the last fifty years directed to community integration for people with ID. Whist they are all commendable, the vital question at the heart of integration is whether to close down specialist services and rely on community resources or acknowledge the ongoing need for those services for certain individuals. It is unclear that *Valuing People* has resolved this. If anything, it may have encouraged the closure of many day centres as was evident in discussion with family carers. One of the main barriers to the concept of inclusion or 'accessing the community' for this population is the dire lack of community changing facilities. The Changing Places (2011)[4] campaign has been making slow, but steady progress since its launch in 2006. However, staff at a day centre in the inner London borough, had concerns about the wider community not being accepting of people with ID. Barriers they encountered the most, were negative attitudes of the general public. The following exchange initially focused on notions of being accepted as being central to an idea of 'community.'

SM: I 'It's where you live, in society. Being accepted. Walking around and working in a place where you are accepted. You see people daily, they are accepting you without saying "I accept you."' (Lyle, 2015, p178)

However, it quickly transpired that the workers had real concerns about how little their SU's were accepted. I started to ask, 'Do you think' and a worker interrupted me with 'No, the answer's no, but carry on.' I continued, 'No?'

You're gonna ask do you think they're included. Inclusion, as in we try and access it, the community. But whether it is accepting? If you mean are they accepted?

(SM:I)

I asked if she meant people were not very accepting and the worker replied 'not in our lifetime.

(SM:I)

At this point I referred back to the filmed excerpts in particular the one where Odyssey visited the arts organisation. I explained the same worker had taken my daughter there every week for some years now. The general public were not always accommodating. For example, they often had to wait for the disabled toilet because an able person was using it. There was a rush of responses and it was evident they had quite pent up feelings that they had had no opportunity to discuss at any length. They discussed indirect discrimination and outright negative attitudes.

> A key word I would use associated with people with LD in the community, is tolerate. It's not whether they're accepted it's about being tolerated. A business or whatever will tolerate in that they will allow people in, but are they accepting?
>
> (SM:I)

Another worker chimed in, 'yeah, people seem to find ways to not accept … more subtle ways like the hours they open or not.' (SM:I, p. 179)
    And another added.

> They don't want to socialise they think it might be catching. Like if you sit near them they will get up and walk away.
>
> (SM:I)

Yet another worker confirmed.

> Yeah, we get this all the time. Like if we go to the park, they walk away from us. If we go to a cafe they get up and walk out.
>
> (SM:I)

There sentiments echoed the staff at the other inner London day centre. One worker noted,

> It's a pity they didn't tell the community we were coming.' People's attitudes 'don't change overnight.
>
> (SM:I)

The two inner London day centres were very focused on negative attitudes from the public. In contrast the outer London day centre told me,

> our clients don't recognise what we are doing. But they know if they have pleasant sensory experiences, so we concentrate on that type of approach, rather than some idea of accessing the community which is meaningless to this group.
>
> (SM:O, p. 175)

Another joined in,

> Why would they want to be dragged around the high street or into Mac Donald's? They need therapeutic interventions and support and that is what we believe is the best thing for them.
>
> (SM:O)

This particular centre was purpose-built for people with PIMD. The staff explained the previous local day centres had all closed soon after *Valuing People* was published. However, a few years later the local authority realised there were many people who needed the specialist daytime support a day centre could provide. Or perhaps they were prompted to by local residential care providers who had lost their day centre provision?

> We were specifically designed as a service for twenty-two people......
> and yet now, barely four years later we have roughly double that each day. There is an increasing population with High Support Needs. PEG feeding has led to greater life expectancy as well and we seem to have many clients with Rhett's disease
>
> (SM:O)

This is in contrast to the inner London day centre, which was also purpose-built. It has a gym, a soft play area, a sensory room, music room, specialist music-making technology called Soundbeam, various individual training rooms, staff rooms, offices, a communal room, a dining room and a large kitchen. There is a reasonable-sized garden to the rear, with access to a local park. All of these areas are underused now, since the community activities commenced. While most of the workers were keen to describe the new activities (going swimming, bowling, cycling, to the park, local cafes and library) one worker questioned if these opportunities were new or if it was simply the idea of leaving the centre that was novel.

> I know you said that and spoke about choice, but how many times can our service users go to the same park? Not being funny but I know that park like the back of my hand now. What must K think? Here again.
>
> (SM:IL, p. 176)

OVERVIEW of storyline with particular reference to PIMD

Across the entire white paper document there appears to be confusion about what PIMD actually is and a reticence to acknowledge the specific needs and financial implications of meeting those needs. *Valuing People* (VP) makes clear from the outset, as was previously noted, that a range of people were involved in consultation over the year prior to publication. Unfortunately, there is no indication that any people with PIMD were present or accounted for at any of these meetings (DH, 2001, p. 10). The document throughout, illustrates sections with quotes by people with ID, good news stories and narrative accounts. The only narrative employed to specifically illustrate these final sections, dealing with 'people with severe and profound disabilities' (but oddly no mention of multiple) is an account of the life of a woman Margaret, now deceased (DH, 2001, p. 100). It states that although she had not acquired language or formal signing skills, nevertheless she was

> very well able to make her wishes known.
>
> (DH, 2001, p. 100)

It does not expand further. This is a shame as those of us who work with people who do not have language skills are always eager to learn of new ways of communicating. We must unfortunately assume the statement refers to her wishes being discerned via her behavioural reaction to various events. For example, the story lists some of the things she enjoyed doing with the advocate 'she acquired' after her mother died (DH, 2001 p. 100). How did she acquire an advocate? It seems unlikely Margaret sought out and retained the advocate herself. It also states that

> she lost contact with her family when her mother died.
>
> (p. 100)

Surely, it's the other way round and the family lost contact with her? She had no formal language skills, therefore could not use phone or write letters. How was she going to sustain contact with her family? It is not clear what Margaret's diagnosis was. The story mentions her enjoyment of long walks, so she did not have mobility problems. There is no mention of additional health issues such as epilepsy. Nor is there any mention of sensory impairments or autistic spectrum disorder. And although the story concludes with her death, there is no mention of age-related illnesses or impairments. All of these are associated with *Valuing People's* own definition of 'additional and complex needs' (p. 100). Therefore, it is unclear why her story illustrates the section 'People with Additional and Complex needs.' Was no living person with PIMD involved at any stage of the consultation? If so, why was their story not used? The example concludes by telling us the advocate was the one person, who was 'there for her' and was with her when she died. So, this is really a story about advocacy not about Margret at all.

As stated Personalisation is the new approach to providing social care and support (Glasby, 2001, pp. 36–42). No more service-led, this new system, can supposedly deliver support tailor made to an individual's need. This is possible via the provision of an individual budget or direct payment. The individual might then choose what support they need, how it is delivered and when they receive it (see for e.g. Alan's story DH, 2001,

p. 49). The person receiving the support is considered to be at the centre of the process and in control of this aspect of their lives. The difficulty with using words like choice, control and user empowerment in the context of services for people with PIMD, is that they tend to overlook the reality of increased family carer involvement in planning, management and day-to-day delivery of said services. This has been highlighted by a number of providers e.g.

> There should be strong self-advocacy and family and carer support and involvement. We believe it is vital to involve family, carers and advocates in this process to ensure people are really able to tell us what they want and what works best for them.
>
> (Creative Support, 2011)

The examples provided by VP, tend to gloss over this detail. They also demonstrate the informalised nature of this new style of support.

The first example discusses how

> a man, living with his parents, receives a direct payment to employ a support worker from an agency for short breaks. Breaks can be a few hours in the evening and weekend or longer.
>
> (DH, 2001, p. 48)

It is unclear if there is anything else in this man's life, such as attendance at a Day Centre or access to continuing education or training for employment. Therefore, it suggests his family provide the bulk of his care. It also states that he employs a support worker, but this could mean his parents do the formal side of employing and managing the staff. Clements (2011) has noted

> the disabled or older person (or perhaps more commonly his or her family carer) takes control.
>
> (Clements, 2011, p. 2)

The second example seems to confirm the shift to informalised services. It states that this man

> wanted to move on from the day service.
>
> (DH, 2001, p. 48)

However, the direct payments only help in accessing leisure facilities in the evening. So, what is he doing the rest of the time and who is providing the support? Is it solely his mother? Both these examples were provided by Hampshire Social Services to illustrate their new flexible direct payments scheme. It is unclear if the men provided the statements themselves, or if they had been a part of the consultation. Therefore, it must be assumed that this is further evidence of no people with PIMD being included in these illustrative narratives. Another example is Susan. The report outlines the process by which her circle of support enabled her to live independently

> with a rota of support workers.
>
> (DH, 2001, p. 50)

Is this a good news story about a woman with PIMD? Demonstrating she was unhappy with her existing care arrangement

> by actions, facial expressions, verbal responses and moods.
>
> (DH, 2001, p. 50)

conveys to the reader the profound nature of her ID. It is therefore confusing to read that,

> her expressions and views guide how the money is spent, so she is in control of the money.
>
> (DH, 2001, p. 50)

This may well make sense to people working closely with her. However, stretching the language to accommodate a discussion of her within this framework feels deeply problematic. To present her story in this manner, to a policymaker or commissioner, or to someone who is not acquainted with her, is highly disingenuous. It lays claims to capacity she clearly does not have. How can this be described as a person-centred approach? Surely it is denial not acknowledgment? Is she really 'in control' or are the financial decisions, ultimately made by her circle of support, based on their combined assumptions about her Best Interests?

Finally, David's story is an example of an individual becoming known to services, after the death of his mother. He inherited the lease on the bungalow, so rather than being moved somewhere else, the LA was able to provide the personalised care package and his life was not further disrupted. Of course, the inclusion of a reference to his siblings living nearby and providing 'emotional and practical support' (DH, 2001, p. 70) hints that the arrangement would not be possible without them. The fact that he is also receiving 'some intensive support ... ... to improve his cooking and domestic skills' (DH, 2001, p. 70) demonstrates the man is unlikely to have PIMD.

Conclusion

There was clear consensus from families and care workers in both boroughs about the lack of awareness and understanding of the needs of those with PIMD at policymaking level. This echoed my original CDA findings. People also believe the lack of understanding was reflected at the level of local commissioning. The main issues raised by family carers were to do with a lack of specialist services, primarily physiotherapy and specialised support especially in the light of the move to informalised community service provision. Residential respite was also a major concern, as was the lack of choice of support, service provider, care worker or travel escort.

British Asian families in the outer London borough did not believe their cultural needs were acknowledged or understood; despite the fact that their borough has a high percentage of British Asian residents. There was no comparative complaint from the (mostly) African Caribbean families in the inner London borough. This suggests more effective cultural awareness in place across services. It could also mean people had given up complaining.

As stated there was general agreement amongst care workers across all three sites, that policymakers seemed unaware of the needs of people with PIMD. The constant refrain of, 'they don't get it,' was voiced by family carers and care workers alike. This included managers. It is my contention that this lack of awareness at commissioning and policymaking levels impacts negatively at practice level. This was confirmed by some care worker's approaches, which were at odds with the mental capacity of the service users. By promoting generalised ideas and insisting they are applicable to all people with all levels of ID, *Valuing People* (DH, 2001) has inadvertently caused 'on the ground' difficulties for carers, care workers and service users alike. These difficulties were compounded by the concerns of paid care workers that the new approach was not reflected in public attitudes. In the next chapter I will focus on my daughter's journey, these past ten years.

Because of the Winterbourne View abuse scandal there has been much discussion about Assessment and Treatment Units (ATU's). As a parent I have experienced the often frightening, violent responses to extreme distress described as 'challenging behaviour.' When Odyssey was an adolescent I had never heard of an ATU, had no idea what 'challenging behaviour' was. I simply knew my daughter had gradually become, what? Unmanageable sounds awful, but is probably the best description. School couldn't cope, I couldn't cope, the respite centre couldn't cope. After one particular incident her doctor prescribed haloperidol, an anti-psychotic drug. Seeing my daughter transform into a listless, drooling shadow of herself was even more scary than her wild behaviour. I took her off that drug. Coincidentally around the same time I had found a specialist residential school for Multi-Handicapped Visually Impaired children (MHVI). The psychology team began talking about admitting her to the local mental health hospital for observation. I chose the school.

Notes

1   www.cqc.org.uk/sites/default/files/CQC_Transition%20Report_Summary_lores.pdf
2   www.newstatesman,com/blogs/politics/2012/10/george-osbornes-speech-conservative-conference-full-text

3 www.aboutlearningdisabilities.co.uk/human-rights-act-learning-disabilities.html
4 www.changing-places.org/news/£2_million_for_changing_places_toilets_.aspx

Bibliography

Bartlett, C. and Bunning, K. (1997). 'The importance of communication partnerships: a study to investigate the communicative exchanges between staff and adults with learning disabilities.' *British Journal of Learning Disabilities*, Volume 25 (4), pp. 148–153. Wiley-Blackwell, UK.

Blumer, H., (2010). in King, N., and Horrocks, C. (eds) *Interviews in Qualitative Research*. pp. 61–62. Sage, London, UK.

Clements, L. (2011). 'Social care law developments. A sideways look at personalisation and tightening eligibility criteria.' *Elder Law*, Volume 1, pp. 47–52. New Square Chambers, UK.

Clements, L. (2012). *Carers and Their Rights. The Law Relating to Carers*. Cargo Publishing, Glasgow, UK.

Concannon, L. (2005). *Planning for Life Involving Adults with Learning Disabilities in Service Planning*. Routledge, London, UK and New York, USA.

Cook, D. (2016). 'Southern Derbyshire service for people with profound and multiple learning disability.' *PMLD Link*, pp. 34–36. Northampton, UK. Available at www.pmldlink.og.uk

Creative Support. (2011). 'Opportunity support and wellbeing.' Available from www.creativesupport.co.uk/

Dean, H. (2010). *Understanding Human Need*. The Policy Press, University of Bristol, Bristol, UK.

Dean, H. and MacNeill, M. (2003). 'Re-conceptualising welfare-to-work for people with multiple problems and needs.' *Journal of Social Policy*, Volume 32 (3), pp. 441–449. Cambridge University Press, Cambridge, UK.

Department of Health. (2001). *Valuing People: A New Strategy for Learning Disabilities for the 21st Century*. HMSO, London, UK.

Department of Health. (2009) *Valuing People Now*. HMSO, London, UK.

Department of Health. (2009). *Valuing Employment: Now real jobs for people with learning disabilities*. HMSO, London, UK.

Department of Social Security. (1998a). 'A new contract for welfare.' in Powell, M. (ed) (1999) *New Labour, New Welfare State? The Third Way in British Social Policy*. pp. 13–16. Policy Press, Bristol, UK.

Emerson, E. (2009). *Estimating Future Numbers of Adults with Profound and Multiple Learning Disabilities in England*. Centre for Disability Research, Lancaster University, UK.

Fischer, F. (2003). *Reframing Public Policy Discursive Practices and Deliberative Practices*. Oxford University Press, Oxford, UK and New York, USA.

Gaffney, D. (2012). 'Dependency and disability: how to misread the evidence on social security.' in Davison, S. and Rutherford, J. (eds) *Welfare Reform the Dread of Things to Come* Soundings. pp 22–36 (online) Available from www.lwbooks.co.uk/journals/soundings/contents.html

Glasby, J. (ed) (2001). *Evidence Policy and Practice: Critical Perspectives in Health and Social Care*. Policy Press, Bristol, UK.

Hall, S. (2012). 'The neo-liberal revolution.' in Davison, S. and Rutherford, J. (eds) *Soundings on the Neoliberal Crisis.* (online). pp. 8–26. Available from www.lwbooks. co.uk/ebooks/The_Neoliberal_crisis.pdf

Harper, D. (1998). 'Visual sociology: expanding the sociological vision.' *The American Sociologist*, Volume 19 (1), pp. 54–70. Springer, USA.

Henley, C. (2005). *Learning Disabilities. The Rise and Potential Demise of Structured Day Services for Adults with Learning Disabilities 1955–2005.* The Minster Press, Dorset, UK.

Joint Committee on Human Rights (JCHR). (2008). *A Life Like Any Other? Human Rights of Adults with Learning Disabilities.* HMSO, London, UK.

Keeley, B. and Clarke, M. (1999). *Consultation with Carers. Good Practice Guide.* The Princess Royal Trust for Carers, London, Lancashire, Glasgow, UK.

Kittay, E. (1999). *Love's Labour: Essays on Women, Equality and Dependency.* Routledge, New York, USA.

Kittay, E., in Carlson, L. (2010). *The Face of Intellectual Disability. Philosophical Reflections.* Indiana University Press, Bloomington, Indiana, USA.

Lapenta, F. (2011). 'Some theoretical and methodological views on photo-elicitation.' in Margolis, L. and Pauwel, E. (eds) *The Sage Handbook of Visual Research Methods.* pp. 201–213. Sage, London, New Delhi, California, Singapore.

Lyle, D. (2015). 'Policy to practice: a critical analysis of the "valuing people" strategy.' Available from eprints.mdx.ac.uk

Nind, M. and Sheehy, K. (2005). 'Emotional well-being for all: Mental health and people with profound and multiple learning disabilities.' *British Journal of Learning Disabilities*, Volume 33 (1). pp. 34–38. Wiley-Blackwell, Oxford, UK.

Nussbaum, M.C. (2006). *Frontiers of Justice Disability Nationality Species Membership.* The Belknap Press of Harvard University Press, Cambridge Massachusetts, London, UK.

Osbourne, G. (2012). 'George Osbourne's full speech to the conservative conference. Full text.' Avaialable online at www.newstatesman.com/blogs/politics/2012/10/george-osbornes-speech-conservative-conference-full-text

Pawlyn, J. and Carnaby, S. (eds) (2009). *Profound Intellectual and Multiple Disabilities Nursing Complex Needs.* Wiley-Blackwell, Oxford, UK.

Pink, S. (2004). 'Visual methods.' in Seale, C. (ed) *Qualitative Research Practice.* pp. 361–376. Sage, London, UK.

Powell, M. (ed) (1999) *New Labour, New Welfare State? The Third Way in British Social Policy.* Policy Press, Bristol, UK.

Prosser, J. (1998). *Image-Based Research: A Source Book for Qualitative Researchers.* Routledge Farmer, Taylor & Francis Group, London, UK and New York, USA.

Reindal, S.M. (1999). 'Independence, dependence, interdependence: some reflections on the subject and personal autonomy.' *Disability & Society*, Volume 14 (3), pp. 353–367. Routledge, UK.

Rose, G. (2007). V*isual Methodologies. An Introduction to the Interpretation of Visual Materials.* Sage, London, New Delhi, Singapore.

Samuel, J. and Pritchard, M. (2001). 'The ignored minority: meeting the needs of people with profound learning disability.' *Tizard Learning Disability Review*, Volume 6 (2), pp. 34–44. Emerald Publishing Limited, UK.

Schneider, A. and Ingram, I. in Fischer, F. (2003) *Reframing Public Policy Discursive Practices and Deliberative Practices.* Oxford University Press, Oxford, UK and New York, USA.

Schwandt, in Denzin, N., and Lincoln, Y. (eds) (2003). *Strategies of Qualitative Enquiry*. Sage, Thousand Oaks, CA.

Slowie, D. and Hebron, C. (2016). 'Raising our sights, combating nihilism to improve outcomes for people with profound and multiple learning disabilities (PMLD).' *PMLD Link*, Volume 28 (3, 85), pp. 5–7. Northampton, UK.

Vehmas, S. and Makela, P. (2010). 'A realist account of the ontology of impairment.' *Journal of Medical Ethics*, Volume 34, pp. 93–95. BMJ Publishing Group, UK.

4   All in the same direction or 'it's not about you'

Introduction

The last chapter considered the impact of current UK policy, *Valuing People* (DH, 2001, 2009), for people with PIMD. Examining family carer and care worker responses to questions and discussions about the core drivers of 'rights, independence, choice/control and inclusion' and setting these against an initial deep analysis of the white paper itself, revealed a number of concerns. Family carers felt there was an overemphasis on people with lower support needs. Formal (i.e. paid) care workers especially at the outer London day centre felt the policy had little relevance for their client group. Care workers in the inner London borough were understandably confused. After all, *Valuing People* was telling them, for example, that assistive technology can improve cognitive functioning (DH, 2001, p. 52). Likewise the unclear use of language suggested people 'may' need help, 'may' need support, 'may' have difficulty, when in fact the people this book is focussing on will always have difficulty, will always need help and will always need full support in every aspect of their lives. This is not me, deliberately saying mean things about people and their limitations. This is a plea for scrupulous language and clarity when discussing this group's needs. This has a direct impact on their quality of life.

We do not particularly value care work in this country. People are usually paid minimum wage and often work on zero hours contracts. Training can be haphazard, often 'in-house,' e-learning and far from specific. I visited many residential settings with inspectors from the Care Quality Commission (CQC), over a number of years, working as an expert by experience. I was often asked to talk to the support staff about their most recent training. It was common for people to tell me they had completed a particular module that held no relevance for those they were supporting. Training was usually demonstrated by a list of modules that had to be completed. Workers advised they were tick box exercises, most commonly by e-learning. It's fair to say I rarely encountered enthusiasm for this side of their job. It always seems a shame to me, a lost opportunity somehow. Clinical supervision or formal reflexive practice is rare. How then can we expect workers, including generic agency workers, to provide good care and support if we only equip them with the most basic understanding and knowledge to do their job? There is a breadth of difference between supporting someone who can relay their wants and express their needs with words, language, symbols or technology and someone for whom we can only ever make assumptions, based on our knowledge of them. Where does this knowledge come from? How do workers learn about the people they are supporting? Those interviewed in the previous chapter spoke about 'keeping their choices in their Individual Service Plans.' I would query just how 'live' these documents are. I have visited countless residential homes and assessment and treatment units (ATU's) in my role as expert by experience. Sadly, these documents are often filed away and rarely read. Workers have advised me they get to read the files for their induction, but have rarely been able to show me how these documents are incorporated into someone's accessible Daily Living Plan or Daily Diary. I always queried this absence. How is someone to know what each day entails? Surely we all keep a daily diary or at least have some idea of what we will do each day? I am often reminded of the Learning Disability nurse who helped us with managing my daughter's behavioural support needs. He would always point out, 'Odyssey just wants to predict what will happen next.' It sounds so simple but how to support her, and those like her, in this very basic goal?

This chapter will recount the turnaround a truly person-centred and therapeutic approach has made to her life. Of course one cannot generalise and make claims for the same level of turnaround for anyone else. However, anyone in any setting can adapt their own behaviour to be more empathetic. This is the person-centred approach in a nutshell. I will however argue, that a 'person-centred' approach has to first and foremost acknowledge this particular woman's multiplicity of impairments, including the manner in which their *gestalt* impacts on her day-to-day life. I will demonstrate how it is possible to move beyond discussion of 'placement breakdown' due to 'challenging behaviour' to issues of comprehension and communication. When I discuss communication, I include health professionals and managers and the manner in which they relay support strategies, to on-the-ground care workers. Why have bespoke support guidelines written by professionals if they are filed away and never used? Could the reason be because no one has thoroughly explained the rationale behind the guidelines to the manager or the support staff? This chapter will outline a number of domains and describe ways staff and families can work together to support people towards 'a good or better life' (see Johnson and Walmsley, 2010). Practical guidance is offered in the areas of communication, personalised support, healthcare support, therapeutic support, team building around ownership of activities and goals and ongoing reflexivity.

Background

> If we don't know who we are talking about how can we know what the issues are.
>
> > Samuel and Pritchard (2001, pp. 34–44)

Ten years ago the organisation providing support to Odyssey for two days a week, could only deliver 40% staff cover, even though they were a specialist organisation and managed an average of 98% cover with their other clients. Why was this? Why did people not want to work with this woman? In fact over the past 30 years or so a particular narrative had developed around Odyssey. She was often described as 'violent,' 'aggressive' and 'extremely challenging.' 'Refused' was the word most used in any communication with staff at her former day centre.

> 'Odyssey refused to go out,' 'Odyssey refused to engage,' 'Odyssey refused her lunch,' 'Odyssey refused to get on the bus,' 'Odyssey refused to get off the toilet.'

What has happened in these intervening years? Why do people now want to work with my daughter? Why do I have such good staff retention and rare absences through sickness? What are we doing that people were not able to do in the past? Why do I, only now, have to recruit for the first time in seven years? Why is this working so well? Odyssey is still the same person, with the same diagnoses and conditions. She still has her meltdowns and crises, although these are not nearly so frequent as before. Rather than try to quell her behaviour we now try to support her to manage her feelings. We try to understand the world as she experiences it. Although he has now moved on, she had a wonderful support worker for over five years. He was with her long enough to see this difference. He described her accessing the local Saturday Stories group after two years of attending as 'tolerating' it. This was a sensory story/massage session set up especially for people with PIMD. Odyssey would often become agitated and distressed and have to be taken out of the room. Gradually though this reduced to her simply standing up and vocally expressing her concern and then with prompts sitting back down again.

Then an even greater change occurred. It wasn't until she had been attending for almost five years that her worker would come back, eager to tell me how much she enjoyed her day. She was starting to join in, to clap, to sing, to express her joy. And this worker noticed in the others who attended. Many of them came from local residential homes and often with different workers, who did not know them well. But Odyssey's worker had grown to know them. He would tell me how one woman would make excited vocal sounds as she came into the room and the worker supporting her thought she was upset. He would tell them no, she wasn't upset. She was excited and looking forward to the story. She was able to predict what was going to happen. He used to get quite annoyed with the support workers who moaned, 'why do we have to have the same story each week, it's boring.' We would both laugh about this later as we said, 'because it's not about you.' How many times have I found myself saying this over the years? How often have people queried why we do something in some particular way? 'I wouldn't like that,' they will say. 'Well,' I always reply, 'it's not about you.'

Communication communication communication

There are many guides, toolkits and approaches to communication with people with ID. These include online resources available to individuals, families, managers and care workers. I have included a number of links in a Resource list at the end of this chapter. I am pleased to see 'communication' is usually included as an item. I wish it could always be the first item. Surely communication is the most important aspect of supporting someone?

How does Odyssey communicate? This question is asked often, appears on many forms and plans. How does she communicate? I have been told so many times, 'oh she understands everything I say.' Yet when I ask how they know this, the usual response is laugher and something like 'oh she knows.' This has always troubled me. This narrative often builds around an individual who does not have a typical communication style, based on language and comprehension. I believe it is a kind of wish fulfilment. It is almost as if the idea that somebody does not understand us is too overwhelming, too painful to consider for some people. The only way they can deal with it is through denial. Valerie Sinason (2004) has written about,

> the magnitude of defensive manoeuvres used by people to evade this reality, i.e. the sheer painfulness of having a learning disability, to all concerned.

Psychoanalytic accounts are less in favour these days, although they do offer us insight. Readers may be taken aback by the statement 'sheer painfulness.' If we are trying to be open, honest and scrupulous in our efforts to understand life for adults with PIMD, perhaps we ought not to shy away from confronting our own defensive manoeuvres. If we are employing people to undertake 'emotional labour' we have a responsibility to help them to manage this, in order that they may carry out their work anxiety free, or as close to this as possible. I strongly believe if someone does not understand words and language, they can still discern emotional intent. This means they can sense anxiety. It's not difficult to see how these feelings can escalate. Imagine an unsure worker, feeling anxious about how Odyssey will react today? Is she going to lash out, screech or attack? I know workers have panicked with her in the past. I don't blame them. It is a perfectly understandable response to a difficult situation. However, if workers have an understanding of what gives rise to this anxious behaviour, in themselves as well as Odyssey, they are on the first step to developing empathy. Hence when describing an empathetic approach, the first step is to being fully present. This is not as simple as it sounds. This is actually quite hard to do. Focussing on this moment, right here, right now takes practice. It is all too easy to be distracted. But you need to be fully present in order to attune to the quiet, tiny 'real' words from Odyssey and her myriad of non-verbal communication attempts.

Odyssey cannot see you smiling at her, but she will certainly smile at you. Often, just at the moment you turn away. We always need to remember processes are so much slower for people like Odyssey. They need time to respond. I think it is enormously important for workers to spend time simply BE-ing with Odyssey. Just having that quiet time together, when they can work on attuning their relationship. Using Odyssey's name in the third person is a good way to help allay her anxieties. She responds well to people describing what they think she is feeling and encouraging her with a positive tone. For example, 'I hear Odyssey had a really good day at music.' (Body language of little excited shudders.) 'I heard she joined in this week' (more shudders and wiggles). 'Odyssey played the guitar ... and the drum.' Usually by this stage she will be vocalising in a to and fro mode with whoever she is having the conversation with. Her confidence levels have increased enormously since we focussed on ways to include her that are not confrontational. I call it being mentally side-by-side with her, rather than face-to-face.

Odyssey has always tended to refuse. As a child and adolescent, she was always curled up in a ball, physically withdrawing from any contact. Her answer to everything for many years was 'no.' She was tactile defensive, to the point that she now appears double-jointed as she can bend her thumb and fingers back to her wrist. Nowadays, 'okaaaaay' has entered her vocabulary. So, when we do get a very forceful, 'no,' we tend to respect that this really is a 'no.' And how truly empowering for her? She can affect some control.

As I write I can hear the 'knocking' game going on in the living room between Odyssey and her care worker. When Odyssey sits at the table to eat, she has developed her tapping to include tapping or knocking on the side of the wooden seat. So her worker has developed this into their interactive game. One of Odyssey's echolalic phrases is 'Knock it off.' This gets included, then we have 'Is Odyssey knocking?' again. The worker knows it may take a while before the knock happens, but she waits, encourages and sure enough ... there is another knock. Sometimes it is so faint, you wouldn't notice, but those faint movements are intentional. Without intentionality there is no communication. We want her to want to engage with us. We want her to want to join in, to 'join the party.' This is something I have been trying to encourage in her for the last forty years. And bless her she really is finally, 'joining in.' Even I have been amazed at her 'developmental spurts' as her neurologist describes them.

The subject of communication within the context of supporting Odyssey involves much more than me relaying to workers her communication style. How do I communicate with those workers? How do the professionals involved in her life communicate with me and how do I then relay this to the workers as well? Support guidelines are essential. These must be clear and easy to understand. These are a resource for workers and should enhance their practice. I do think the onus ought to be on the professional, be they occupational therapist, psychologist, physiotherapist, speech and language therapist or learning disability nurse to see these are fully understood. If health professionals are devising guidelines that care workers will be expected to observe, they need to ensure the workers are on board. The way to do this is by engaging with workers and explaining the rationale behind their guidelines. Too often guidelines are prepared but who relays them to the support team? If they were instigated some time previously, who ensures that new staff members gain a thorough understanding of the rationale and importance of executing these support strategies? They also need to be regularly reviewed to see they are still fit for purpose and tweaked if necessary.

Of course the most important aspect of communication is how we communicate with Odyssey. I describe the way we engage with her as using an Intensive Interaction approach. One of the key elements of this is to first and foremost acknowledge the transactional nature of our attempts at interacting with someone who has profound communication difficulties. Nind et al. (in Firth, 2016) describe the way we have historically attributed the difficulty entirely to the person with PIMD. Hence interventions always seek to develop or enhance their communication competencies, via, for example Objects of Reference. Since communication is at least a two-way process, oughtn't we find ways to enhance our communication ability? It has been shown that the use of 'motherese,' whereby we adopt more straightforward language but with exaggerated pitch, can lead to increased engagement. Vocalising in unison and turn-taking by imitating the various sounds someone makes are really at the core of the Intensive Interaction approach.

Culture of personalised support

I cannot impress how important it is for staff to try and understand the world as Odyssey experiences it. Of course it is impossible, but the first step to understanding is to acknowledge the impact of her multiplicity of conditions and impairments on her health and wellbeing. This is a woman who is totally neurologically blind, with a profound learning disability and autism. She has hyperacusis (see Tantum, 2012, pp. 256–257) and epilepsy. She also has cerebral palsy (CP), sensory integration disorder (SID), polycystic ovary syndrome (POS), a non-specific, evolving skin disorder and latterly has developed haemorrhoids after a lifetime of chronic constipation. All of these ten diagnoses combine and impact on her health and well-being to varying degrees from one day to the next.

For example her hyperacusis varies from day to day. This means her hearing is extremely sensitive. A revving motorbike, helicopters or workers using their strimming machines to trim the hedges that surround our block, can leave her so distraught she will violently self-injure for the rest of the day. Another time, we get ready for her distress when we hear certain sounds and she doesn't even notice them. Her workers very quickly acclimatise to the sounds that affect her the worst. Odyssey tends to simply lash out or head butt when she cannot cope with the noise. If workers are not aware of her hyperacusis or have no understanding of it, it seems reasonable for them to be confused and hurt by suddenly being attacked for no reason, as they see it.

The Samuel and Pritchard (2001) quote is a favourite of mine as I believe one of the reasons staff have developed a keen insight into Odyssey's needs is because I have given them so much information about her various diagnoses. This is not to say I view my daughter as a collection of labels, rather it is to help staff understand her behaviour is not 'naughty,' 'deliberate,' 'vindictive' or any of the other multitude of negative reasons I have been told in the past.

I want staff to understand what motivates her, what her levels of understanding, cognition and capacity actually are. And I also impress on them that we can only ever make assumptions about what we think she is feeling or experiencing at any particular time. We can never presume to truly know. How many times have we all heard people say

> (s)he knows how to wind me up' Or, 'we don't need a communication passport, I know what (s)he means'. I have had both comments from various workers in various settings.

I believe this is so important. I never make presumptions for my daughter. Professionals often ask me 'what does she mean?' or 'what does she want?' I tell them truthfully, I have no idea. But I can make a guess based on knowing her for so many years. I may get it right I may also be completely wrong.

Consistency & clarity = trust

The first step to helping Odyssey was to develop trust. Prior to the services of the specialist organisation, she had been removed from her local adult shared-care placement for her own safety. We will never know what happened, as she cannot tell us. Her behaviour clearly demonstrated she no longer trusted anyone. Apart from whatever verbal, physical or sexual abuse she had endured, she also experienced years of lying. People (including me) lying to her in order to get her to eat, get her to stand, sit, get washed, dressed or get on board the school bus or later the bus to the day centre, or to have her blood tests done, or for any other number of procedures throughout her life. Her entire life was inauthentic in a sense. Everybody around her was acting *as if* she understood everyone perfectly. I still have reams of Communication Books, letters and cards written in the first person, supposedly by Odyssey, telling me all about her school days, holidays and respite breaks. Why do we persist in this lie? I decided enough was enough and from now on, even if it meant adding an extra word or ten, we would be very clear about what Odyssey's actual perspective was in any given situation. Because her mood, feelings, sensory acuity, levels of anxiety or any other number of factors can be 'all over the shop,' we need to provide her with a sense of consistency. She needs repetition in order to predict what will happen next. She needs to know that when 'A' happens 'B' will follow. There is nothing predictable about Odyssey. In fact a psychiatrist (LF) once told me,

> the thing that is predictable about Odyssey is her unpredictability. We need to worry when she becomes unpredictably unpredictable.

Therefore we must provide the predictability. We started off with a careplan entitled 'TIME.' The reason being that time as a construct does not actually exist for her. Her body clock is often thrown out of whack due to her total blindness, but combined with her ASD she can have weeks of the experience of being jetlagged. Studies have shown that people with autism experience atypical sleep patterns (see Limoges et al., 2005). Also, I was determined to allow her the time to do as much of anything that she could. We were not going to rush her to finish anything. We were not going to overpower her to complete a task. I impressed on her supporters from the outset, that this was all about us empowering her to attain the most independence and control she could.

Imagine how frustrating and frightening it must be to have everything in your life foisted on you, often with no forewarning, especially if you are totally blind? We often hear the expression 'learned helplessness' (Seligman, 1972).

But is it any wonder people are passive if this is all they know? And how interesting that any resistance to being pulled, moved, fed, washed or dragged is perceived as 'challenging' or a 'choice' NOT to do something. What if this person is demonstrating very clearly that they do want to do something, just at a pace they prefer? Yes, they may take forever to pick that piece of food off the plate. Their hand may hover over for some time, but wait and see how confident someone is when you let them take the time to do it. Yes, you may feel it is like watching paint dry and you can do it so much better and so much quicker, but please remember the title of that book I want to write, '*It's Not About You*' and allow someone some precious time.

Rights was, 'the lack of specific reference to human rights' (JCHR, 2008, Paragraph 39, p. 19) in the original Valuing People white paper.[3]

Families were also concerned about the lack of any reference to specific rights such as the right to social welfare provision (Dean, 2010) or the right to local, specialist Intensive Support Units (ISU) or adult college provision. There is no mention of the right to trained support and care workers or of the right to the range of specialist support such as physiotherapy, occupational therapy, speech and language therapy and psychological support, which the strategy acknowledges as being key to good outcomes for this group. Nor is there any mention of the right to provision of equipment such as wheelchairs, home adaptions or hoists. And there is no mention of the right to visual impairment aids or hearing aids. This list is not exhaustive, simply an indication of the range of support an individual with PIMD may need during their lives. In their handbook outlining nursing care needs of people with PIMD, Pawlyn and Carnaby (2009) describe the above and also include dental care, respiratory care, dysphagic support, continence support, specific implications of epilepsy support and nutrition and hydration support (Section 2: Chapters 8–18).

One of the sibling carers interviewed spoke about lack of respite in terms of his mother's rights.

> I know they use those words, that Valuing People thing … I think it should be more about my mum's rights. She's on dialysis now three times a week. She's an elderly woman, she should get help. Look how long since we had respite. Others, there's others that are easier to manage than my brother. They go on outings, on holidays. Remember S took us to see that place? They expected to get my brother in to a shower, that bloody toy shower. How were they gonna support him? It takes two people to lift him. How were they gonna get him from his wheelchair to that little plastic shower seat? It would have just collapsed. He's a big man and he cannot support himself, he needs you to help him. All these ideas, they need to meet him then they would see.
>
> (WD:I)

Part three 'Delivering Change' (DH, 2001, p. 106) states that local Partnership Boards will need to

> ensure the availability of service options to meet people's assessed needs.
>
> (p. 106)

However, the Boards were never statutory or strategic so they had no power to agree what service was funded or even where the funding would come from. Now the situation is one of flux as many Partnerships Boards have

From the outset we have stuck to a fairly strict routine of indoor and outdoor activities including specific outings. Leaving or entering a building could be immensely anxiety inducing for Odyssey. Ten years ago it could take anywhere between forty minutes to two hours for her to cross a threshold. Often it would end by Odyssey being manhandled over the threshold, or even carried. Nowadays we have a routine that everyone observes. It is quite straightforward, but the most important aspect is that everyone observes the routine. No one has the attitude, of

knowing how to handle her.

That is not what we are seeking to achieve. We don't want to 'handle her' we want her to want to engage with us.

As an example I arrived home one day and a newer member of the team was concerned that she had not been able to leave the house. Odyssey had refused. So I asked the worker to talk me through the routine that she had been taught. She told me she had advised Odyssey they would be leaving the house in ten minutes. (Check) Ten minutes later the worker had simply tapped her knee and Odyssey had leapt up from the couch. (Check) She had directed her with one word 'toilet.' (Check). After the toilet she had put on Odyssey's coat. (Check) Then her … And as she opened her mouth the worker realised,

Oh no, I forgot her backpack.

She has never forgotten that backpack since. Odyssey does not understand that the weighted backpack supports her proprioception needs. But she does understand it as part of the routine she undertakes before leaving the house. One aspect left out and the whole routine fails. People with ASD experience high levels of anxiety. We know this. When someone is anxious and frightened, surely we ought to be trying to reassure them? Surely the best way to reassure them is to help them feel safe? And surely one of the ways we can feel safe is with another human focussed entirely on supporting us?

We read that someone has 'twenty-four hour supported care' or 'one-to-one care'. Families provide this kind of continuous support, but of course when support is provided elsewhere it will be by a team. Time and again we hear how important it is for the team to have background information and knowledge from families to enable them to provide good support. We hear that organisations need to work in partnership with families. This partnership working can also be rather patchy. I have heard differing accounts over the years from family members. Interviewing them for feedback for the CQC inspectors was always illuminating. Many though have been extremely enthusiastic about their daughter or son's life in a particular setting. It was always a joy to speak with these families. During our induction as experts by experience for the CQC, we were told to consider, 'Would I want my daughter/son/mum (etc.)

living here?' Some places just had a 'feel' the minute you entered. Of what exactly? Of calm, unhurried approaches, with time for those little interactions and opportunities that are essential to good support. Insight into people's needs, but spoken about respectfully. And a sense that workers wanted to be there, that they actually enjoyed their jobs. These workers would tell me they felt supported by management. In those instances there was always the evidence to support this. I would observe clear outlines of roles and responsibilities and signs that people who lived there were also meaningfully involved in the general running of their home.

Routine = consistency of approach

In order to establish and maintain a consistent approach that all those supporting an individual will adhere to, it is helpful to establish an agreed protocol. How does each worker commence and finish their shift? And what are the activities they will be engaging in with Odyssey on that particular day or evening? Certainly for a newer worker this will involve clear guidelines and comprehension of why they need to be in place. People need to understand that contextual understanding and verbal comprehension are not the same. In the past I have had workers comment that Odyssey often looks as if she is about to make a profound statement, it doesn't mean that she will. People who do not use language may become adept at contextual understanding. This is why it is so important we keep our routines and approach consistent.

Workers will always change, either shift wise, or away on holiday or moving on. As long as we keep a general consistency of approach these changes are less difficult for Odyssey to manage.

When 'no' means 'no'

Odyssey's use of words is primarily echolalic, rather than to create language. In other words, she echoes or parrots words, phrases, singing and vocalisations she has heard. It is quite uncanny to hear her suddenly burst into a line or two of '*Do the Right Thing*,' which was the theme tune for an anti-litter campaign in Sydney, Australia during the early 1980s. Mostly she is seeking the sensory sensation of playing with sounds. Try it. See how much you can make your lips tingle, just by making a long 'V' sound. It is quite a pleasant sensation. Notice if you focus on the sensation, the way it becomes a sensation in your ears as well? Notice you can vary it, by the amount of breath you use. Or block out other noises by really focussing in on the 'Vvvvvvvvvv.' Odyssey also used to have a wide repertoire of various squawks and screeches although this is much reduced now. When she says 'no, no, no,' (which she will say prior to the escalation of screeching) people try to understand if it's a 'no,' because everything is 'no,' or if there is a reason behind it. For example ... there is a routine (there is a routine for everything to be fair) around mealtimes. For some reason, Odyssey will happily sit at the table for breakfast and lunch, but sometimes no amount of encouragement will help her to move from the couch to sit at the table for dinner. She will respond to a suggestion, with her 'no.' This can escalate to a point where she becomes quite distressed. We will see in the section on food and eating how mealtimes became a confrontational exercise in the past, eventually leading to her diagnosis of anorexia. We have discussed this as a team and decided it is actually a good thing for Odyssey to express a clear preference. Who doesn't occasionally like to sit on the couch with their food on a tray for dinner? It's not all the time, and not with only one particular worker for example. But food and eating have been where she seeks to find some level of control so I am happy she is able to express this and have her preference accepted by us.

Echoed words rather than language

Odyssey uses five or so words, like 'bed' or 'couch' in a truly functional sense. Everyone will tell you, walking home, to '*sit on the couch*' is always at a much faster pace, because she actually knows and understands where she is going.

She has keen contextual awareness which everyone working with her needs to understand, as well as the implication of her levels of understanding. There is no point offering her open-ended choices such as,

> What would you like to do today Odyssey?

This is completely meaningless to her as it is way beyond her capacity to comprehend. In fact, she tends to the most basic choice making which is 'accept' or 'reject.' Someone whose capacity is at an extremely early level of development may literally swallow or spit out food. The next level is 'either/or.' We have struggled with this. We try to offer her a meaningful choice of 'couch' or 'bed' after her bath routine. It's always 'bed,' even if we switch the order.

Also there is a fine line between joining in her word-salad sensory game, by echoing what she says and perhaps adding another word or tone and talking over her, or not hearing some quiet word which might be the only one with real meaning or significance for her. Her previous music therapist always told me that although people think Odyssey is loud because of the way she sings; her real voice is the tiny almost a whisper voice. She described it as 'a very shy voice.' This is so true. Odyssey sometimes whispers, 'and an egg sandwich,' which is very clearly asking for food. Considering she was anorexic at the start of this current journey, it is a joy to hear such a request. Unfortunately, we are more likely to hear,

> Sit there and do as you ARE told,' or 'If you do that again I am going to thump you.

Or any other number of negative utterances. These are always in very loud, forceful tones and very much echo something I recently read by Phoebe Caldwell (2014).

> ... when placed in situations that they find stressful, producing with extra-ordinary accuracy the verbal assaults they have endured previously in similar instances. Through them we hear the voices of those in whose care they have been placed – one cannot say by whom they were supported since these vignettes are almost always negative, critical or repressive, with no understanding of what led up to a particular behaviour. If we listen, we will hear the history of verbal misunderstanding and abuse to which some have been subjected, accurate echoes of the voices from their past.
>
> (p. 108)

I had read this, but it really stuck a chord with me recently. As we were making our way to the local shop, we had to turn around which became confusing for Odyssey. She immediately launched into a stream of, 'Stop it Kenny stop it.' Exactly as Phoebe Caldwell describes, she was 'placed in a situation she found stressful' and immediately echoed the care workers' admonitions from the past. I feel desperately sorry for this man, Kenny. Imagine if all you ever hear are people telling you not to do things. It brings to mind the parent who told me,

> They're always acting as if the choice she makes is wrong. Saying, 'Where are you going? Sit down. Don't do that.
>
> (FG:I)

If staff do not have a clear understanding of the individuals they are supporting, how can the individual feel safe? How can they trust you? I will return to this concern in the final chapter, as it seems more and more people are being admitted to hospital and often sectioned, based on their behaviour. The behaviour is inextricably linked to their conditions, yet it appears we are punishing them for this.

The clarity I describe is about clarity in our verbal overtures to Odyssey and clarity in our own understanding of what we are doing to support her and why.

This is why ideas around communication ought to be all pervasive. Not simply 'How does Odyssey communicate?' How does she make sense of the world and how can we enhance that understanding? This is why I take issue with a statement in *Valuing People* (DH, 2001) about a woman called Margaret. We are told,

> She acquired neither language nor formal signing, but was very well able to make her wishes known.
>
> (p. 101)

No, she was not. The statement really needs to be unpicked because it tells us much more about the person writing this that the subject of the story. Why do people like Odyssey lash out, self-injure, screech and wail? It is not because they are perfectly able to make their wishes known. The behaviour is a sign of distress resulting from the fact that they cannot make their wishes known.

Guidelines, charts, feedback sheets

To reiterate, there is no point obtaining specialist input from speech and language teams (SALT) or functional analyses of behaviours by psychology/ behaviour support teams, culminating in the newly introduced Positive Behaviour Support (PBS) plans, if the guidelines they produce are not understood or followed. Certainly, in my work with the Care Quality Commission (CQC) or on the NHS Care and Treatment Reviews (CTR's) it was not uncommon to see extremely comprehensive guidelines and strategies stored in box files and rarely used. I often saw frustrated, overstretched, poorly qualified teams at a loss what to do beyond 'maintain' or in many Assessment and Treatment Units (ATU's) 'restrain.' I was also shocked there was no clinical supervision for the support staff. No regular space for reflection and discussion with peers and a clinical facilitator. I believe this is essential to ensure workers feel psychologically supported and valued in their role. I used to work for a third-sector organisation, delivering the National Autistic Society's early intervention programme for children newly diagnosed with autism. We provided ongoing mentoring to families, to help them manage the programme. I found our quarterly clinical supervision sessions enormously helpful in understanding why I was not making progress with particular families or children. These days I always work through the specialist guidelines with staff, explaining why we use them and impressing on them how important it is to follow them to the letter. I cannot impress on people enough how the recording of, for example, incidents of 'challenging behaviour,' can of itself reduce the behaviour. I know this, because I have experienced it. I know what it is like to be utterly ragged and raw from years of interrupted sleep and no respite. I know what it is like to be exhausted physically and mentally from struggling to understand your child's extreme behaviour with no one offering help. I know how I reacted the first time someone advised me to keep a diary of Odyssey's behaviour. Probably explosively and riddled with expletives. I told them,

> my daughter is ripping the gas fire out of the wall, she's punched the glass out of her window and you are telling me to keep a diary!

If you are there, trust me dear fellow parent, diaries help. They really do. By keeping a diary you can keep track. I found those small memo books ideal. You may have been advised to include the ABC, or the antecedent, behaviour and consequence. In other words what happened before an incident, what was the actual incident and what happened after? It is useful to just write down as much as you can recall or think is connected. These memos help in a number of ways. Firstly, to ascertain just how frequent incidents are and secondly to see if there is a pattern. Do incidents always occur at certain times? A certain place? With a certain person? Often, just the act of keeping this diary seems to help. Sometimes I thought, maybe the act of writing in the diary helped to calm me down and in some way this helped Odyssey as well.

Having clear evidence that incidents were occurring, for example, every time you entered the supermarket you can then work on strategies. Maybe avoiding supermarkets if possible, or shopping at more quiet times or even finding another entrance. With adults behaviours are usually well entrenched and can often be a reaction to something that happened a long time ago. Hence, when filling out your ABC diary, you might want to consider how something from the past might be impacting on a person's life now. If this is a person who has moved from family home into residential care or supported living when their parent died, how was their grief managed? The first Care and Treatment review I was asked to join, concerned a young woman whose grandmother had died and no one seemed to have taken this into account. All we heard from professional after professional was how extreme this young woman's behaviour was. Indeed. Grief is extreme.

Keeping ABC charts or diaries is also a way to allay staff concerns. As I said earlier people were refusing to work with Odyssey because they found her behaviours too extreme. So when we devised our own Incident Feedback Sheet, we asked people to grade their injury, from 1 (no mark) to 10 (drew blood). In this way people will consider and describe what happened in factual detail. We always talk through the chart and try to understand what happened and why. Incidents of any kind can be frightening. I never belittle that experience for the worker. Nowadays we have people who have worked with us for long enough to recognise particular behaviours and be confident in their understanding and response.

We were involved in the pilot of the Disability Distress and Assessment (DISDAT) tool, which can be completed over time and reviewed and updated as necessary. This is actually designed for a number of people to fill in. Hence providing a more complete picture of an individual. The tool can help, especially when people have unusual ways of signalling distress. Some people might smile or grin excessively. I know we all can do that when we feel nervous or anxious. Imagine if you cannot communicate this anxiety in any way other than a frozen grin? And imagine if those supporting you simply responded by, 'Oh someone's happy.'

Imagine if you were feeling sharp sudden stomach pains? The kind associated with IBS? If you were holding the arm of your support worker and suddenly felt gripped by pain, might you not try to alert them? If you had no way to do this other than physical response, might you not lash out or head butt their arm? Think for a moment of all those little niggly aches and pains we all experience. Headaches because we have forgotten to drink water, muscle aches, because we have sat in the one position too long, pins and needles, sudden numbness, shooting pains, buzzing in our ears, ear ache, sudden itch in a really awkward position, dull dragging ache of period pain.

Sore throat, heartburn, or any other myriad of unpleasant feelings. We can make sense of them. Imagine if you couldn't? If you had no way of rationalising what you were experiencing? Imagine if you were experiencing more serious symptoms? Very many people with PIMD have respiratory illnesses. How do those supporting you recognise when you need medical support? And if you are admitted to hospital how will the staff there be able to interpret your idiosyncratic ways of communicating your pain and distress?

The tool is also useful for care workers to use their observational skills and work together to understand people more fully. For example, someone who knows an individual well may have filled in sections relating to when someone is 'content.' A newer worker may not be sure if the person they are with is distressed or not. By noting their own observations they can compare and are then better able to decide if there is something amiss. I found just working through the baseline with our team is a really good way of unpicking certain behaviours and encourages people to feel confident in their own understanding. We have an almost shorthand language now. In fact the tool does what families have done over many years. As an example, my whole family joke about their scars. Odyssey has experienced chronic constipation all her life. Her way of letting us know she needed to poo was to scratch us on the forearm. I would trim her nails, file them smooth, but this woman could always find a way to dig those nails into our skin. And yes, draw blood. One of my sisters has always had cats; many cats and stray kittens. She would joke, that she could never tell the difference between the scars from her kitten scratches and those from Odyssey.

We also devise our own guidelines when teaching indoor tasks, or for accessing a particular activity or for travelling on the underground or simply walking to the park. We regularly unpick them to see where we can tweak something or alter it entirely. But we all agree and understand that the consistency of our approach is essential for Odyssey.

We have an extremely comprehensive Feedback Sheet for staff to complete at the end of shift. The items covered include morning routine, (everything from whether or not we had to wake her, to how slowly she ate her breakfast) afternoon and dinner routine and water intake are also observed and recorded. Specific items include: Mood (scaled 0–5, from upset/anxious to happy/confident); Bowel Movement (including Bristol stool chart observations, time and any additional notes); Vocal (scaled 0–5 from very quiet to very chatty); Physically active (scaled 0–5 from being still to lots of rocking and bouncing); Sensitivity to noise (scaled 0–5 from not sensitive to highly sensitive); Walking outside (Confident/Quick, Average or Slow); Face tapping (scaled from 0 for none, to 5 for severe); How Present was Odyssey (from 0 for being very distant, to 5 for being very present).

Bodywork: How did she respond? Cooperative or resistant? And 'Any other notes,' where staff will feed back anything they feel the rest of the team ought to be aware of.

Staff spend the first fifteen minutes at least of their shift reading through the prior notes. In this way, even if they haven't worked with Odyssey for a few days, they can get a picture of how she has been. It is quite common to hear them talk about Odyssey being in a slow phase or a bit in 'lala land.' Everyone is keyed into her BMs, as they are now very aware how much her chronic constipation affects her mood. Shockingly in the UK, constipation is one of the lead factors in early deaths of people with ID. It is awful to think it has taken these deaths to alert us, but it also worries me how easily professionals brushed aside my concerns about Odyssey's constipation. She was regularly faecally impacted but no one seemed to think this was particularly worrying. 'Just give her some more lactulose' was the usual response. No one investigated further. No one acknowledged that chronic constipation is more likely if someone has cerebral palsy (CP). In fact no one actually paid much heed to her CP, including me. It only appeared to affect her right leg. Within the context of all her other diagnoses it seemed minor.

Now as she is an adult, the fact that she did not really walk until she was in her twenties has an impact. We are starting to see other evidence, including dysphagia. We had wondered what the odd facial movements were. Was it a tic, was she having some kind of seizure, was she simply trying to hold water in her mouth in an odd fashion? No, it's a mild form of dysphagia.

Physical, intellectual and sensory access

One aspect of life for someone with PIMD and those supporting them is the amount of preparation that is necessary for everything. It is impossible to do things on a whim. Everything has to be prepared and considered. For many, this will be knowledge of the nearest Changing Places toilet (see www.changingplaces.org). This campaign started in 2006 and has been growing ever since. It was recognised that there were people who needed more than simply an accessible toilet. They needed somewhere with a changing bench and a hoist. Recent government initiative the Disability and Society Inter-ministerial group describes forthcoming:

> ... action across government to tackle the barriers disabled people face realising their full participation in society ... including access to sport, culture and transport.
>
> (McVey, 2018)

Changing Places believe enhanced toilet facilities need to be provided in addition to standard accessible toilets. Surely all people with disabilities ought to be able to visit the shops, attend hospital appointments, enjoy community life socialise and travel with the same dignity as everyone else? Latest figures show 1,248 Changing Places on their official map. They also have a commitment from a major supermarket to incorporate more than thirty Changing Place into their stores across the UK.

PAMIS (Promoting a More Inclusive Society)[1] describe 'intellectual access' for people with PIMD as a route to increased social inclusion. They describe a new project they are embarking on as aiming to increase awareness and understanding of people with PIMD/PMLD. They want to offer more life-long learning opportunities by developing multi-sensory storytelling resources. The Senior Director of Family Services at PAMIS announced the funding they would receive to facilitate access to heritage sights by those with PIMD.

> We are delighted to receive this award and excited to begin this project which will open up our communities for people with profound and multiple learning disabilities and those who care for them. There will be more opportunities for meaningful activities and this will improve the quality of life for everyone.
>
> (Phillip, 2019)

It is increasingly recognised that people with sensory processing difficulties may find sounds, lights, textures or other experiences extremely uncomfortable. They can be anxiety inducing and even painful for individuals with for e.g. ASD, Down's or Fragile X syndromes. Many local cinemas offer 'autism friendly' sessions, where the lights may be dimmed and sound turned down. Often they will avoid screening advertisements or trailers, as these can be noisy and over-stimulating. Some movie theatres offer a chill-out zone and there is always freedom to move around and sit where you like during the screening. The cinema staff are usually trained in autism awareness as well.

Food and eating

Odyssey was an extremely premature baby and weighed barely a kilogram when she was born. She had reflux problems early on even though I had managed to breast feed her. On reflection the fixation on her bottle, her drinking cup, bananas as sole source of food, followed by peanut butter sandwiches for her early years, including the onset of food storing, were all early indicators of her autism. However with no diagnosis I was in No Man's Land with no specialist guidance or support. I simply used constant trial and error. Nowadays we have wonderful speech and language therapists with amazing insight and skills who devised 'Food and Eating Guidelines,' that I was determined staff I employed would observe. Unfortunately in the past the guidelines were ignored. I never ask or expect staff to do anything I would or could not do myself. I induct all new workers as well as have them observe other member of the team on their shifts. They observe us going through the process of 'alerting Odyssey to the idea of a meal time,' for example.

This is so very important. Imagine you are totally blind, lost in your own sensorial world, curled up in a ball on a couch quite happily listening to music, when suddenly someone grabs you and forcefully attempts to walk you, by telling you to

get in the kitchen.

The kitchen has a different floor surface (noisy laminate compared to carpet in the rest of the house), there is a radio badly tuned to a station staff prefer, blaring out loudly and staff are also shouting to other people to

get in the kitchen, now.

How does any of this signify that a meal is about to take place?
Compare the above scenario to one where someone is standing near to the same woman and musing aloud in exaggerated tones, for example,

Oooh I'm feeling so hungry. I wonder if it's nearly lunchtime. Who's going to make some lunch I wonder.

And then, in order to gradually include her, but not confront her,

I wonder if Odyssey is feeling hungry, maybe we could both have something to eat. Maybe a cheese sandwich.

(DL)

Depending on Odyssey's anxiety levels you could encourage her with an Object of Reference (i.e. an actual olive or lump of cheese) or suggest she joins you in the kitchen as you prepare her meal. This is done with constant description and occasional olives or cheese as before, until you are ready to sit at the table to eat your meal. This is the gist of her guidelines and I would suggest a meaningful way of alerting this woman to the notion of food and eating. And guess what, it works. Ten years ago Odyssey weighed around 35 kilos today she weighs around 55 kilos. Surely proof that Guidelines work when they are understood and observed by all involved. Odyssey must become accustomed to the idea of food and eating, before we actually offer her any food. Indeed she must become accustomed to the idea of any activity before it can take place. We saw earlier how the routine with her backpack enables her to get used to the idea of 'leaving the house,' which is a fairly abstract concept for Odyssey. Feeling safe and contained are paramount.

Sometimes people tell me they feel self-conscious speaking in exaggerated tones, or having a conversation with themselves. This is common. We all feel self-conscious at times. Of course, doing something new and oddly exaggerated will feel strange to us. Some people more than others. Practice and repetition help. I am often at home, especially in the early days of a new worker in post. I will happily engage with the worker to demonstrate and help them see that the style does work. Exaggerated tone of voice, clear signals and plenty of time for Odyssey to process information are very important to her.

I have had conversations with managers of services about how they manage people's inhibitions. I was recently talking to someone who was delivering Intensive Interaction training within a large provider organisation. I was really impressed to hear she was using video as a way to assess how embedded the approach was. She told me how she had met quite a bit of resistance from staff at first. I know what she meant. I spent ten years struggling to convince the manager of a service that this would be a really good method of relaying information about how to support Odyssey. I had experience of using it formally in the manner of *Video Interaction Guidance* (VIG) (Kennedy, 2011). I know how invaluable a tool film can be. The trainer explained how she conducted the sessions, but later would turn up to observe and film people and their interactions. Once people recognised how unobtrusive the filming could be and how viewing interactions really did aid their learning, there were less objections.

I also loved the attitude of a manager of a residential respite service who always advised new applicants, 'this is hands and knees work.' I use that description myself now, when interviewing. It encapsulates the idea that you certainly need to be fairly agile and physically fit, but you also need an element of playfulness. You cannot take yourself too seriously when crawling about on the floor and this includes worrying about how you might look or sound when reviewing a segment of filming.

Water and aloe vera juice / digestion and elimination

Everything we do with Odyssey is based on an incremental approach. And bear in mind all the work I am discussing commenced when she was in her early thirties. This is a woman who would not drink any liquid other than tea, throughout her adult life until now. She has had constant chronic constipation all her life. Doctors always told me not to worry about the fact that she only drank tea, so long as it was weak and milky. They talked about her diet advising me to increase fibre intake. Hmmm. Healthy food was always the norm. I have always used brown rice, wholegrain bread, porridge, unsweetened muesli, vegetables, beans and pulses. I do suspect she could really taste the difference between my food and the processed food other places offered. But it was not the food causing her constipation. It was the lack of water that made it so bad. We discovered this almost by accident. We had started to introduce juices to her and we found that using small bottles was ideal, as they did not overwhelm her. She could hand them back if/when she had had enough. We decided to use the same bottles with water and aloe vera juice and latterly simply full of water. At first, she simply put the bottle to her mouth and handed it back straight away. So we would hand it back to her and she would take the tiniest sip. This might to and fro for a while or she might sit there with the bottle to her lips and be playing with the feel of liquid but not swallowing. No matter, we continued to offer. This is the point. Someone asked me once how long I was going to attempt to teach her to use the toilet.

'How long?' I replied, 'Forever, obviously.'

I used to talk about the difference between 'active' care and support and 'maintenance' care. I must have been onto something, as coincidentally I came across a book recently, which gave a comprehensive overview of 'a proven model of care' called Active Support (Mansell and Beadle-Brown, 2012). To my mind we should all be focussed on active support. Any manager ought to be developing their staff along these lines. Developing relationships with those you are supporting is key. Using interactions as an opportunity for building rapport is a good start. Then constantly appraising what you are doing with someone and thinking about how you can extend that individual's involvement, however minute. A care worker I know, who works in a Special Needs school during the day, was telling me about her colleagues.

It seems they all disappeared as soon as the students needed their personal care. Most of the students were profoundly physically disabled. At first this woman was annoyed at being left to do so much on her own, but then she told me, she realised it was a great opportunity to build more rapport with the students. Perfect one-to-one time, when she could encourage some movement, involvement and turn-taking conversations, away from the classroom. How much more pleasant must their personal care time be? Time spent with someone who wants to be there and who wants to find a way to make it a moment for meaningful engagement with them.

So, there we all were, offering the bottle of water to Odyssey constantly and more often than not having the almost full bottle handed back. Until the constant offering eventually paid off, to the point where this woman would, at times drink a full bottle. She has progressed to glasses now and often finishes a whole glass of water, a number of times a day. As I mentioned we keep Daily Feedback sheets so we can monitor all the basics like bowel movements (BM), mood etc. As of course they are all interlinked. By careful monitoring and keen analysis we now understand her cycles more. A slowed down state, sleep disturbed, manic, constipated and prone to sensory sensitivity can change radically to excellent appetite, normal sleep patterns, coping with motorbike noise and a desire to engage via chatting games or singalongs. And it is usually as simple as Odyssey managing some regular BMs.

I know chronic constipation is quite common with people with ASD. I believe the 'holding back' is about being so tense all the time and almost afraid to let go. Whenever Odyssey went away on respite, she never had a BM. On her return, sometimes even before she was actually home, we always had a massive evacuation of her bowels. Faecal matters may not be the nicest sub-ject to discuss but they are so very important. Another parent when writing about her son Gabriel devoted an entire chapter to 'Shit Happens' (Rankin, 2000, pp. 175–184). She shares my query about the 'holding onto' aspect. She managed to establish toileting at the urinating stage, but not for BMs. Whilst Odyssey is still not fully continent we describe her incontinence as 'accidents,' as they are less frequent than her use of the toilet. She has a toilet stool and we find using that at a regular time each day does help her.

Physiotherapy and deep tissue massage

This next section needs to be in HUGE letters, screaming out of the page. I thought the introduction of water and aloe vera was so important as it brought about such a change in Odyssey's life. The woman who would be contorted in pain in order to 'deliver' gigantic BMs every two or three or more weeks, now has regular motions. The toilet still gets blocked but not nearly as often. Hurrah for water and aloe vera juice and proper colonic massage. Who would have believed that this woman would love her massage so much? Again, this came about almost by acci-dent. I had a new worker, who was in her final year studying osteopathy. She had that special knack, and knew exactly how to massage Odyssey's colon with excellent results. She recommended a physiotherapist she knew who then joined our team. We already had a final year osteopath so the two of them assessed Odyssey's muscle groups. For many years Odyssey was on a waiting list for physiotherapy. I had always thought her only need for treatment was for her hunched back. All those years curled up into a ball and because of being totally blind she always had her head bent forward. The result being she had quite a distorted body shape.

When I first took over managing her care, the social worker suggested we invite a mainstream physiotherapist to her first review meeting. This woman did not even examine Odyssey. She simply observed the way she was sitting and advised that physiotherapy would be of no use as Odyssey's vertebrae in her spine 'were probably fused together.' I was not convinced and insisted on an appointment at their hospital clinic. Ultimately I was told the clinic could not treat her, that she needed to be seen by the Specialist team. So I was back where I started. The specialist team was usually a part-time appointment and the waiting list so long, my daughter was always at the bottom and never received a treatment programme.

It was a huge shock to me when on examination, it was discovered that every single muscle group in Odyssey's body was tight to the point of spasm. It seems her default position is the opposite of relax. Everything is tense to the point of tight. No wonder she can be spikey and grumpy. She's been in pain and not only doesn't understand what pain is, but she cannot tell us either. How often do I moan to people about my aching back, my sore neck or my various arthritic hotspots? And I can do something about it. I can walk. I can stretch. I can exercise. I can visit the sauna. I can even relax with a glass of red wine. None of these options are open to Odyssey.

With immense insight, patience and skill this dedicated physiotherapist worked diligently with Odyssey once a week for over five years. She started off barely able to touch Odyssey as she sat on the couch. She came the same day each week for the same two hours. The same attempts to approach were met with lots of screeching and squawking, lots of lashing out and a general air of extreme anxiety and fear. The therapist simply withdrew and waited. I have never seen such creative use of cushions and pillows. Gradually, gradually as Odyssey grew to trust her, pillows would be removed and she would be lying down. Firstly this was on the couch, later (years later) onto a mat on the floor, until finally she accessed the massage bed. I cannot describe the joy I still experience watching this woman roll over onto her stomach and relax herself down onto that bed with a slight shudder of complete delight. She actually groans with pleasure as she is massaged.

We have lived in the same flat now for over twenty years and my daughter is well known in the neighbourhood. Strangers come up to me in the street saying things like,

Your girl has come on, isn't she lovely and straight these days.

Or,

I remember when she'd just lie down in the road screaming. That's all changed hasn't it?

Yes it has. Rather than lie down in the middle of the main road she has discovered the same experience, but in the safety of her living room. She now lies on her special mat every day for stretching and relaxing. Her wonderful physiotherapist has moved back to Poland, but the effect on Odyssey is well embedded. She knows deep tissue massage relaxes and makes her feel good. And because she had that magic number of five years with the same therapist the trust has remained. It has taken much less time for her to access the massage table for her new therapist. Probably most importantly her trust has generalised. She had to have a number of scans recently, in two different hospitals. Both times the staff were amazed at how swiftly and confidently she accessed their benches. The massage table has become her most important Object of Reference.

Blood tests

Possibly the most amazing add on benefit has been with regard to blood tests. I know this is a minefield for many people. For years just having her blood pressure taken was impossible. She hated that Velcro sound and the weird sensation if anyone did actually manage to wrap it around her arm. We have managed that by buying a BP machine and letting her hold it, feel it, press the button on it herself. But blood tests were always difficult. Like many others, we would use instances of dental treatment by general anaesthetic as an opportunity to retrieve some blood samples. Not anymore. With careful preparation and after discussion with her doctor, we now manage them in his surgery. We apply the cream at home to numb her arm and take her favourite blanket and squiggly snake for squeezing. On arrival she happily hops onto the surgery bed and the procedure is managed. My mind often flashes back to those desperate times, when she was having monthly blood tests at our local hospital. I was always instructed to 'hold her down, mother' and I did. I like to think I am an assertive woman, but somehow in hospital settings, surrounded by specialists telling me what to do, I would meekly comply. Finally though, on one occasion when there were already seven people attempting to hold her down and the doctor was motioning to two security guards to come and help, I did find my voice, saying something like 'I'm sorry, but this is abuse, we have to stop.' These days we have Reasonable Adjustments. Most hospital and medical staff have some basic understanding of these. I doubt they would extend to provision of five years of deep tissue massage to allay someone's fears and anxieties, or would they?

Music therapy

Odyssey has been attending a weekly music therapy session for a number of years now. She attends with her older sister (who is also a qualified OT and a musician) and according to her therapist the progress she has made was not expected at all. If you can imagine someone who had real difficulty entering the building four years ago, compared to the woman now, who on a good day will excitedly chatter or even burst into pealing song when she hears her therapist's voice. The real breakthrough came when they decided to respond differently when Odyssey got upset. Calming her down meant she physically slumped and would curl up again and become very unresponsive. They decided to match the level of her upset to show it was OK. So when she would suddenly leap up screeching the therapist would sing louder or really bang the piano keys. And a strange thing happened. After a moment or so, Odyssey would just sit back down and rather than slump she would engage. Was she learning to contain her feelings? It certainly seemed so. And one of her supporters reported back that she was better able to cope with her Saturday group session. The noise was not so distressing and sometimes she was able to access the entire sessions. This was a vast improvement. It seems the effect of the Friday music session was generalising to her Saturday session. It is a pity they are not able to offer her a continuous therapist for more than a year at a time. And sadly we lost her fantastic Saturday worker (and osteopath) as well. As much as I regret she could not have that magic five years with her music therapist, I have to recognise things will always change. This is the nature of life and certainly something we must continuously help Odyssey to manage. After all those years of struggling to manage an apparently simply change, from indoors to outdoors, managing the change of activity session or therapist is now well within her capabilities.

Behavioural support needs: where does the 'challenge' lie?

The strong aversion to change developed in early childhood and during adolescence this withdrawal behaviour increased. The small child who would roll herself up into a ball like shape, to avoid touch or attempts to interact with her, now physically and vocally resisted any attempts to encourage her out of bed. She developed a particularly blood curdling scream. The local psychology team became involved. Their plan was to physically drag her out of bed. They were a team of three, plus my older daughter and myself. Every morning, five days a week this battle would ensue. Again, like the hospital wanting to use security staff to restrain her, this did not feel right. Most mornings we gave up exhausted. What were we achieving? Looking back I do wonder why I ever colluded with that team. Because of course I believed they were the experts and knew what to do. This overpowering and physically restraining approach was also the choice of the headmistress at her local special needs school. If I did manage to get her up and ready I would drive her to school. Once there (can you guess?) she would refuse to get out of the car. Cue another battle. The schools' response was to provide a sheet that we could roll Odyssey into and then four of us would drag this poor wee kicking and screaming creature into the school auditorium where she would roll about flaying and screaming for another few hours. Fast-forward a number of years. I was working part-time with a third-sector organisation, mentoring families of children with autism. My daughter was in a shared-care arrangement, whereby she was at home half the week and spent the rest of the week in a local residential home. Since there are seven days in a week, it meant for over five years I had to manage an eight-day week. The upshot being I had to take Odyssey to work with me one day a fortnight. By this stage she was attending a day centre two days a week. She still had her major difficulties accessing that building. She had also developed a new strategy for dealing with her anxieties. She would simply refuse to get off the toilet. She would even scream that '*She needs to do a poo,*' so people would leave her. On many, many occasions the manager would ring to tell me Odyssey had been on the toilet for hours. They were all wanting to get home so could I please come and get her off the toilet.

On one particular day, during a training session at work my colleague was discussing a new type of soft restraint for use on children. I was not convinced. I'm still not. My concern is that any type of physical overpowering of a child is possible, easy even. But the child grows and their resistance to being restrained also grows. Eventually you reach the point where security guards and even police are involved. At core is still a frightened and terrified individual being blamed for their condition. Whilst we were having the discussion, I had to take Odyssey to the toilet and guess what? 'She needs to do a poo.' Okay, I thought. Let her have some space and give her ten minutes. Maybe she does need to. Ten minutes later, no. Another ten minutes passed and another. Eventually hours later everyone had gone, apart from my colleague and one other member of staff who was waiting to lock the building. And eventually for whatever reason Odyssey decided to let me assist her off the toilet.

This became a kind of shorthand for my colleague and me. It was a shared understanding that simple restraint was not always the answer. Of course, in situations of danger one had to. But the rest of the time we decided to put more effort into thinking through what might be going on. What else could we try other than restraint? Whenever we were in a situation with a particularly robust child, my colleague would look over to me, with a twinkle in her eye, saying, 'She needs to do a poo.'

Too often we see people described as 'challenging.' The challenge lies with us, not the individual in distress. Once the narrative of 'challenging' is established, it is hard to erase. A negative feedback loop is established. Support become reactive and crisis led, rather than proactive and consistent.

All it takes is time. Time is seemingly such a precious commodity that it cannot be extended to people with complex support needs. I don't understand this.

Surely allowing someone time in the first place is a worthy goal? Time to carry a cup to the sink, time to hover over a plate and eventually pick up a sandwich, time to let all the auditory and verbal cues settle and process and time to respond in a turn-taking game. Surely any of these examples are what the Valuing People driver of 'control' represents for people with PIMD? No Odyssey is not in control of her finances or even her support team. Currently her locus of control is her cup or glass. Is it such a huge ask to allow her the time to decide when she is finished? Recently someone new was visiting. They had said hello to Odyssey and noting she was holding her cup to her face immediately started asking was she finished. I intervened and explained that we afforded Odyssey the courtesy of allowing her to decide when she was finished. I know this person wasn't quite sure what I was trying to explain, but they certainly understood about ten minutes later. Odyssey placed her cup on the floor with much excitement and lots of positive noises. Puffed up with confidence is a recent development in her repertoire and I welcome it wholeheartedly.

Containment

I want to raise the notion of 'containment' after Bion (1967). Without going into the theoretical background, it is worth observing that people like Odyssey may have great difficulties dealing with or containing their emotions. I always remember a young man I met in a residential hospital, whose first (and only) words to me were 'I want to go home.'

Initially the staff did not want me to visit him, as they feared he was 'too challenging.' Bless him, when I entered his apartment, he was lying on the floor in restraint harnesses that were barely done up. Staff explained that he wanted to be restrained. I saw this a number of times in different settings with different individuals. They were all people with severe-profound learning disabilities and autism. Some had the capacity to request the restraints. Some did not use words. They were all seemingly intuitively seeking out some kind of firm hold. They wanted to be wrapped up and contained.

Temple Grandin (2005) not only understood this for herself but generalised her own experience to animal science. She initially designed her famous chute or 'hug machine' (www.grandin.com/inc/intro-squeeze.html) as a deep pressure device for calming hypersensitive people. Later it was used in animal husbandry for more humane slaughter of animals. As a child Odyssey did appear to seek out the same contained feeing. We often found she had somehow made her way into the toilet. Literally inside the bowl, facing the cistern, with her legs stuck down the S bend and her arms kind of hugging the sides. Nowadays we have found that weighted blankets have the same effect. In fact, we have now progressed from the weighted blanket to a soft throw, which we wrap her in head to toe, especially when she is very fixed on her 'nose tapping.' This has increased in perseveration and intensity and we have been at a loss what to do about it. She has a constant red lump on the bridge of her nose and sometimes the skin will break and bleed. What started as a simple sensory feedback style activity has progressed to a point where she was injuring herself. Latterly, I have discovered I don't need to wrap the blanket around her, I simply wrap her hands. Or, if she is wearing a dressing gown at breakfast, I slip her hand into the pocket. It's quite uncanny to see her sitting very calmly with her hands wrapped in a scarf or inside the pocket. I always remember our clinical supervision sessions with the psychotherapist who facilitated them. He often talked about using pockets for children to metaphorically zip in their feelings. More recently we have an even better solution and one Odyssey will reach out for. My friend brought us some knitted muffs from the hospice she works at. The volunteers make them for the patients with Alzheimer's. They can display quite agitated behaviours and fidget with their hands. The muffs are knitted and soft, but they have buttons and other objects stitched into the lining, so someone can still fiddle in a contained way. She brought them because she had seen how calming they are. Again, it is quite amazing to see this adult woman, who has experienced so much extreme distress throughout her life, siting relaxed and calm with her hands inside this woollen muff.

A truly person-centred approach recognises the times when everything is just a little too heightened or too overwhelming and we respond appropriately. Some days Odyssey and her worker have barely left the house and have to return. This particular worker has been with her for seven years, so has a good understanding of her cycles and anxieties. She can judge when it is just too much to bear. Odyssey's default mode is not to be distressed and aggressive. If she displays this kind of behaviour, it is a sign there is something wrong and we need to respect that and do our best to find out what it is and how we can support her to a calmer state.

Building a team

This must be live and ongoing, as people will always leave. Certainly staff turnover can be a problem, especially living in London. This is why a thorough understanding of approach is paramount. If staff change, but routine remains constant the change is not so problematic. Of course this still needs keen oversight by a team leader or a manager. I have a routine to staff induction, which relies on much observation, shadowing and shifts commencing in the home and only later extending to outside. I want new staff members to feel confident in their approach, before working alone with my daughter. Where possible they will observe all of the team at various times, to give them a good oversight of everyone's individual style and the overall approaches we use. From the outset I encourage a reflexive attitude to their work. So rather than staff telling me 'Oh she knows how to wind us up' they are thinking, 'What step did I miss out' or 'I wonder what noise upset her.' In this way they are problem solving in a positive way and when feeding back to me, will be confident in their analytic skills. I encourage lap over of their shifts. Even half an hour is time to catch up and relay what has been going on, rather than simply reading the feedback entry. Working with one person can be isolating for staff. It is different to working one-to-one in a residential home for example. There is no opportunity for a break. For this reason, people always start on short shifts and they are only increased, as workers feel more confident with Odyssey. The longest shift is seven hours in the day and nine hours for a waking night shift.

Training/development

I am a big believer in appropriate and specialist or bespoke training. But this has to be manageable. Apart from one worker, everyone else in our team works for us as their second job. This makes sense for short shifts, which suit Odyssey and workers. It does make for difficulties when accessing training and development. Over the years the team have benefitted from some great initiatives. They really enjoyed the Intensive Interaction training that was delivered locally over a six-month period. I am very pleased they all understand it and use it as an approach to their way of working, rather than an activity they engage in only at certain times. They have been to a number of seminars, specifically with Phoebe Caldwell whose books I find illuminating and invaluable. (I have included references in the resource list.) They have also attended a number of one-day events, specifically for people with PIMD who are visually impaired and described as deaf-blind due to their communication impairment. These are enormously helpful and inspiring to them. Working with adults with PIMD does not suit everyone. There is a special knack one needs to acquire. The ability to think quickly, to be mentally alert, whilst supporting someone who is extremely slow can feel unnatural at first. One is almost impelled to 'help' someone finish a task. Oftentimes workers feel they have to be seen 'doing,' when I am asking them to simply 'be.' They feel they have to demonstrate achievements. One way to manage their expectations is to talk through our goals for Odyssey and encourage them to choose a task they can work on together.

Goals

Our goals for Odyssey overall are to encourage her to initiate, to learn to manage her feelings and to experience shared joy. Considering she spent so much of her life in an extremely withdrawn state and her most common response to any verbal overture was 'no,' I did not hold great expectations for this first goal. It was one of those goals (like full toileting) that I never expected her to attain, but still thought it worth actively pursuing. My 'join the party' mantra has often been echoed, but would she ever initiate anything?

If she is stuck or she appears to be more distressed more frequently we pull back. Back to basic language, basic one word commands and basic activities until she feels confident enough to start again.

Here the 'TIME' of her care plan comes into play. Everyone understands we are not in competition with Odyssey. If she responds to us with increasing distress we simply back off. Sometimes people think if they keep asking her to do something in an entreating tone, she will. She is more likely to be feeling overwhelmed in those instances. I encourage the less is more approach at these times. I tell people to literally turn their back and focus on looking out of the window or even watching the clock for ten minutes. I want their focus to move, physically and mentally. In the past, the ten-minute rule sometimes extended to thirty or even forty minutes, but that is extremely rare these days.

We even go back to the original guideline from the Learning Disability nurse. He would say, 'If she only makes it to the corner of the street and back again, that's fine.' In other words, let her set the pace and respect it. These days Odyssey has her Daily Plan, which includes a number of structured sessional activities such as music therapy and yoga. She also has her individual routines with particular workers. These can be adjusted depending on how she is. These individual routines will include an activity each particular worker has decided they will do together.

Task breakdown

This 'task breakdown' is something we have used a lot. It is surprising how many steps a simple task might comprise. Initially staff will work through all the components of an activity and what part Odyssey might play in completing that process. They usually start off with something tangible, that she understands. For someone who has rarely drunk any other liquid since milk, tea was very important. As a result of this Odyssey now participates in the following: Pressing the button on the kettle > placing cup on floor > to carrying cup to kitchen > carrying plate to kitchen.

Giving support staff the opportunity to choose a task they want to engage in with Odyssey also encourages a sense of ownership of the process. Too often I believe support staff feel they have to do things to individuals rather than with them. This subtle shift in approach automatically creates a sense of partnership between Odyssey and her care workers rather than them seeing her as a passive recipient of care. Using this approach she has attained these listed skills.

Will place her cup/glass on the floor, without prompting when finished.

Will carry cup/plate from couch in living room to the sink in adjoining kitchen (open plan hence no doorway to negotiate) with verbal and audio prompting. Skilled staff will understand how often to use prompts and will test how long they can extend the time with no prompts. Since there are no time constraints, this has been known to take 4–60 minutes, especially if it's a 'cup pressed to bridge of the nose' day.

A recent modification of this has come about since Odyssey sometimes does not want her cup of tea. (It is hard to believe the 'tea as sole liquid refreshment choice' appears to be waning, but this woman now drinks water and juices fairly regularly). When she doesn't want it, she;

Will seek out whoever is supporting her and actually place her cup in their hand.

Will press the button on the kettle with verbal and audio prompting.

Will pick up her clothes from bathroom floor (meaningful exercise for her knees) and carry them down hallway and place in laundry basket with verbal and audio prompting.

Will respond to doorbell and make her way from couch to door with verbal and audio prompting to answer it.

This last achievement is one of those activities that make so much sense to her I am still kicking myself for not thinking of it sooner. As a totally blind person, Odyssey has always had 'things' magically occur at her fingertips. It occurred to me that the people who support her always 'appear' out of nowhere. So I came up with the idea of Odyssey bringing the outside in. It has had such a positive impact. Odyssey even contributes her own element. When she opens the door and people say 'hello' she reaches up her hand in a high five for them. Latterly someone walked in with her, and was facing her holding her hand. Odyssey started to rock, so this worker joined in and as the rocking progressed, Odyssey started to sing, 'see saw Marjory daw.' This became a delightful moment of shared joy between the two of them.

Odyssey tolerates household sounds much better since we have encouraged her to be in control by pressing the 'on' button on hoover and toothbrush. She 'hoovers' the hallway/lounge with her evening worker. She has yet to master the art of pushing but will happily stand and/or be guided to push.

The toothbrush use has generalised to the dentist. She happily presses the button and since she loves her sensations will tolerate the electric toothbrush very well. Equally pillow and toothbrush are excellent Objects of Reference for her at the dentist. She will sit in the chair, but sit forward awkwardly and clenched. Just touching the back of her head with a pillow is enough for her to relax and lay back. People have always been keen to tell me Odyssey *'understands everything I say,'* but she doesn't. A clear example of this at the dentist is the 'open your mouth' approach. Dental nurses do it, I do it and dentists themselves do it. We all use cheerful, pleasant, cajoling tones and Odyssey just clamps her mouth tighter and tighter shut. In the past dentists have simply given up, advising 'She'll have to come in for general anaesthetic.' This is always seen as default option, even though it is not without danger. On one visit however a very clever dental nurse simply held a toothbrush to her mouth and hey presto, she opened so wide we were all taken aback.

Contextual understanding and comprehension are not the same. We need to exercise much clarity with people who do not use language. Just because someone 'looks as if they are on the verge of making a profound statement,' does not mean they will. Sometimes the workers will tell me, she said something like, 'Yes let's do that.' I always tell them to let me know when she says it a second time. I came across a letter I had written when she was still a teenager. I talked about how proud I was of teaching her to say 'yes.' Of course, she never did say it a second time.

Conclusion

My reason for this chapter's title 'All in the Same Direction' is because I believe the most important aspect of any attempt to instigate truly person-centred approaches is an emphasis on team working. Everybody must be on board. Firth et al. (2010, p. 204) discuss with honesty, some of the difficulties of getting people on board. We ought not to shy away from this discussion as we are all aware of the difficulties encouraging people to work in different ways might engender. We need to be proactive in our recruitment and development of suitable support staff. This means being clear and honest about an individual's needs. I do believe my daughter has an exceptional team of people working with her. Yes, unfortunately people move on, happily not too often. We had the aforementioned physiotherapist, who trained in Poland. Her emphasis was on a holistic full body approach as opposed to UK/NHS style, which is more often targeted to specific areas. We had an osteopath who has done much additional bodywork with her and her sister the OT who is great at working on her sensory issues and devising those very small individualised tasks that make sense to Odyssey. The rest of the team are all university graduates, one is qualified in Special Needs teaching. Another was a final year medical student, who spent two years with us. Overall there is a high standard. Having said that, one of the PA's who was with us the longest period and who worked long hours with Odyssey, had no qualifications, was very young and came to us from her job as a waitress.

I believe the most important aspects of supporting someone with PIMD are following guidelines and developing a relationship. Once the relationship is established the guidelines can be ever so slightly stretched or tweaked, depending on Odyssey on the day. She will always be a woman with profound intellectual and multiple disabilities. That will not change. Her fundamental needs will never change. She will always need full support in all aspects of her life twenty-four hours a day. However that old adage that we cannot change other people, but we can change ourselves, rings so true for her and those like her. We can always check ourselves, check we are not overloading her with questions, check we are not making excessive demands on her, check we provide her with an atmosphere of structure and consistency, check we are patient with her and mostly see her as Odyssey, a beautiful, musical, lively and affectionate woman.

The penultimate chapter commences with a discussion of the late Professor Mansell's report and the then coalition government's response. 'Raising Our Sights' (Mansell, 2010) found that families of people with PIMD often had to struggle to gain the services they need. This is echoed across the UK and almost ten years later families still struggle to obtain appropriate specialist services and competent staff.

Note

1   http://pamis.org.uk/news/changing-places-toilets/pamis-receives-funding-to-improve-intellectual-access-to-heritage-for-people-with-pmld/

Resources

Bristol Stool Chart. www.suttonccg.nhs.uk/vanguard/Resources/PublishingImages/Pages/default/Bristol%20Stool%20Chart%20-%20A3%20poster.pdf

Caldwell, P. (2003). *Crossing the Minefield Establishing Safe Passage through the Sensory Chaos of Autistic Spectrum Disorder*. Pavilion Publishing, Brighton, UK.

Caldwell, P. (2014). *The Anger Box*. Pavilion Publishing, Brighton, UK.

Caldwell, P. with Horwood, J. (2007). *From Isolation to Intimacy Making Friends without Words*. Jessica Kingsley Publishers, London and Philadelphia.

Coia, P. and Handley, A.J. 'Developing relationships with people with profound learning disabilities through intensive interaction' in Zeedyk, M.S. (ed) (2008) *Promoting Social Interaction for Individuals with Communication Difficulties*. Jessica Kingsley Publishers, London and New York.

Disability & Distress Tool. Available from http://www.disdat.co.uk

Grandin, T. and Johnson, C. (2006). *Animals in Translation the Woman Who Thinks Like a Cow.* Bloomsbury, London, Great Britain.

Grandin, T. (2006b). *Thinking in Pictures and other Reports from My Life with Autism.* Bloomsbury, Great Britain

Higashida, N. (2013). *The Reason I Jump.* Sceptre, Great Britain.

Leicestershire NHS Partnership. (2013). 'If you listen you will hear us.' YouTube https://youtu.bc/Hp4PW17U_h8

Mansell, J. and Beadle-Brown, J. (2012). *Active Support Enabling and Empowering People with Intellectual Disabilities.* Jessica Kingsley Publishers, London and Philadelphia.

Mariott, A. and Emly, M. (2016). 'Making reasonable adjustments for people with learning disabilities in the management of constipation.'

The Public Health England Learning Disabilities Observatory (PHELDO). Available from www.ndti.org.uk/uploads/files/Constipation_RA_report_final.pdf

Mencap. (2013). A Day In The Life -PMLD available online at https://www.youtube.com/watch?v=-8kDzelLSgc

Mencap and PMLD Network. 'A series of ten how-to guides.' Available from www.mencap.org.uk/advice-and-support/pmld/raising-our-sights-guides

PAMIS: Promoting a More Inclusive Society. 'Supporting people with PMLD and their families, carers and professionals.' www.pamis.org.uk

Wing, L. (1996). *The Autistic Spectrum.* New Updated Edition Robinson, London, UK

Bibliography

Bion, W.R. (1967). *Learning From Experience.* Rowman & Littlefield Publishers Inc., Lanham, Boulder, New York, USA and Oxford, UK.

Department of Health. (2001). *Valuing People a New Strategy for the 21st Century.* HMSO, London, UK.

Department of Health. (2009). *Valuing People Now.* HMSO. London, UK.

Firth, G. (2016). *Intensive Interaction: The Published Research Summaries Document.* Leeds & York Partnership NHS Foundation Trust, Leeds, UK.

Firth, G., Berry, R., and Irvine, C. (2004). *Intensive Interaction Context and Concepts for Professionals and Families.* Jessica Kinsley Publishers, London, UK.

Grandin, T. (2005). *Animals in Translation.* Bloomsbury, London, UK.

Johnson, K. and Walmsley, J. with Wolfe, M. (2010). *People With Intellectual Disabilities towards a Good Life?* Policy Press, Bristol, UK.

Kennedy, H., Landor, M. and Todd, L. (2011) *Video Intraction Guidance A Relation Based Intervention to Promote Attunement, Empathy and Wellbeing.* Jessica Kinglsey Publishing, London, UK.

Limoges, E., Mottorn, L., Bolduc, C., and Godbout, B. (2005). 'Atypical sleep architecture and the autism phenotype.' *Brain*, Volume 128, (5, 1), pp. 1049–1061. Oxford University Press, UK.

Lyle, D. (2015). 'Policy to practice: A critiacal analusus of valuing people policy'. Available at www.http://eprints.mdx.ac.uk/15731/

Mansell, J. (2010). *Raising our Sights Services for Adults with Profound Intellectual and Multiple Disabilities.* Department of Health, London, UK.

McVey, E. (2018). Disability and Society Interministerial Group. Available at https://www.parliament.uk/business/publications/written-questions-answers-statements/written-question/Commons/2018-10-08/176680/

Ockleford, A. (1994). *Objects of Reference*. RNIB, London, UK.

Philip, M. (2019). 'PAMIS: Promoting a More Inclusive Society.' www.pamis.org.uk

Rankin, K. (2000). *Growing Up Severely Autistic They Call Me Gabriel*. Jessica Kingsley Publishers, London, UK and Philadelphia, USA.

Samuel, J. and Pritchard, M. (2001).'The ignored minority: meeting the healthcare needs of people with profound learning disability.' *Tizard Learning Disability Review*. Volume 6, (2) pp. 34–44. Emerald Publishing Limited, UK.

Seligman, M. (1972) 'Learned helplessness.' *Annual Review of Medicine*, Volume 23 (1), pp. 407–412. Annual Reviews Palo Alto, USA.

Sinason, V. (2010). *Mental Handicap and the Huan Conditon An Analytic Approach to Intellectual Disability Revised Edition*. Free Association Books, London, UK.

Simpson, D. and Miller, L. (eds) (2004). *Unexpected Gains Psychotherapy with People with Learning Disabilities*. Karnac, London, UK and New York, USA.

Sinason, V. (1992, 2010). *Mental Handicap and the Human Condition An Analytic Approach to Intellectual Disability* Revised edition. Free Association Books, London, UK.

Tantum, D. (2012). *Autism Spectrum Disorders through the Life Span*. Jessica Kinsley Publishing, Philadelphia, London, UK.

Zeedyk, M.S. (ed) (2008). *Promoting Social Interaction for Individuals with Communication Difficulties* Jessica Kingsley Publishers, London, UK and New York, USA.

5 Raising our sights

Introduction

This chapter focuses on the lived experience of adults with PIMD. From where people live, to what they do during the day, to whom they spend their time with and who provides their support. There is analysis of the report Raising Out Sights (Mansell, 2010) and evidence that families still have the same concerns highlighted there. While Odyssey's life has been significantly turned around what are the lessons learnt? Clearly the constant yo-yoing between extreme distress and withdrawal throughout her childhood and young adulthood left little room for joyful exchanges with anyone apart from close family. The expectations of those involved in her care and support were fairly limited. What did they see in Odyssey? Looking through the comments in her old Communication Books and Handover Sheets, it is striking how little there is regarding actual communication. The focus as ever was very much on her behaviours, mostly described as negative. For example, when she repeatedly communicated she was not enjoying an activity, by screaming and sticking her fingers in her ears, no one thought to change the activity. Or thought about how she was being prepared for the activity, or even how she knew the activity was taking place. If someone does not like whatever is taking place and expresses that by behavioural means we are told '*Oh he knows how to wind me up,*' or '*She knows exactly what she's doing.*' Or the advocate in *Valuing People* describing someone with no language skills as, '*very well able to make her wishes known,*' with no explanation as to how. Why is this?

Valerie Sinason (2010) uses a psychoanalytic approach to 'Finding Meaning Without Words.' In her recently updated book, '*Mental Handicap and the Human Condition*' she describes the despair unsupported workers experience, when confronted with self-injuring individuals (pp. 185–212). My sense is that this defence mechanism occurs where there is no reflexive practice at work. This is different to training and staff development really depends on it. When staff are not encouraged to reflect, they become stuck. When no new ideas are being presented old ideas are maintained. When there is a lack of understanding fear prevails. When people are afraid they react differently.

Readers will recognise those last two sentences refer equally to a worker or to someone like Odyssey. A setting where everyone is on edge or constantly fearful is not going to be pleasant. Is this one of the reasons for high staff turnover? Workers can leave, but what must it be like for the people who spend their time in these settings? In fact what are common settings for people with PIMD?

Settings and services

Most people live with their families. They may attend a building-based day centre, but as we have seen it is rare nowadays for anyone to be offered a five-day week. Those whose families manage their care may have individualised activities that occur in formal and informal settings. For example, Odyssey currently attends a formal music therapy session once a week and a yoga session also. Both these sessions are specifically designed for people with complex and multiple needs. She has a home visit massage 1–2 times per week. She also has regular times she will go to the local park for a walk and to use the swing and to local cafes for lunch. She has a daily mat exercise routine, which is regularly supervised by her private physiotherapist. Much of her time at home involves practical care including the infamous manicures and pedicures. Most of her time is spent one to one with a worker or me. The opportunities for her to explore social interactions with others in a safe environment are limited. The only formal activity where this might be possible is Saturday Stories with the PMLD group, Carousel.[1] Unfortunately, staffing issues have meant she has recently ceased attending.

In a report carried out by Mencap and I Count in 2010, it was apparent people did not have a wide range of meaningful activities.

> Assuming people with PMLD spend around nine hours sleeping, and the majority are spending between 3 and 5 hours outside the home per day, this leaves between 12 and 15 hours per day that they are spending on activities in the family home. How does the person spend their time at home during the week? The number of hours individuals spent doing different activities in the place they lived varied from person to person.
>
> How time was spent on different activities:
>
> 1 person was spending 48 hours per week 'chilling' (around 7 hours per day).
>
> 1 person was watching 35 hours of television per week (5 hours per day).
>
> 1 person was spending up to 28 hours per week listening to the radio (4 hours per day).
>
> 1 person was spending 6 hours per week doing therapeutic activities (around 1 hour per day).

1 person was spending 12 hours per week helping to prepare food (around 2 hours per day).

1 person was spending up to 8 hours helping with gardening (around 1 hour per day).

Family carers and paid staff said that personal care and eating were activities that took up a number of hours per week.

(Mencap, 2010, p. 40, see also Putten and Vasclamp, 2011)

As the list shows, only two people were involved in activities with others. The rest were passing their time passively. Watching television, listening to the radio or 'chilling.' We all enjoy the notion of 'chilling,' but for seven hours a day, every day? It is not clear if there were activities on offer, if this person might prefer them. It could be the constant time and effort involved in personal care and feeding leaves both the carer and their son or daughter in need of relaxing time. Or it could be that the family have worked out their own routine based on many years of coping. I really liked the routine at a residential home I visited with a CQC inspector. Sunday was their 'chilling out' day. Every other day was mapped out with various activities and outings. However, they had decided to make Sunday a day for relaxing. Residents were left to sleep in. Who doesn't love a lie in on Sundays? Meal times were more relaxed and there was plenty of time for 'chilling.' Staff felt they had more opportunity on Sundays for prolonged interaction and engagement. Rather than being focused on getting someone ready, with all that entails for someone who needs full support in all aspects of their care, they could simply be with each other. They felt this had led to a deeper understanding of the people they supported.

The most common 'settings' therefore for people with PIMD are the family home, residential or supported living arrangements, day centres, residential respite and of course hospitals. Who was tasked with ensuring the basic *Valuing People* drivers of 'rights, independence, choice/control and inclusion' were met in these diverse situations? In fact there was a growing concern by various stakeholders about the lack of representation of people with PIMD as a distinct group within the *Valuing People* strategy. This concern led to the Department of Health commissioning a review of services by the late Professor Mansell.[2] This was also published in 2010 in response to the refresh of *Valuing People* (DH, 2009), and acknowledged progress of change in service provision for people with complex and high support needs, had been too slow. Eight years on have (m)any of the recommendations been met? Why not? This penultimate chapter focuses on that services review report 'Raising Our Sights.' Mansell (2010) found that families of people with PIMD often had to struggle to gain the services they need. This is echoed across the UK and almost ten years later families still struggle to obtain appropriate services and competent staff. The implications of the continuing marketisation of social care are critical for people with PIMD and those who care for them. The manager of a building based specialist day service in an outer borough of London confirmed attendance is now four times the original capacity. Rather than opening a new centre, the local authority has outsourced the service. New referrals are being offered more informal domiciliary care by agency workers. Families are allocated to the agency with no choice. The workers are unskilled and not trained in any specialist approaches. Redley (2009) argues that services are now

> 'being consolidated in the hands of fewer and larger providers,' who are, 'subject to economic pressures to be efficient.'
>
> (p. 499)

Personalisation

> Person-centred planning is a process of life planning for individuals, based around the principles of inclusion and the social model of disability ... Person-centred planning replaces more traditional outmoded styles of assessment and planning which are based on a medical model approach to people's needs.
>
> (Circles Network, 2005)

Personalisation is seen as the new approach to social care provision (see for e.g. Gladsby, 2011, pp. 36–42). No more service-led, this new system can supposedly deliver support tailor made to an individual's needs. This is possible via the provision of an individual budget or direct payment. The individual might then choose the support they need, how it is delivered and when they receive it.

> Alan is in his 50s and now lives in his own terraced house. He wasn't happy living in a hostel nor in his own flat with support from a key worker. He met someone who was getting a direct payment and decided '– yes that's for me! I like the idea of employing my own personal assistants who I could ask to do what I wanted when I wanted.' His social worker put him in touch with the local independent direct payments support agency. They helped him apply for a direct payment, advertise for personal assistants and prepare job descriptions and contracts. They arranged training about direct payments and employment. Alan said 'Without the training I wouldn't have been able to cope with a direct payment.' Now he gives talks to social workers and people with learning disabilities about how to get a direct payment.
>
> (DH, 2001, p. 49)

This excerpt from *Valuing People* is a great example of someone being supported to take control of his life. Alan appears to have a happy and fulfilled life, a home he is happy living in and meaningful engagement with his peers.

He directly employs his assistants and is clearly '*very well able to make his wishes known.*' Alan certainly appears to be at the centre of the process and in control of this aspect of his life. But our focus is on people with PIMD.

> Susan, who is in her early 20s, is severely disabled. She makes her views known through her actions, verbal responses, facial expressions and moods. Susan's circle of support realised she was unhappy with her existing services and put together a package of money to enable her to live independently. Direct payments are part of the package. The circle formed itself into a user controlled trust fund, which manages the direct payment. Susan's expressions and views guide how the money is spent, so she is in control of the use of the money. Direct payments mean Susan can live in her own house with her own rota of support workers. She is relaxed, confident and content with a full social life and is very much part of the community.
>
> (p. 50)

In this case study we do not know who comprises Susan's Circle of Support. But they are the drivers of the support package. They must ensure staff are in place and available for work. The difficulty with using words like choice, control and user empowerment in this context is they tend to disregard the volunteer input, usually family. Their involvement in planning, management and day-to-day delivery of services is key.

> There should be strong self-advocacy and family and carer support and involvement. We believe it is vital to involve family, carers and advocates in this process to ensure people are really able to tell us what they want and what works best for them.
>
> (Creative Support, 2011)

Carers in an inner London borough reported reductions in service evidenced by reduced attendance at the day centre (Lyle, 2015). Carers overall had little enthusiasm for the self–directed approach to service provision. Only one of the families interviewed had chosen this route. They explained it had been a pragmatic decision to ensure their daughter's continuity of care. A newer larger conglomerate had outbid the local provider. They simply paid their budget to the new organisation, which then provided the care. All families reported a perceived pressure from their LA's to adopt the individual budget's on offer. The majority did not want the extra work. And I can confirm that it is a lot of work. This includes recruiting, inducting, training, developing and managing a team of workers and all for no pay. Being the 'expert' Mansell (2010, p. 9) describes is much different to being the lynchpin. There needs to be more analysis of the input of family carers. As a family carer wryly observed at a recent conference, '

> take a break from caring, become an employer.
>
> (Parent R)

We become the care manager and by default the bank worker. What happens when staff are sick or on holiday or caught out by some emergency? What happens when staff leave and recruitment is problematic? Only one of the case studies in Mansell's report described their use of a local not-for-profit organisation for backup and support. Not all families will have access to such a service (Clements et al, undated) warns that,

> personalised services have both the potential to improve support for carers and, if misapplied, to undermine it.
>
> (p. 1)

And later

> There is also a risk that what is intended to be a liberating experience of being 'in control' is overlaid with anxiety and paperwork in order to comply with rules and procedures.
>
> (p. 15)

Organisations working with carers have expressed concern that the decision was taken before the impact of the pilot programmes on carers had been adequately assessed. This concern, essentially that carers were not seen as central to the implementation of the new programme, is also born out in the Ibsen (2009) report which notes that in a number of Individual Budget pilot areas, the officers with lead responsibility for supporting carers had not been involved in developing the pilot. As the Report notes, this was justified in one case on the grounds that

> the IB team had spent so much time and effort developing and implementing IBs for service users that there was no time to consider carers' issues and in any case it was expected that IBs would have no impact on carers.
>
> (p. 28)

As the Report goes on to explain, this view must be mistaken, since the programme has a direct impact on carers.

> Whilst many family and carers will willingly take on such roles and responsibilities, it is of concern that so little attention has been paid to this question – given that in many of the examples advanced by the proponents of the scheme this is proving to be a crucial – and unpaid – function.
>
> (p. 9)

The concept of personalisation is of course two pronged. Self-directed support is key, but also person-centred approaches. All families are adamant that current services appear to be delivered in a one-size-fits-all approach, which is clearly at odds with individualised approaches. During a focus group discussion (Lyle, 2015) care workers in a day centre told me,

> The trouble is now there is no equal opportunities. Everyone's gotta be treated in the same way. They don't seem to recognise everyone is different. That's why this one size don't make no sense.
>
> (Lyle, 2015, p. 190)

The discussion had turned to ways in which policy impacted on their service. The issue of Individual Service Plans (ISP) arose. Workers were sceptical about completing these on behalf of the users of their service.

> You mean the way we have to fill out their aspirations and dreams and stuff on the ISP? We have to imagine what a service user's dreams and wishes are, based on what we know about them.

I asked, 'So, it's your assumption of their aspiration?' 'Exactly,' they replied. I then asked,

> Can you tell me about person-centred planning?

A worker replied,

> Yes, it's about putting the person in the centre of the planning.

However, when I asked for an example there was lots of nervous laughter, but no one had an example they could relay (p. 191).

Why film is important

Since this book is an attempt to understand more about the lives and needs of adults with PIMD, this definition is a helpful recap.

Adults with profound intellectual and multiple disabilities:

- have a profound learning disability
- have more than one disability
- have great difficulty communicating
- need high levels of support with most aspects of daily life, may have additional sensory and/or physical disabilities, complex health needs or mental health difficulties, may have behaviours that challenge

But does this help us create a mental picture of someone with PIMD? After all we saw earlier a number of family carers describe their son or daughter as having 'high support needs' (HSN) and the day centre manager who felt all people with an intellectual impairment could be described as having 'complex support needs.' In their own way all of them are right of course. The experience of having a child born with a disorder resulting in this 'thing' we describe (variously) as learning disability or intellectual impairment, might also be considered profound. These children have a profound effect on our lives undoubtedly. And compared to her neighbour's daughter of the same age, the carer who describes her own daughter as having 'high support needs' has a point. Yes, her daughter can 'travel independently,' but the 'independence' is conditional. She needs supported training for some time before she can travel alone. She needs clear instructions and assurance that the timetable is correct. Difficulties arise when a bus is late or cancelled, not an uncommon occurrence. Often, she has to ask for help and is indeed dependent on '*the kindness of strangers*' (Williams, 1947).

The people I want to focus on are also 'dependent on the kindness of strangers,' although the strangers are most likely to be paid care workers. People with PIMD are less likely to have a circle of friends or peers, especially now day centres offer less attendance days and people increasingly spend much of their week at home, be that the family home or their residential or supported living accommodation. This is why film is becoming increasingly important for understanding the lived experience of people with PIMD. We saw how it can be invaluable as a tool for eliciting deeper discussion. It is also increasingly being used in training and development of care staff. For example, to assess how embedded Intensive Interaction approaches are in a care worker's practice. Promoting empathy and building positive relationships can certainly be enhanced by the adoption of *Video Interaction Guidance*. (VIG) This is based on Video Home Training (VHT) which itself was developed in the Netherlands and is based on the study of what happens in 'moments of vitality' between people. In the UK, Professor Trevarthen describes the 'communicative dance' between a parent and child. The principles of his work on attunement refer to,

> a harmonious and responsive relationship where both partners play an active role.
>
> (Kennedy et al., 2011, p. 23)

When thinking of the care worker's role, surely this description would describe the moments of shared joy I believe are immensely important to the relationship between cared for and care giver.

The Central Office of Information produced an accompanying film used to illustrate the issues addressed in the Raising Our Sights report. It was recognised that not everyone reading the report would know a person with PIMD and therefore would not necessarily understand what needs to be done and why. The link between government policy and people's real lived experiences is often not clear. People with PIMD are such a small population it is highly unlikely that every reader of this book would have met someone or know someone with PIMD personally. A list of characteristics is much less effective than a short film portraying someone living their life. To this end, I have included web addresses for these films and others on various platforms such as YouTube and TED talks (see resource list at end of chapter). It is hoped by viewing them readers will understand more fully how diverse the population is and most importantly how vital and engaging. Before viewing readers who do not know someone with PIMD, may want to re-look at the definition at opening of this section and after viewing, consider if they feel the films matched their expectations.

Raising our sights

The report 'Raising Our Sights' (Mansell, 2010) was originally commissioned by the Department of Health as a service review to accompany the refresh of *Valuing People* (DH, 2009). It had been acknowledged that the new policy for people with ID published originally in 2001, had not best served those with PIMD. At that time Mencap's then National Officer for PMLD, Beverley Dawkins OBE and the Foundation for People with Learning Disabilities formed the PMLD Network. They brought together a group of third sector organisations and family carers with a specific interest and expertise in working with people with PIMD (PMLD). Their first task was to write a response to *Valuing People*, called 'Valuing People with Profound and Multiple Learning Disabilities' (PMLD Network, 2001). This demonstrated that people with more complex needs were missing out on the government strategy of 'including everyone,' not least because of their lack of specific representation.

> In many ways it could be said that Valuing People accurately reflects the problems facing children and adults with PMLD – we don't know how to describe them and therefore we don't know how to accumulate the information we require to gain an accurate picture of their needs.
>
> (p. 2)

This echoed European concerns,

> People with complex dependency needs are little known to the general public. Nor do authorities responsible for social policy and programmes and even the disability programmes in many countries properly know them. They are the excluded among the excluded.
>
> (European Disability Forum, 2000)

As we saw these concerns were also acknowledged in the later cross-departmental report, 'Improving the Life Chances of Disabled People' (DWP, 2005). Unfortunately, people with PIMD were entirely ignored as a specific group in the subsequent report, 'Fulfilling potential Building a deeper understanding of disability in the UK today' (DWP, 2013).

There was a note about people with 'learning disabilities' although clearly this is not referring to someone like Odyssey.

> People with some types of impairment, for example learning disability are likely to be excluded from surveys that do not make reasonable adjustments for people with cognitive impairments. They may also be less likely to self-identify as having a disability or a long-standing illness.
>
> (p. 17)

Unfortunately, there is no acknowledgment of people with multiple impairments, or specifically profound intellectual and multiple impairments.

> LOS collected data on the level of difficulty people experienced with each impairment and how often they experienced this level of difficulty. Some impairments (for example mobility or learning) are more likely than others (for example hearing, sight) to result in difficulties, which are experienced often or always.
>
> (LOS Wave 1 2009/11, Appendix Table 1)

Yet my daughter Odyssey experiences constant and enduring 'difficulties' with her neurological visual impairment as well. She has been totally blind since birth. Apart from the 'difficulty' that entails, she has also experienced cataracts, keratoconus, and enucleation of one eye. The point is, her various impairments are all interlinked. In order to *'Build a Deeper Understanding'* we do need to know certain people exist in the first place. This seems a missed opportunity to include a discussion of the barriers to inclusion people with PIMD face. The only reference to 'multiple learning difficulties' in the entire document, is in relation to young people moving from education to employment, or not.

> The proportion of disabled apprentices completing their framework has increased from 49% to 70% but success rates for those with mental ill health, emotional/behavioural difficulties, multiple learning disabilities and moderate learning disabilities are consistently lower than for other groups.
>
> (Department of Business Innovation and Skills, 2011)

Perhaps the remit was constrained, as the report was prepared by the Department for Work and Pensions, rather than the cross-departmental approach of its predecessor. Surely this would have been an ideal opportunity to explore the 'complex dependency needs' the European Disability

Forum describes for example? The DWP conversation is ongoing, so future reports might well incorporate more intelligence on this population.

In the meantime, the Mansell report, Raising our Sights (2010) sets out a series of specific principles, focussing on vision, values, visibility, rights and representation. These underline the recommendations the PMLD Network believes need to be enacted if people are to benefit from the *Valuing People* strategy. The network further contributed to the Raising Our Sights report by providing examples of good practice in services for people with PIMD and also feedback from families. Professor Mansell and the then minister Paul Burstow MP, agreed this group of people is,

a   relatively small (approx. 16, 000 out of population of fifty-five million),
b   easily identifiable, with,
c   undeniable need for lifelong care and support

(Burstow, 2011)

Readers may well query why families report such difficulty in accessing services. Put bluntly, why do families still have to fight? Mansell highlights examples of good practice in his report, but also recognises this is the exception not the rule. The norm appears to be a lack of support for family carers, with many families reporting twenty-four hour days, or having to wake multiple times during the night to tend to someone's needs. Lack of respite was also a major concern as noted by the Mencap report, 'Breaking Point' (Mencap, 2006), with 70% of those responding citing a lack of respite services. Families also have to co-ordinate many different agencies, including adult services, DWP, housing and education, on top of the often multiple health professions involved in someone's life. All too often health services do not extend Reasonable Adjustments (Michael, 2008), which ought to make services more accessible. Families report being seen as '*over protective*' or '*too demanding*' when often they are more likely to have a keen early insight when something is going wrong. The 'Breaking Point' report highlighted worrying figures. Of those interviewed only 6% believed there was effective planning for transition to adult services. 92% were concerned at the lack of therapy in adult services compared to children's. Only 3% believed there were sufficient services for their son or daughter. In terms of major obstacles, the report highlighted the disincentive to providing suitable housing, the problems with wheelchair provision and maintenance and the lack of further education opportunities.

Five years later the views of family carers interviewed for Lyle (2015) echoed those in the report. Families still described their experiences in terms of 'battling' for services, whilst many were resigned and overwhelmed from the physical and emotional effects of this. They still referred to the lack of trained staff, of appropriate therapeutic services and of suitable respite. They also referred to poorly planned transitions to adult services. If the government acknowledge there will be a 'lifelong need for care and support' why, for example do local authorities insist on separating Children and Adult services for people with PIMD? Where is the joined-up approach people have talked about for as long as I can remember?

The following sections will look at aspects of the report in depth, including families, respite, community specialist health teams and training.

Families

> 74.3% of carers of a person with learning disabilities had been in a caring role for more than 20 years, compared with an average of 20.1% for all carers in England.
>
> (Public Health England, 2015)

Mansell's report describes in more detail what those twenty plus years might entail. Ten or more hours a day spent on physical care was common for 60% of carers interviewed. A further 33% provided continuous round-the-clock physical care. Almost 50% received no outside support. In my own case the first seventeen years of my daughter's life were mostly spent washing up to eight loads a day of nappies, bedsheets, towels and clothes. I was woken numerous times during the night and never slept for longer than three hours at a time. On top of which was a continuous round of hospital appointments or home visits by various professionals. Having a child with multiple complex health and support issues is still deeply problematic. During my daughter's early life, the lack of services were explained away by, '*There's no one else like her,*' '*She's too complex*' or my favourite, '*If you think there's nothing for her in children's, wait till you get to adult services.*' Twenty years later despite 'a new strategy for learning disability for the 21st century' (Department of Health, 2001), families are still denied services for the same reasons (Mansell, 2010 p. 5). Why? Mansell argues it is the low expectations of the past coupled with discrimination of the present, whereby those with PIMD are deemed,

> as not worth bothering with, as too difficult to support well and as people for whom the poor standards of the past are all that can be achieved.
>
> (p. 6)

The Foundation for Learning Disabilities describes family carers' intentions; often perceived by service providers as oppositional.

> An essential difference between many family carers of people with learning disabilities and other carer groups is the lifetime experience of caring with different needs arising at different times. The majority of family carers are parents, although there are increasing numbers of siblings, grandparents

and other relatives, partners and friends who are also caring. Most of these family carers have been involved with the person since birth and their lives are usually centred on the needs of the person with the learning disability. It can be easy for people to make assumptions that the needs of all family carers are the same – but this is clearly not true. Families often find themselves in situations where they appear to be focusing on the negatives rather than the positives. This is often misinterpreted by people working in services as obstructive and over-protective. However, family carers have often found their own ways of coping over many years. They can feel they are not listened to or have their experience recognised when they are trying to get the support their relative needs. Whether speaking up in meetings, reviews or filling in paperwork, it can be exhausting and frustrating to be perceived as the person(s) who will always be negative when your intention is quite the opposite!

(Foundation for Learning Disabilities, 2009)

In my own study (Lyle, 2015) 40% of the family carers believed service providers perceived them as overprotective. They felt they were seen as somehow holding their adult children back or impeding their independence. This could be in conversation with support workers, who might constantly say, '*He always does it for me,*' or in the Communication books sent home from the day centre. One family wondered, as it was the same account each day, was the book for the family or the support workers.

> According to the workers he did so much when he was at the centre. I always felt I was doing something wrong, because he never did the same at home.
>
> (EP:I)

Another was worried,

> they're always telling me he knows how to wind them up. They say it in a jokey way, but I know they really believe it.
>
> (WD:I)

More worrying were the families who tried to raise concerns. One family had complained to their local adult services department about declining standards at the care home their son had lived in for many years. They were told,

> if you don't like it there are plenty of other people on the waiting list.
>
> (BL:O)

When discussing the issue of 'choice,' one of the key drivers of the Valuing People policy, a parent recounted an exchange.

> My daughter only has her behaviour to communicate. She does 'speak,' but no one is listening. Certain people just cannot get her to do things, so she's saying she doesn't want them. When I tried to take the manager aside and tell him this, they just said, 'Oh I don't want to get into an argument on a Wednesday.'
>
> (G.H:I)

So much for working in partnership with families. This parent felt her daughter was not being heard and neither was she. The residential care home her daughter lived in had no formal carers group or meetings, so there was no formal space to air her concerns and have them responded to. In common with many parents I have spoken to, in my recent role as expert by experience for the Care Quality Commission, she was wary of saying too much or formally complaining, as she was concerned it would negatively impact on her daughter's care. An NHS study (undated), 'Ask, Listen, Do.' found 26% of family carers of children and adults with 'a learning disability, autism or both,' who responded, did not make formal complaints as they were worried that it might negatively affect how their family member was treated. Bearing in mind, these are parents of people who cannot self-report in any conventional sense.

> With my son, certain people he is not accepting. These people are strong in their nature. If they were gentle, doing it calmly, he would let them. But they are in a rush and they know everything, so my son is blamed. They say he is very challenging.
>
> (TU:O)

As the Foundation for Learning Disabilities points out these parents are too often perceived as being constantly oppositional when, as with the parent above, all they want is to help services provide the best life for their son and daughter. And as Mansell (2010) states,

> Good services treat the family as expert.
>
> (p. 9)

Unfortunately it seems the best outcomes still occur to those who shout loudest for services. Raising Our Sights uses case studies to demonstrate the personalisation agenda can extend to people with PIMD. However it is unclear how these examples would have fared without the dynamic and steadfast determination of the family carers.

This point cannot be reiterated enough. Not all family carers are willing or have the capacity to take on the additional responsibility of managing a care plan and therefore a team of workers. Not all have the mental and physical energy either. Many adults with PIMD still live with their families who work for long hours over many years providing increasingly complex health care and support. These families represent enormous savings to local authorities. It seems sound economic sense for LA's to properly support these carers so they might carry on their role as long as possible. Worryingly many carers believed they received fewer services because they were living with the family member. The Royal Commission on Long Term Care (Sutherland, 1999) did in fact report that those still living with family carers were seen as a low priority by their local authority. During discussion with a group of family carers living in London, one sibling stated,

> Well it's my mum really. She's the main carer, bottle washer and nappy changer. She's got tired of the constant battle for any support, so she just gets on with it. It's like she's been doing it so long, it's all she knows.
>
> (Lyle, 2015, WD:I)

In a recent poll, Carers UK[3] found that 60% of the family carers providing more than fifty hours of care per week are in fact women. One in four of those aged between 50 and 64 care for a family member. The vast majority, 72% are in receipt of Carers Allowance. They highlight one woman's story. Patricia has been caring for her daughter for thirty-eight years. When asked what she would like to see change for carers, she says,

> I want carers to be taken out of poverty. Before carers go into meltdown I want the Government to help like they promised, and to stop cutting the services of our loved ones, which in turn makes our lives even worse. I want to stop being ignored by the Government.
>
> (Patricia, Carers UK)

Do historical assumptions about caring in general mean it is still seen as menial 'women's work' and therefore not a task one should be paid for? Feminist writers discuss the free family care provided by women and the 'public patriarchy' of the paid care sector (see for e.g. Daly and Lewis, 2000, Szehebehely, 2005). In the UK only 16% of the care workforce is male. In a review critically appraising current developments in the theory, policy and practice of care, in six European countries, it was noted that in the UK,

> care ideology has favoured a female part-time worker/carer model, with family care shared with the state and increasingly residual and rationed access to formal long term care: political support for 'family care first' is strong despite there being a choice of publicly funded care options and locally determined eligibility for care services and some regional differences in eligibility to long term care.
>
> (Rummery and Fine, 2012, p. 333)

The move to less formal care and support is now inextricably linked to the UK Conservative government's austerity agenda. Changes to day services, ostensibly described as more flexible, usually result in less attendance. Carers have queried how this is a response to individual need, which has not changed.

> When she started at the college it was better. But they changed to this 'one-size-fits-all' approach. They had a routine before. Suddenly they were just taking them out to wander round the streets
>
> (Lyle, 2015, EP:I)

A parent was asked if she had been involved in devising her son's new care-plan after the review of his day service.

> What care-plan? He does nothing. Activities nothing, opportunities nothing. He doesn't go out. He sits in his wheelchair. He sits there all day in front of the television.
>
> (BL:I)

Leyin and Kauder (2009) conducted a small-scale study monitoring the community activities of a group of older adults with PIMD, before and after the closure of two day centres. They found that there was no significant increase in their community activities or social inclusion. This echoes concerns of the families interviewed in 2015. As one told me,

> He used to go to the day centre five days a week. Now, it's just one. The rest of the week it's supposed to be this new community life. But he does nothing. He goes nowhere. They just don't take them out. They tell me nothing.
>
> (BL:I)

'R'espite or 'r'espite

> The support carers receive is still viewed as evidence of the state's beneficence rather than as compensation for the discrimination they experience from the non-carer majority, and in consequence they are still not seen as 'rights holders.'
>
> (Clements, 2011 p. 3)

Some 70% of family carers interviewed felt they had reached 'Breaking Point' because of a lack of respite (Mencap, 2003). I recently came across a letter I had written to the Editor of one of our daily broadsheets in the early 1990s. I don't think it was ever published. I do think I had probably reached 'breaking point.' Reading through this, well over twenty-five years later I wonder how I survived. I am also struck by how similar my concerns were then, to the concerns of parents interviewed in successive years, right up to the current situation. Respite, and staff training do not seem such a big ask of services in return for voluntary round-the-clock care and support.

> There is no local suitable respite option for either of our children. The eldest has had forty four nights away in twenty-one years. Thirty nights between sixteen and eighteen years at a hospice in the country and four nights at another charity in another part of the country. None of this cost our local authority a penny. This is a real problem and one we have faced all their lives. The money allocated for a respite service specifically for those with PMLD/complex needs was divided up between three local charities, to provide short breaks for a greater number of families. None of these were able to take either of our children. Now the same thing has happened in adult services.
>
> (Lyle, 2015 HN:I)

This family need a respite space equipped with the right facilities and with staff trained in working with people with higher support needs. Others need regular predictable dates, as opposed to one–off opportunities.

> My son needs structure he needs to have a routine. You can't just suddenly offer him a week away to somewhere he's never been, with staff who don't know him. And then complain about his behaviour so he never gets offered again.
>
> (NN:O)

A sibling carer spoke about respite in terms of his mother's rights.

> I think it should be more about my mum's rights. She's on dialysis now, three times a week. She's an elderly woman she should get help. Look how long since we had respite. Others, there are others who are easier to manage than my brother. They go on outings and on holidays. Remember they took us to that place they thought would be suitable for a holiday? They expected to get my brother into that tiny shower. How were they going to support him? It takes two people to lift him. How were they going to get him from his wheelchair to that little plastic shower seat? It would have collapsed. My brother is a big man and he can't support himself, he needs you to help him. All these ideas. They need to meet my brother, then they'd see.
>
> (WD:I0)

This family had received no respite since 2003 when their local authority had closed down the existing facility. Apart from three sessions a week, 10.00–3.00 at the local day centre they received no additional help. The local voluntary organisation organising short breaks for families could never offer this family a break as the accommodation was never suitable for people with complex needs. Another family had relinquished care of their son, when the respite centre closed. They had been offered cover in their home, but their home had failed a Health and Safety assessment.

> It was alright for us to manage all those years though.
>
> (NX:I)

They also saw the difficulty with being offered a basic home sitting service as twofold.

> This pre-supposes we have somewhere to go or that we can afford to go somewhere. Sometimes you just want to be able to relax in your own home. You have no idea how quiet this place suddenly becomes when he is away. There is a certain low gurgling noise he makes constantly. It seems to echo through the whole house. Sometimes you want a break from that.
>
> (DX:I)

This family were also concerned that the new idea of informal breaks in the home would deprive people with more profound support needs from stimulating experiences outside the home.

Day/respite services

Attendance at a day centre can also be defined as 'a short break' for the family carer rather than a learning/leisure/day opportunity for the individual. This means local authorities can claim 100% of parents of adults who receive community services are in fact receiving a short-term break. Even and especially those families quoted in the previous section. In the past families might expect their son or daughter would attend a day centre five days a week, with residential respite of some six weeks throughout the year. Families providing fulltime care to an individual with PIMD, to someone with this package, would still be providing 138 hours of care per week. An annual 2 week break and monthly weekends off is the kind of support families used to expect. The move to so-called personalised services combined with massive cost-cutting has led families to believe the two are linked. Sadly they probably are.

As a family carer points out,

> Rob Grieg (author of *Valuing People*) was adamant the strategy was not about saving money. However, if you point out to LA's, as he did, that there is a potential for saving money, then they will adopt the strategy in order to save money.
>
> (NX:1 p. 138)

In a more recent discussion of changing day services in Scotland, Campbell (2012) raises the concern that,

> a move to more flexible 'alternative day opportunities' is driven more by reduced budgets than a policy of modernising day services in response to individuals' needs.

(p. 205)

He describes the negative consequences of a poorly re-designed service for those with PIMD. One of reduced hours where

> the carer will pick up the slack.

(p. 213)

This appears to be happening across the UK. In Mencap's follow up to Breaking Point (Mencap, 2003, 2006) they noted,

> .... our findings show that widespread cuts are being made across the country. These cuts show no sign of slowing, with expenditure in both children's and adults' services reducing, and with a steady rise in the number of short breaks services being closed.

(Mencap, 2012, p. 43)

We are seeing the difficulty with enacting a policy apparently empowering and enabling for Alan (see, Personalisation) but not necessarily for parents of adults with PIMD. A policy so keenly directed towards those adults with the capacity to truly self-advocate, has real difficulties when directed towards those at the profound end of the ID spectrum. This needs to be acknowledged. A policy designed to

> move away from the gift model of welfare delivery towards a citizenship model: whereby disabled and older people are no longer passive recipients of care, but actively involved in their care through designing, commissioning and purchasing services.

(Gladsby, et al, 2009)

Politicians might not know anyone like my daughter. They may have met people with ID and been struck by how keenly they express their desire to be more in control of their lives. Who wouldn't support a policy that could do this? Looking at the above quote, how does this apply to Odyssey? As we saw in the last chapter, all of the team supporting her constantly work on ways she can be 'actively involved in her care.' This may be via backward/forward chaining, whereby she will complete the first or last step of a task. Following audible prompts to press the button on the kettle or pulling up the sock that has been placed over her foot are just two examples.

How does she move from these real and tangible examples to 'designing, commissioning and purchasing' her care? There are those who argue that by expressing preferences and/or choices she is in fact designing her service. I find this a semantic stretch too far. As we saw in previous chapters the notion of 'choice' is fraught with presumption and assumption. In the interests of clarity and scrupulous use of clear language, can we not simply acknowledge that I have designed her service and I purchase her care? After all I was interviewed by DWP officials and as a result was made her appointee when she reached nineteen. This means her disability benefits are paid into my bank account on her behalf. This is because it is acknowledged that she does not have the mental capacity to manage her own affairs. By refusing to acknowledge my involvement in managing her Individual Budget we are denying the level of her impairment whilst making my input invisible in the process. The idea that marketising care services leads to some level of self-determination and increased social participation for Odyssey is clearly a misnomer.

Some local authorities have recognised the need for a physical day centre, after initially closing them down in line with Valuing People ideas. There is however a mixed picture in the UK, with the emergence of a range of service management structures, including third sector and social enterprises taking advantage of the budgets available to individuals via the Personalisation agenda. Hence we may find a LA managed and funded Day Centre in one borough, whilst a neighbouring borough refers people to an independently run charity. These newer independent third-sector organisations offer a range of services, often under one roof. The irony of this is not lost on some older family carers. These newer building based services are reminiscent of the idea behind the original Intensive Support Units (ISU) where everything would be available under one roof. This would include all therapeutic services, including physiotherapy, speech and language and occupational as well as rebound therapy, music therapy and hydrotherapy. Families ruefully explained their day service centre was purpose-built, but the facilities never eventuated.

> I remember when they used to talk about the hydrotherapy pool. We fought for the new day centre, we envisaged and we were promised so much.
>
> (EP:I)

However these newer centres are dependent on fundraising and donations; their longevity is in no way assured and their existence often perilous. And for families, the availability is down to postcodes. If I refer again to Odyssey there is a strong argument that a truly person-centred approach to her needs would recognise how appropriate an old style ISU would be for her. In the absence of such a space her home becomes her day centre and access to any therapeutic activity is limited and problematic. The available local services are run by a local third-sector organisation and in multiple locations. Having to negotiate physical, sensory and intellectual access across a range of sites before any activity commences can be overwhelming for her, especially on days where her sensitivities are high.

Still fighting

This BBC online Panorama (Panorama, BBC, 2018) site leads with a film focusing on families of young children but the language is all about having to fight. Why are families still using this combative language when trying to access services? Why can local authorities not see the short sightedness of reducing respite days, after school activities or transport provision? Unfortunately, the position in the UK politically is still described as one of 'austerity.' In a recent statement the Local Government Association (LGA) outlined the further £1.3 billion cuts in government grant funding for local services for 2019/20. They noted councils across the country were already struggling to balance their books with more in-year cuts and overspending. In a two-year period (2010–2012) councils will have lost 60p in every pound they receive in government funding. Cllr Richard Watts, Chair of the LGA's Resources Board, points out:

> Unprecedented funding pressures and demand for adult and children's social care and homelessness services is pushing councils to the limit. Losing a further £1.3 billion of central government funding at this time is going to tip many councils over the edge.
>
> (Panorama, BBC, 2018)

Sadly, people with PIMD are only one vulnerable group scrabbling for services. Their continued lack of specific representation in policy and consultation is problematic.

Community specialist health teams

In the last chapter, it was shown how beneficial regular physiotherapy and massage has been for Odyssey. How specific therapeutic guidelines when followed can have a life changing affect. This was most evident in her recovery from anorexia via her speech and language guidelines. Helping Odyssey manage her sensory and proprioception issues with input from her occupational therapist (OT) resulted is much reduced anxiety and fear levels. Regular physiotherapy has had a significant impact on Odyssey's body posture. Regular massage has taught her what being 'relaxed' means.

The Valuing People strategy was very focused on mainstreaming services. In an interview on publication of the refresh strategy, the then minister was concerned,

....particularly in ensuring that people with learning disabilities can access mainstream services for health, housing, education and employment – the things that ensure equality of citizenship.

(Department of Health, 2009b)

Considering the refresh document was meant to be taking account of those with more complex healthcare and support needs, the focus on mainstream clearly overlooked their need for specialist services. Mainstream physiotherapy could not work with Odyssey. It took over two years of regular weekly sessions before she was confident enough to access the massage table. Mainstream NHS physiotherapy services do not have the capacity to spend years working with someone incrementally just to get them to the level where they are ready to be treated.

One community specialist heath team are providing the kind of holistic comprehensive support families say they need. South Derbyshire Community Learning Disability team have described how their service was set up in the late 1990s. The Complex Needs Clinic is recognised now as a national example of Good Practice. People are seen regularly over long periods of time. This means the team develop close relationships with families, care providers and importantly acute hospitals. This means they can often advise, liaise, fast-track or arrange provision of specialist equipment following hospital stays. They have also evidenced reduced hospital admissions, length of stay and inappropriate discharge for this group of people. They feed into strategic planning discussions and emphasise the increase in this population can have significant budgetary impact. However they also educate Health Board members, commissioners and other key professionals about the lifelong nature of conditions associated with PIMD and the inappropriateness of using a 'recovery' model with this group. They recognise that due to the complexity of people's needs their cases must remain open for substantial periods of time. And their oldest client is 89.

Training

Families have voiced the concern that workers do not have enough understanding or insight into the particular needs of those with PIMD (Lyle, 2015). They query why staff do not receive training specifically around the needs of this group.

Training has to be effective with demonstrated outcomes. Instead most is a tick box exercise, with no follow-up, say in three months. It just looks good on CVs.

(ND:I)

They also believe staff need to be well managed. They understood the role of a manager included guiding and developing staff in order to enhance the quality of support they provided.

I think at the day centre they'd be happy if everyone just stayed in their wheelchairs. But you know, he can walk and they have the room there, they have that gym for a start, they can help him with his walking, but they don't. They'd rather just load him on the bus, along with everyone else and just drive around.

(WD:I)

The PMLD Network and Mencap published a range of ten guides for implementing recommendations from Raising Our Sights at local level. The guide for workforce training is comprehensive. It outlines the skills and additional training workers will need, as well as required areas of knowledge and understanding. It goes on to list the number of professionals who could well be involved in someone's life and notes that a worker will often be required to carry out their particular guidelines or strategies.

The people involved in meeting the needs of those with PMLD/PIMD can include:

- physiotherapists
- speech and language therapists
- occupational therapists
- dieticians
- community nurses
- school and support staff
- practitioners in postural care
- managers/staff in respite care
- palliative care/end of life care staff
- day centre managers/staff
- local health specialists
- learning disability nurse specialists
- social workers
- dentists
- optometrists
- personal assistants/relief and agency staff.

Some of the skills and particular training people will need to support an individual are:

- High quality communication skills, including an understanding of Intensive Interaction, communication passports, objects of reference and the use of switches for cause and effect
- Know how to engage with the person day to day in a meaningful way
- An understanding that photos and keeping information about people's lives and their stories is important
- Training on complex health needs, for example using suctioning equipment or tube feeding

- Training in nutrition, eating and drinking
- Postural care training
- Training around supporting an individual with behaviour that challenges – which focuses on the principles of positive behaviour support
- Training around assistive technologies and equipment, for example iPads
- Advocacy training
- Person-centred planning training
- An understanding of, and commitment to, the principles of the Mental Capacity Act and 'best interests.'

Each person working with or supporting someone will need knowledge and understanding underpinned by skills that are specific to their area of work such as,

- understanding of issues around consent and medication
- understanding of the importance of hospital passports and health action plans
- understanding of sensory needs and recognition that sensory assessments can be an important part of getting support right
- moving and handling
- managing direct payments
- understanding of the health and social care system.

The guide emphasises how important it is that all support staff respond to guidelines from the various involved professionals. This is especially important as it will be frontline support staff who actually make them happen. Staff need to be supported to do this, ensuring they feel valued and therefore motivated to put the plans into action. Equally their managers must be skilled at ensuring staff adhere to guidelines consistently and over time. Too often staff, including managers are not sufficiently informed about the reasons for guidelines and the time it can take to embed them into someone's support. Leadership from managers is essential in order for workers to feel confident in their work.

> Sometimes my brother can cry out, makes these noises, yes vocal, what you say? Vocalisations. They say in his book he was being challenging. I say no, he is trying to tell you something. Maybe he needs changing, maybe he wants something. No, no, not challenging. It makes him sound bad.
>
> (BL:O)

Those employed to formally support people with PIMD/PMLD will also need important underpinning values and skills such as:

- empathy
- understanding
- shared interests
- assertiveness
- respect
- sensitivity
- commitment
- creativity
- facilitation skills
- networking skills
- ability to work as part of a team and in isolation
- understanding of the importance of relationships with family and friends
- understanding of the importance of developing relationships with the wider community
- understanding of the importance of thinking creatively about paid work and developing opportunities for people with PMLD.

And all of the above for minimum wage, often on zero-hour contacts. As was pointed out in a survey conducted by Fitzroy in 2015,

> I discovered I could earn much more as an office cleaner than a carer, and have so much less responsibility. A carer is lucky to see £6.70 an hour or £8.50 an hour with advanced training. But the responsibility they have, and the criticism they face if they make a mistake, are intense.
>
> (p. 15)

This stark realisation hit me recently, when I had to employ a cleaner. The fact that care workers and cleaners both hold 'unskilled' status regarding their pay surely tells us something about the way we value our care workers? Not very much would seem to be the answer. In the current climate of neoliberal marketisation, care work continues to be low paid and undervalued. As Tronto (1998) warns, those feeling undervalued and under pressure are less likely to be supported to provide responsive and attentive ethical care. She also notes that those being cared for in this manner are more likely to be

> at significant risk of exploitative, low quality care that fails to meet their needs at best and is abusive at worst.
>
> (p. 337)

Recruitment and retention are at crisis levels, although the Chair of the Independent Care Group (ICG) believes this crisis is easy to resolve. Firstly, recognise care workers as skilled rather than unskilled and secondly, the government needs a sustainable funding model, which pays competitive wages. This seems obvious, so why is it so seemingly difficult to instigate? We all recognise there are varying types of care and support, based on people's recognised needs. We talk about those with PIMD as having 'High Support Needs.' Why not have tiered approaches to care work such as, Entry Level, Intermediate and Senior? This would also give workers more incentive to stay in care work. With a clear progression route, which they could attain through additional training and those in senior level positions could take a team leader position within any setting. As the Raising Our Sights guide to workforce training points out, the best workers are going to be those who like their work, want to do it and like the person they are working with. This is so important, but how to ensure we employ the best? The recruitment process needs to be extremely thorough from the outset. Unfortunately, this is not always the case. A senior manager at a leading staff recruitment organisation told me he was shocked when he first started working there. He initially offered meetings with care home managers to discuss their staffing needs, including profile of workers, background knowledge and other specific requirements. No one took him up on his offer. Their response was usually a fairly perfunctory request for X amount of workers. Happily, there are organisations that do understand the recruitment process is key. Regular recruitment drives, including lengthy application processes culminating in full day workshops of various support scenarios ensure a higher quality of candidate. Selecting staff with values and attitudes they can evidence in this way has to be cost effective in the long run. Bigby (2009) described the way certain workers agree with policy drivers like independence, choice or inclusion in a general sense. However, when working with more severely disabled people they tended to adopt a 'doing for' stance, rather than 'doing with.' It has been shown that when staff are encouraged to focus on the interpersonal side of their work, they will deliver the more technical side more effectively. Mansell and Beadle-Brown (2012) describe the *'enabling relationship'* as one, which is

> ... founded in understanding, respect and empathy for the individual being supported, a commitment to and understanding of the possibilities for a better life and a reflective, critical appraisal of how things are going.
>
> (p. 57)

Bespoke training qualification

Families' concerns about appropriate staff training, specific to the support of those with PIMD were further highlighted in Raising Our Sights. In fact previous to Mansell's report these needs had been highlighted in a number of papers and reviews. Healy and Walsh (2007) examined the communication strategies of staff supporting individuals with severe and profound intellectual disabilities. Their interactions were video recorded and analysed to assess the frequencies of their verbal and non-verbal acts. In semi-structured and focus group interviews staff described the communication environment, alternative methods of communication and choice as key elements in communicating with those they supported. However the video recordings revealed no differences in their verbal and non-verbal acts. There were discrepancies between the communication strategies they described and the ones they actually used. Most of the workers failed to adjust their language and overall the study suggested that they did not always use the optimal strategies in their everyday communication with those they supported who used non-verbal language. The report recommended continuing education in communication. By recommending 'continuing education' the authors recognise a one off course, or in-house, online generic training might not be sufficient for workers in this field. Mansell (2007) discusses the value of group and face-to-face training as opposed to online alternatives.

The issue of unskilled and poorly trained workers cannot be ignored. Whilst the Valuing People promise of a skilled, trained and qualified workforce is still far from the norm in the UK, not so in Belgium for example. In a recent study there, the vast majority of workers supporting those with PIMD had university degrees and a background in Special Education (Hostyn et al., 2010). The most prevalent qualification at the same time in the UK was the National Vocational Qualification Level 2 (Dobson and Myers, 2006). Put bluntly, overstretched staff with no specialist expertise or support will construct unconscious psychological defences to cope with, for example, the particular behaviours of their service users. In the absence of real understanding of the implications of various conditions, it is easy to fall back on personal assumptions and attitudes. Workers need specific training in these areas, if they are to provide adequate support.

Currently there is only one nationally recognised qualification, which focuses purely on supporting with people with PIMD. It is the only qualification listed in the 'Learning Disabilities Core Skills Education and Training Framework for Supporting People with PMLD' (Department of Health, Skills for Care, 2016). It is registered with the governmental Office of Qualifications and Examination Regulation (Ofqual). Most importantly and reassuringly it is regulated by an awarding body, therefore set standards must be met. This is excellent news for those family carers who have concerns about generically trained staff. However the increasing use of agency staff, often by families managing personal budgets on behalf of their sons and daughters, does highlight another area of concern.

How can he ever get to know them? A different person comes every time. Sometimes twice a day. All different. It's a vicious circle.

(YW:O)

And another parent describing agency staff,

> these staff, they don't even know about the epilepsy and they don't care.
>
> (TD:I)

As I have reiterated throughout this chapter people with PIMD have complex health and support needs which inadequately or untrained staff cannot be expected to understand. Surely there ought to be a requirement for care agencies to demonstrate to local authorities that their staff are appropriately trained before securing outsourced contracts? Similarly all staff employed directly by the local authority ought to have specific training. Once undertaken the training ought to be monitored and evaluated regularly in order to demonstrate that skills have actually become embedded into practice, rather than the superficial assimilation of new words and phrases we have seen in practice.

Raising Our Sights has a focus on the personalisation agenda and this extends to recruitment of the newly styled 'personal assistants.' With these packages of care the responsibility for training of staff shifts from local authority to the individual family, if they are managing the care plan or the social care provider. In this case,

> it is the responsibility of individual social care employers to ensure that their staff are adequately trained for the role that they perform.
>
> (Department of Health, 2011)

When a family are the employer, they may recognise those individuals who are rare, but who we have all met at some point.

> Often – not always but sometimes – the best people have been people who have come with the right values and attitudes and with no experience whatsoever... That's why it is so important that the person understands and has that ability to build a relationship, to see the person as a person. You can teach all the rest.
>
> (Mansell, p. 12)

My sense though, after ten years of recruiting and managing is that we cannot rely on this innate ability entirely. Ensuring they feel valued helps staff to have a positive attitude to their work. However, even the most empathetic natural workers need ongoing training and development. They need an atmosphere of active reflection, in order to assess their own style. They also need to feel excited by new thinking and new approaches. As Townsend (2018) puts it,

> Experience indicates the importance and direct impact of professional development on staff retention: staff who are more accomplished,

competent and appropriately qualified are more likely to enjoy their work. It therefore stands to reason that if both the person with PMLD and carers or support staff alike enjoy an improved quality of experience and well-being then support will be more effective.

(p. 27)

Conclusion

This chapter sought to probe deeper into the lived experience of people with PIMD. Testimonies by family carers and care workers illustrate where people spend their time and with whom. Analysing aspects of the Raising Our Sights report demonstrated these are still of concern to families. Issues of respite and day activity provision are still paramount. As are the ongoing and often lifelong need for specialist health provision such as physiotherapy. Ideas of self-directed support drew short shrift from many families, who saw this as a money saving tool for cash strapped local authorities. Subsequent reports have identified that the substantial input of family carers in this policy initiative were initially overlooked, unrecognised and therefore unacknowledged. The key to training for workers in this field was seen as best delivered by bespoke packages. And organisations who followed up their training with video observations of staff interactions reported much more effective embedding of that work.

The final chapter will commence with a discussion of the many enquiries, reports and recommendations that have flourished in the last years in response to the continuing abuse, neglect and avoidable early deaths of people with SID, including autism and/or mental health diagnoses and PIMD.

It concludes with a description and discussion of the newly published 'Core and Essential Service Standards for Supporting People with Profound and Multiple Learning Disabilities' (Doukas et al., 2017). These were devised by a group of family carers, practitioners, researchers and providers as an informative and practical resource for health, education and care sectors. The Standards aim to enhance quality and equity of support and service provision for children and adults with PIMD. Whilst they have already been adopted by NHS England and the Royal College of Occupational Therapists the ambition is for them to be adopted nationally.

Notes

1 www.lambethmencap.org.uk/services/profound-multiple-learning-disability/
2 www.theguardian.com/society/2012/mar/16/jim-mansell
3 www.carersuk.org/news-and-campaigns/campaigns/fairer-for-carers

Resources

http://static.carers.org/files/policy-and-resources-pack-final-low-res-4604.pdf

https://assets.publishing.service.gov.uk/government/uploads/system/uploads/attach
ment_data/file/216273/dh_124256.pdf

www.mencap.org.uk/sites/default/files/2016-06/Raising_our_Sights_report.pdf

www.learningdisabilitytoday.co.uk/demanding-a-better-life

https://youtu.be/SP9AiYJ4Gdg

https://youtu.be/CObYhkvjkfQ

https://youtu.be/SSV7UyCdKR4

https://youtu.be/-8kDzelLSgc

www.mencap.org.uk/advice-and-support/pmld/raising-our-sights-guides

www.learningdisabilitytoday.co.uk/project-involving-people-with-pmld-praised-for-its-
life-changing-outcomes

www.theguardian.com/society/2018/aug/22/respite-care-families-of-disabled-children-
at-breaking-point

www.bbc.co.uk/programmes/p06j80tm

https://thebarnetgroup.org/ycb/2018/10/19/need-help-with-respite-care-come-to-valley-
way-open-day-on-25th-october/

https://thebarnetgroup.org/ycb/2018/10/08/disability-dance-and-sports-afternoon/

Bibliography

Bigby, C., Clement, T., Mansell, J., and Beaele-Bren, J. (2009). 'It's pretty hard with our ones, they can't talk, the more able bodied can participate': Staff attitudes about the applicability of disability policies to people with severe and profound intellectual disabilities.' *Journal of Intellectual Disabilty Research*, Volume 16 (3), pp. 205–215. Blackwell Publishing, Oxford, UK.

Burstow, P. (2011). 'Services for adults with profound intellectual and multiple disabilities'. Health written statement. Available online at https://www.theyworkforyou.com/wms/?id=2011-02-10b.15WS.1&iru=99NFE74L3I

Campbell, M. (2012). 'Changing day services. do you agree?' *Journal of Intellectual Disabilities*, Volume 16 (3), pp. 205-215. Sage Publishing, London, UK.

Circles Network. (2005). 'What is Person Cenred Planning?' Available online at http://www.what_is_person_centred_planning.htm

Clements, L., Bangs, J. and Holzhausen, J. (undated). 'Individual budgets and carers'. Available online at http://www.lukeclements.co.uk/resources-index/files/PDF%2005.pdf

Clements, L. (2008). 'Individual Budgets and irrational exuberance.' 11 C.C.L.R. 413-430 A prepublication draft copy accessible at: www.lukeclements.co.uk/page1/page1.html

Clements, L. (2011). 'Social care law developments: A sideways look at personalisation and tightening eligibility criteria.' *Elder Law*, Volume 1, pp. 47–52.

Creative Support (Opportunity support and wellbeing). (2011). (online) Available from www.reativesupport.co.uk/ (Last accessed November 11, 2018 Circles Network (2005).

Daly, M. and Lewis, J. (2000). 'The concept of social care and the analysis of contemporary welfare states.' *British Journal of Sociology*, Volume 51 (2), pp. 281–298.

Daly and Lewis. (2002). 'The concept of social care and the analysis of contemporary welfare states.' *British Journal of Sociology*, Volume 51 (2), pp. 281–298. Wiley-Blackwell Publishing, Hoboken, New Jersey, USA.

Department for Work and Pensions. (2013) *Fulfilling Potential Building A Deeper Understanding of Disability in the UK Today.* HMSO, London, UK.

Department of Business Innovation and Skills. (2011). *Evaluation of Apprenticeship Learners.* HMSO, London, UK.

Department of Health. (1999). *Health Survey for England 1999: The Health of Minority Ethnic Groups.* Department of Health. HMSO, London, UK.

Department of Health. (2001). '*Valuing People: A new strategy for learning disabilities for the 21st Century*'. HMSO, London, UK.

Department of Health. (2009a). 'Valuing people now: from progress to transformation – A consultation on the next three years of learning disability policy.' London – *The Times*, August 10, 2007.

Department of Health. (2009b). Introduction to Refresh of VP. HMSO, London, UK.

Department of Health. (2011). 'The Government's response to Raising Our Sights: Services for adults with profound intellectual and multiple disabilities.' HMSO, London, UK.

Department of Health, Skills for Care. (2016). *Learning Disabilities Core Skills Education and Training Framework for Supporting People with PMLD.* NHS Health Education, London, UK.

Department for Work and Pensions, Department of Health, Department for Education and Skills and the Office of the Deputy Prime Minister. (2005). 'Improving the life chances of disabled people'. Prime Ministers Strategy Unit (PMSU) HMSO, London, UK.

Dobson, J. & Myers, P. (2006). 'NVQ Edexcel Level 2 in health and social care'. May (Issue 2). Available online from http://pearsonwbl.edexcel.com/migrationdocuments/NVQ/N015904-Health-and-Social-Care-L2-Iss2.pdf

Doukas, T., Fergusson, A., Fullerton, M., and Grace, J. (2017). 'Supporting people with profound and multiple learning disabilities Core & Essential Service Standards.' CMG PMLD LINK. The Sensory Projects Choice Support.

European Disability Forum. (2000). *Excluded Among the Excluded. People with Complex Dependency Needs.* www.england.nhs.uk/learning-disabilities/about/ask-listen-do/survey-results/www.fitzroy.org/wp-content/uploads/Who-will-care-after-im-gone.pdf

Foundation for Learning Disabilities. (2009). 'Supporting family carers of people with learning disabilities'. Available online at http://static.carers.org/files/policy-and-resources-pack-final-low-res-4604.pdf

Gladsby, J., Le Grand, J. and Duffy, S. (2009). 'A healthy choice? Direct payments and healthcare in the English NHS.' *Policy & Politics.* Volume 37 (4), pp. 481–497. Policy Press, Bristol, UK.

Gladsby, J.. (ed) (2011). *Evidence Policy and Practice Critical Perspectives in Health And Social Care.* The Policy press. University of Bristol, Bristol, UK.

Glendinning, C., Challis, D., Fernandez, J.L., Jacobs, S., Jones, K., Knapp, M., Moran, N., Netteen, A., Stevens, M., and Wilberforce, M. (2008). www.york.ac.uk/inst/spru/pubs/pdf/IBSEN.pdf

Granville, G., Runnicles, D., Barker, S., Lee, M., Wilkins, A., and Bowers, H. (2011). 'Increasing the voice, choice and control of older people with high support needs. A research findings paper from the South East Regional Initiative.'

Healy, D. and Walsh, P.N. (2007). 'Communication among nurses and adults with severe and profound intellectual disabilities: Predicted and observed strategies.' *Journal Intellectual Disability*, June Volume 11 (2), pp. 127–141.

Hostyn, I., Daelman, M., Janssen, M., and Maes, B. (2010). 'Describing dialogue between persons with profound intellectual and multiple disabilities and direct support staff using the scale for dialogical meaning making.' *Journal of Intellectual Disability Research*, Volume 54 (8), pp. 679–690.

Ibsen. (2009). *Evaluation of Individual Budgets pilot* available online at http://www.kcl.ac.uk/sspp/policy-institute/scwru/res/roles/ibsen.aspx

Jon, G. (ed) (2005). 'Evidence, policy and practice critical perspectives in health and social care.' The Policy Press, Bristol, UK.

Kennedy, H., Landor., M., and Todd, L. (2011). *Video Interaction Guidance A Relation-Based Intervention to Promote Attunement, Empathy and Wellbeing*. Jessica Kingsley Publishers, London, UK.

Kingston, A., Herrera-Comas, A., and Jagger, C. (2018). 'Forecasting the care needs of the older population in England over the next 20 years: Estimates from the population ageing and care simulation.' *PACSim Modelling Study The Lancet*, Volume 3 (9), pp. 447–455. https://doi.org/10.1016/S2468-2667(18)30118-X

Lambeth Mencap and I Count.

Leyin and Kauder. (2009). www.local.gov.uk/about/news/local-services-face-further-ps13-billion-government-funding-cut-201920

Lyle, D. (2015). 'Policy to practice: A critical analysis of the valuing people strategy'. Available online at http://eprints.mdx.ac.uk/15731/

Mansell, J. (2007). *Services for People with Learning Disabilities and Challenging Behaviour or Mental Health Needs (revised edition)*. Department of Health HMSO, London, UK.

Mansell, J. (2010). www.mencap.org.uk/sites/default/files/201606/Raising_our_Sights_report.pdf

Mansell, J. and Beasle-Brown, J. (2012). *Active Support: Enbling and Empowering People with Intellectual Disabilites*. Jessica Kingsley Publishing, London, UK.

Mencap. (2001). 'No ordinary life: The support needs of families caring for children and adults with profound and multiple learning disabilities.' Royal Society for Mentally Handicapped Children and Adults, London, UK.

Mencap. (2003). 'Breaking point a report on caring without a break for children and adults with severe or profound learning disabilities.' Mencap, London www.mencap.org.uk/sites/default/files/201607/campaigns_breaking_point_0408.pdf

Mencap. (2006). 'Breaking point – families still need a break: A report on the continuing problem of caring without a break for children and adults with severe and profound learning disabilities.' Mencap, London, UK.

Mencap. (2012). 'Short breaks support is failing family carers: Reviewing progress 10 years on from Mencap's first breaking point report.' www.mencap.org.uk/sites/default/files/2016-07/Short%20breaks%20support%20is%20failing%20family%20carers.pdf

Mencap, I Count. (2010). 'Lambeth PMLD project Understanding the lives and needs of people with profound and multiple learning disabilities in Lambeth.'

Michael, J. (2008). 'Report of the independent inquiry into access to healthcare for people with learning disabilities.' Independent Inquiry into Access to Healthcare for People with Learning Disabilities, London, UK.

National Assembly of Wales. (2000). www.england.nhs.uk/learning-disabilities/about/ask-listen-do/survey-results/

Network, P.M.L.D. (2006). Unpublished survey www.pmldnetwork.org

Panorama, BBC. (2018). Online available at www.bbc.co.uk/programmes/p06j80tm

Patricia's story. (2018). 'Carers UK.' available online at www.carersuk.org/news-and-campaigns/campaigns/fairer-for-carers

PMLD Network. (2001). 'Valuing people with profound and multiple learning disabilities.' Mencap, London, UK.

Public Health England. (2015). '*Learning Disabilities Observatory People with learning disabilities in England in 2015: Main Report.*' HMSO, London, UK.

Putten, A. and Vasclamp, C. (2011). 'Day services for people with profound intellectual and multiple disabilities: An analysis of thematically organized activities.' *Journal of Intellectual Disabilities*, Volume 8 (1), pp. 10–17.

Redley, M. (2009). 'Understanding the social exclusion and stalled welfare of citizens with learning disabilities.' *Disability & Society*, Volume 24 (4), pp. 489–501. 10.1080/09687590902879122.

Rummery, K. and Fine, M. (2012). 'Care: A critical review of theory, policy and practice.' *Social Policy & Administration*, Volume 46 (3), pp. 321–343.

Sinason, V. (2010). '*Mental handicap and the human condition an analytic approach to intellectual disability revised edition.*' Free Association Books, London, UK.

Stalker, K. (2003). 'Carers.' *Research Policy and Planning*, Volume 21 (2).

Sutherland, S. (1999). 'Free personal care for the elderly' royal commission on long-term care.' Scottish Executive. TSO Scotland.

Szehebehely, M. (2005). 'Care as employment and welfare provision: Child care and elder care in Sweden at the dawn of the 21st century.' in Dahl, H.M. and Eriksen, T.R. (eds) *Dilemmas of Care in the Nordic Welfare State: Continuity and Change.* Ashgate, Aldershot.

Townsend, S. (2018). 'Understanding the needs of individuals with PMLD – A bespoke qualification.' *PMLD Link*, Volume 30 (No. 2 Issue 90), pp. 25–28.

Tronto, J.C. (1998). 'An ethic of care.' *Generations, Journal of the American Society on Ageing*, Volume 22 (3), pp. 15–20. ASA, USA.

Verdonschot, M.M., de Witte, L.P., Reichrath, E., Buntinx, W.H., and Curfs, L.M. (2009). 'Community participation of people with an intellectual disability: A review of empirical findings.' *Journal of Intellectual Disabilities*, Volume 53 (4), pp. 303–318. Sage, UK.

Warner, M. (1993). 'Objectivity and Emancipation in Learning Disabilities. Holism from the Perspective of Critical Realism.' *Journal of Learning Disabilities*, Volume 26(5), pp. 311–325. Hammill Institute on Disabilities. Austin, Texas, USA

Williams, T. (1947). *A Streetcar Named Desire*. Heinemann, USA.

Williams and Robinson. (2000). In Stalker. (2003) see above.

6 Raising the bar

Beyond the 'burden of non-productiveness'

Introduction

Throughout the writing of this book, I have covered many aspects of the lived experience of people with PIMD. There is so little literature available, specifically looking at adult life I wanted to try and comprehensively include as much as possible. I opened the book with a thorough examination of the various terms and definitions in use in the UK today. I have illustrated the areas of confusion around definitions and ideologies underpinning delivery of care and support. Finding some clarity seemed very important, especially in light of family, care worker and care manager concerns that people with PIMD are not visible in policy, locally or nationally. I have argued that *'the ignored minority'* (Samuel and Pritchard, 2001) are a heterogeneous group, who all share one commonality at least and that is the profound nature of their intellectual disability. This means their difficulties with communication are developmental in origin. Their communication is described as being at a 'pre-verbal' or 'pre-intentional' stage (Bunning, 2009). In other words, people with PIMD cannot 'speak up' (in the self-advocacy parlance of People First), as they do not have the mental capacity to express themselves with language. They need a 'communication partner' and ideally an advocate. This has to be someone who knows them very well. Someone who has a relationship with them formed over a minimum period of two to five years. This is how long it takes to attune. Commissioners of advocacy services need to bear this in mind. I will include a section in this final chapter exploring the urgency of advocacy need through the prism of 'Paul's' shocking death.[1]

Chapter two posed the question, how can people with PIMD be meaningfully included in a strategy based on independence. And further why do we shy away from discussions of dependence in this country? I have shown that a strategy based on self-advocacy, independent living and employment was always going to be problematic for this group of people. I have warned against the dangers of over-ascribing capacity and queried the belief that in order to have 'value' an individual must fulfil society's normative assumptions. Acknowledging difference is problematic in policy frameworks and service provision when ID is constantly framed *'as if'* everyone with ID has low support needs (p. 22) and would benefit from a one-size-fits-all approach. The chapter sought to understand the apparent lack of fit between social model of disability ideas and the broad ranging, often complex and specialist needs of individuals with PIMD.

In chapter three, I examined the four cornerstones of the Valuing People strategy within the context of the lived experience of PIMD. Initially I was interested to see how well people with PIMD were represented in the original policy document. I noted their lack of visibility echoes a theme of Gaffney's (2012) paper, exploring the manner in which current narratives are 'air brushing long-term disability out of the picture' (p. 22). The chapter went on to examine ways families and paid care workers understand the notions of rights, independence, choice and inclusion. And how these cornerstones are embedded in current practice or not. I refer to the illusory and almost idealised Valuing People representation of individuals with ID, which holds little relevance for the families interviewed and has led to some confusion for care worker's understanding of their client group.

I have included a chapter based on the work I have done managing my daughter's care these past ten years via a personal budget. I focus on the challenges to providing truly personalised support in any setting. I have included practical approaches to reframing behavioural support within a therapeutic environment. I describe in detail the varied benefits that accrue from incremental work and demonstrate the efficacy of mindful and reflexive practice.

Chapter five was concerned with understanding services and settings for people with PIMD. What did people do, where do they spend their time and with whom? How were new approaches, such as the personalisation agenda impacting on their lives? How did families, who were still the primary carers feel supported or not by the new frameworks? Had their needs changed significantly or were they still struggling to obtain the basics of well-trained staff and respite breaks in order that they could keep contributing extensive provision of care? In light of the current conservative government's continuing austerity agenda there does appear to be an increasing lack of appropriate and specialist support available. In fact people with PIMD ought not to be so affected by the policy of austerity, which has seen funding to local authorities diminish year on year, as their needs are statutory and therefore their services cannot be cut. Lyle (2015) carried out interviews with families prior to the real force of national government funding cuts and found the same concerns. And Breaking Point the original Mencap report was first published in 2003, five years before the international banking crisis. The paucity of ambition for what someone can achieve is often directed to their support staff. It could equally be attributed to local commissioners and government ministers.

In this final chapter, I cannot shy away from including some discussion of the abuse, neglect and avoidable deaths of people with ID, (including PIMD) in this country. The latest significant scandals emerged in Assessment and

Treatment Units (ATU), where vulnerable women and men with ID and additional mental health issues including ASD were supposedly being 'treated.' I believe there is a degree of crossover in the cohorts. Many individuals I have met in ATU's when I have been specialist advisor on Care and Treatment reviews were able to use language verbally. Indeed, I clearly remember a conversation with a young woman, who we were advised was 'unable to communicate.' However, I also remember the first CQC Inspection I joined as an expert by experience. It was to a medium-secure unit. I only heard about a man living there, I never met him. I was told he 'has PMLD, but we are starting to think he may be schizophrenic as well.' He had been in the unit for some years. He was described as extremely challenging, a big man, who needed up to seven people to restrain him. A member of staff pointed toward one end of a corridor where two people were sitting outside his door. I was told he was too dangerous for me to meet. Later during the day, when I was in another section of the unit I heard some alarms going off and a general commotion. One of the other in-patients told me it was this man 'kicking off.' What stayed with me, apart from the fact I never actually saw or met him was the discourse around him. The staff, other patients and even the inspector I was working with all accepted this. He was someone who could not be controlled or contained, so was basically living in solitary confinement with guards at his door.

Abuse

The Winterbourne View abuse scandal, emerged in 2011 but not as a result of safeguarding concerns being raised at the time.[2] Rather the abuse finally surfaced through the actions of the BBC television programme, *Panorama*. A former nurse who could not get authorities to respond to his concerns had approached the producers. In fact workers at the privately owned taxpayer funded hospital had raised concerns nineteen times, all unheeded.[3] The BBC programme installed an undercover reporter who gained employment access and then secretly filmed the abuse. Ultimately, after many arrests eleven people were charged with wilful neglect and the ill treatment of people with severe learning disabilities and autism (SLD/ASD) and sentenced in 2012.[4] The investigation led to the Department of Health's Transforming Care (2012) programme. Unfortunately, this programme's initial specific target of transferring the thousands of people in hospital Assessment & Treatment Units (ATU) across the country was missed. The care minister at the time described this as '*an abject failure*' (Lamb[5]). The limited success in bringing people back into local communities included a lack of government understanding of the complexity of its own commitment. For example the initial promise was issued without knowing the numbers of people needing bespoke community placements. Increasing local capacity needed assurances from commissioners that these placements could be provided. Again, this was not simply a physical space, but the support to provide personalised care plans designed to manage risks and prevent re-admission. There had been no analysis of why people had been referred to hospital or even quantification of the resources needed for such an ambitious idea to be completed in a relatively short space of time. Notwithstanding the final report comprehensively outlines ambitions for improving the quality and safety of care, tightening regulation and inspection of providers and strengthening accountability and corporate responsibility for quality of care. The interim report reviewed how best to improve local provision in order to encourage the continuing movement of people out of hospital and into more appropriate community settings (Bubb, 2014; ADASS et al., 2015). It summarised good practice guidance by referring to reports, revised and updated, but essentially saying the same thing since 1993 (Mansell, 1993, 2007, 2011). That people ought to live in their communities. That services ought to meet their needs and those of their families and carers. Those services ought to be commissioned in the knowledge that the high level of support needed for people with complex or challenging needs would be met. And there ought to be a focus on preventing re-admission to hospital via delivery of personalised care and support. The proposed key principles of a model of care were based on the individual themselves, services and outcomes (see DH, 2012 Annex A, pp. 50–55). NHS England commissioned a twelve-week consultation, resulting in the government's response, a Green paper, 'No voice unheard, no right ignored' (DH 2015). This outlined (yet again) very basic, clear ideas about an individual's right to personalised services, inclusion and independence, accountability and responsibility.

Death by *indifference* (MENCAP, 2007)

So much appears to have been investigated and reported on. Over the years there have been many publications with long lists of recommendations. The original Mencap report, 'Death by *Indifference*' was published in 2007. This report detailed the life stories of six people, all of whom had died in hospital. One of the parents, stated at the time,

> We believe that Mark died unnecessarily. Throughout his life, we encountered medical professionals who had no idea how to deal with people with a learning disability or what it is like to be a parent of someone with a learning disability – to know their suffering, to see their distress. If only they would listen.'
>
> (Allan, 2007)

Indeed all six people had family advocating on their son's and daughter's behalf and still medical staff did not respond to their concerns. One family even described what they thought the problem was (appendicitis and a blocked bowel) and were ignored. Tragically they were right. Mencap believe the real underlying cause of all these deaths is, the widespread ignorance and indifference throughout our healthcare services towards people with a learning disability, and their families and carers. We say that this is a national disgrace. We say this is institutional discrimination.

(Mencap, 2007)

As a result the Local Government and Parliamentary & Health Ombudsman carried out six investigations of complaints made on behalf of the six families against a total of 20 public bodies. They all concerned the quality of care provided. The majority included concerns about the way subsequent complaints had been handled at local level, and by the Healthcare Commission. The response (Local Government and Health Ombudsman, 2009) was comprehensive and scathing. The 'Six Lives' report describes significant and distressing failures in both health and social care, which in turn led to prolonged suffering for the six individuals. The report is sufficiently in-depth to include much evidence, such as first-hand accounts from a range of people involved. The investigation revealed,

maladministration, service failure and unremedied injustice in relation to a number, but not all, of the NHS bodies and local councils involved
(p. 12)

They found this was for disability related reasons and also in some cases the public bodies concerned had

failed to live up to human rights principles, especially those of dignity and equality

(p. 12)

The areas of concern included, communication, partnership working and co-ordination, relationships with families and carers, failure to follow routine procedures, quality of management and (in my view most importantly) a lack of effective advocacy. The report describes this as notable by its absence. It points to the investment in advocacy outlined by *Valuing People* (DH, 2001) and is puzzled by the fact that there was no use or availability of independent advocacy for any of the six people whose deaths prompted the enquiries. It agrees families advocate strongly, but recognises independent advocates may have been able to support the families and might even have affected the outcomes. The overriding concern was that the very basics of care and support were not being met. Guidelines and policies were evidenced, yet they were clearly not being observed. As they point out, the use of independent advocates,

could have provided an additional safeguard for the rights of a very vulnerable group of people

(p. 27)

Apart from the glaring omission of independent advocacy the report recognised that changing attitudes and service culture requires strong leadership. This needs to be across all areas of an organisation, not simply a top-down process. People need to be identified who

> recognise the hallmarks of good quality services in everyday practice and have a real empathy for and understanding of the situations of others – particularly those who cannot easily communicate, and are prepared to challenge consistently the acceptance of poor outcomes

(p. 27)

The untimely and shocking death of Connor Sparrowhawk[6] occurred in an NHS ATU in 2011. Just a few years after publication of the Health Ombudsman's report 'Six Lives: the provision of public services to people with learning disabilities' (2009) but surely long enough for the recommendations to have been embedded in practice? Thanks to Connor's mother's tireless campaigning, an independent audit was commissioned by NHS England (Mazars, 2015). This demonstrated there had been at least 1,000 deaths of people with learning disabilities and mental health issues in the NHS, which had not been properly investigated. Speaking to BBC News following publication, Connor's mother, Dr Sarah Ryan said the authorities were showing a 'systematic disregard' for some people.

> Certain people simply don't count – you can't dress it up as anything else,' she said. 'We have so much evidence now of a complete dismissal of the human-ness of people labelled with learning disabilities and I don't actually want to live in a society in which this just goes on and the government does nothing about it.

(Ryan, 2015, 2018)

Improving health and lives

This Bubb (2014) and Mazars (2015) reports resulted in the establishment of IHAL.[7] The Learning Disabilities Health Observatory, known as Improving Health and Lives (IHAL) was set up in response to The Mencap report Six Lives (2007). This collaboration between the National Development Team for Inclusion (NDTi), Public Health England and the Centre of Disability Research at Lancaster University aims to reduce the health inequalities experienced by people with learning disabilities (ID) in England. It does this by providing high quality data and information (see below*) to commissioners and providers of health and social care. This in turn helps them to understand the needs of people with learning disabilities, their families and carers, and, ultimately, to deliver better healthcare. Several government departments collect this national statistical information. The Observatory produces an annual report and best practice guides. They have also produced a series of reports looking at reasonable adjustments (RA) in specific service areas. These include, epilepsy, end of life care, primary care, dementia, diabetes, eye care dentistry, cancer screening and latterly constipation. Sadly it took yet another death of a young man to prompt work with a focus on chronic constipation.[8] An inquest into Richard Handley's death found gross failure in the response of the hospital finally treating him. It also recognised changes to Richard's diet and a decrease in monitoring of his bowel movements contributed to his worsening condition and ultimately his untimely death. There seem to be two underlying issues here. One is a general squeamishness from people. I have heard health professionals say they didn't like to discuss 'it' for example. But a general dislike for discussing bodily functions also needs to be understood within the context of 'independence' and 'choice.' There may well have been an assumption by those supporting Richard that in the newly changed status of his care home, monitoring and awareness of diet were no longer their responsibility. Rather like the member of staff who told me, 'We encourage the service user to be independent, so they do it themselves' (Lyle 2015, p. 188).

This detail is so very important. Of course we want to encourage and develop people's independence. However, this is not a blanket state we confer. It has to be an ongoing relationship, whereby we negotiate Best Interests. Person-centredness is meant to be the focus of all service provision. All people with a learning disability (ID) are supposed to have a person-centred Profile/Plan, Communication Plan, Health Action Plan, Communication and Hospital Passport. If they are living with family, these may be less formal. However, if someone is living in a setting, paid for by the local authority, surely these must be in place? Too often the development and maintenance of these plans are seen as extra work, which already pressed staff have to complete. There is not enough recognition of these documents as living plans.

As an expert by experience, accompanying Inspectors from the Care Quality Commission (CQC) my role was to meet with residents. The first thing I would ask to see would be an individuals' plan. In many places, residents and staff alike were more than happy to share them with me. Too often, though staff would have to retrieve them from the office. On rare occasions they were kept by the resident themselves in their room. Why are they so underused? Managers ought to recognise these various plans are a valuable tool, especially in organisations and areas where staff turnover can be high.

An account by Richard's sister is written in the Foreword of the 'Making Reasonable Adjustments' guide to constipation (Public Health England, 2016).

As she points out that the support her brother needed to manage his constipation was actually quite basic, yet it had stopped.

> Slight changes to practice by staff in various roles would have ensured good bowel management. It is hard to understand why this didn't happen but I suspect that it reflects a combination of 'poo aversion' (it isn't glamorous!), diffused responsibility towards physical health amongst

professionals, diagnostic overshadowing, health inequalities and institutional discrimination, all of which are experienced too often by people with learning disabilities.

(p. 7)

Commencing in 2011–2012, NHS Digital has been conducting annual surveys of those adults who use personal social services. Random samples are selected via requests to local authorities. Most of those sampled however, are meant to be people with learning disabilities who can either read easy read versions of the survey, or who can respond with support.

> The experience of social care reported by adults with learning disabilities As Figure 7.16 shows, people with learning disabilities reported markedly more positive experiences of social care services and of their own health (with the exception of present state anxiety/depression) than other groups (this trend is also noticeable in other indicators not reported here). This was particularly noticeable in the proportion using the extreme positive end of possible response options. These differences may partially be accounted for by the easy read version of the survey completed by the majority of people with learning disabilities. Another difference is likely to be that people with learning disabilities were less likely than people with physical disability or people with mental health problems to have completed the survey by themselves (7% vs. 27% and 37%), and more likely to have had help to complete the survey from a care worker (52% vs. 18% and 25%)
>
> (Learning Disabilities Observatory, 2016, pp. 70–71)

My concern is that care workers may well have filled in the survey entirely, if on behalf of someone with PIMD. My worry is that they will be unlikely to record anything that may reflect back as negative care. What is the point of seeking out data, to be used to improve people's lives if the data is less than robust? There is little point in gathering data if it is merely a tick box exercise.

Good leadership, of the kind promoted in the Six Lives report would surely find a better way to respond. For example a guided focus group with an independent ID advocate might better inform people's answers. Good leadership would also develop their care-workers ability to creatively discern individual's preferences and provide opportunities for choice making. Most importantly, good leadership in an organisation supporting people with PIMD specifically would ensure the form was indeed completed with an advocate, who knows the individual and who is completely independent, *'outside the service system'* as Monaghan describes it (Monaghan, 2005). Unfortunately even now, two decades after publication of *Valuing People* (DH, 2001) this type of advocacy, so necessary especially for people for whom we must make assumptions/presumptions about their health, is rare to the point of non-existent. Good leadership would ask constantly, why?

CIPOLD > LeDR

The need for advocacy was rightly flagged up by the Confidential Inquiry into the premature deaths of people with learning disabilities (CIPOLD).

This work took place over the period 2010–2013, reviewing the deaths of 247 people with learning disabilities within five Primary Care Trusts in the South-west of England (Heslop et al., 2013). In the Foreword the writers referred to their dismay that lessons had not been learned and recommendations not implemented from the Six Lives report by the Health Ombudsman (2009). It should also be noted that Mencap published an updated report 'Death by *Indifference* Five Years On,' in which the number of reported premature deaths had risen from six to 74 (2012).

The CIPOLD report found that the lack of reasonable adjustments (RA) to facilitate healthcare of people with learning disabilities, particularly for attendance at clinic appointments and investigations, was a contributory factor in a number of deaths. In addition, professionals in both health and social care commonly showed a lack of adherence to and understanding of the Mental Capacity Act 2005, in particular regarding assessments of capacity, the processes of making 'best interest' decisions and when an Independent Mental Capacity Advocate (IMCA) should be appointed. Many instances were identified of inappropriate or poorly documented DNACPR4 (Do Not Attempt Cardiopulmonary Resuscitation) orders. Record keeping was commonly deficient. Areas highlighted include fluid intake, nutrition, weight and seizures. Predicting potential problems did not occur. For example, knowing when a person was fearful of contact with medical professionals.

As a parent attending various hospitals, including a specialist eye hospital in London, I am constantly dismayed by the lack of awareness of my daughter's need for basic reasonable adjustments. The whole process of attending a clinic can feel as if it is designed to increase her anxiety rather than allay it. And this is all before she actually meets with the clinician. When she was a child I was always advised to hold her firm for examination. And often this would work, simply through my use of brute force. Nowadays I am aghast when clinician's try to instruct me to do the same to my adult daughter or when they try to use swift force themselves. This never ends well. In the most recent example my daughter reacted very badly to her head being suddenly grabbed. It occurred so quickly I couldn't quite believe it was happening. The clinician had seized hold of my daughter's head and attempted to force it onto her machine for eye examination. My poor daughter reacted by resisting. I had to firmly instruct the clinician to stop and advise them the appointment was definitely over. In contrast, we returned at a later date to a different clinic (in fact the wrong clinic as it transpired) but the clinician we saw could not have been more different. She had a very calm demeanour, whereas the previous person had appeared hurried and flustered. Most importantly she spoke directly, to my daughter. She allowed me the time to settle

Odyssey into the chair and let her feel the machine before edging it closer to her face. Unsurprisingly the examination proceeded smoothly.

In order to contextualise the CIPOLD findings, the investigation reviewed a number of deaths of people who did not have an intellectual disability. Analysis of this sub-set comparator group found the number of premature and unexpected deaths was similar, although causes differed. In the non-disabled group causes were potentially preventable conditions. For example, if the individual had given up smoking. People with ID however had died from causes associated with poor basic health care. They had more difficulties with diagnosis and treatment, including care planning, coordination and documentation. And families felt that professionals did not listen to them. The quality and effectiveness of health and social care given to people with ID is described as deficient in a number of ways. Despite numerous previous investigations and reports, many professionals are either not aware of, or do not include in their usual practice, approaches that adapt services to meet the needs of people with ID. As we have seen these needs for reasonable adjustments are often quite minimal. Being afforded ten extra minutes can make the difference between succeeding in an examination or procedure and abandoning it altogether. The CIPOLD study shows how necessary it is to identify people with ID in healthcare settings, and to record, implement and audit the provision of 'reasonable adjustments' to avoid their serious disadvantage. There has been a reluctance to identify people on hospital records. I clearly remember conducting interviews for a research project by the EU Fundamental Rights Agency. I had to interview an advocate based in a hospital, who told me this was a data protection issue and that there was a concern over '*labelling.*' Later when interviewing women with ID, I asked how they felt about being identified on hospital records. One told me, '*Well they're gonna find out sooner or later.*' She raised an excellent point about her experience. As she pointed out, many people with ID cannot read. She was concerned that the Health Care Assistant's would offer her a written menu. They never had the time to talk through what someone wanted, so unless she had family visiting had no way of ordering her food in hospital. How much easier if the hospital records had flagged her as needing a picture or symbol based menu. In fact I have seen hospitals that only use picture-based menus. It can be done Bear in mind this young woman was able to speak up. Martin could not.[9] Despite the fact that speech and language therapists and community nurses had tried to intervene, nobody took any action to feed him. And as the Ombudsman later observed,

> He was not fed for 26 days and it is an indisputable fact ... that without sufficient food people weaken and die.
>
> (Carvel, 2009)

The CIPOLD report identified three factors that enhanced the vulnerability of people with ID in regard to care pathways related to investigation, diagnosis and treatment. These include a lack of reasonable adjustments, a lack of co-ordination across and between the different pathways and service providers, and a lack of effective advocacy. The report identified examples where professional advocacy had worked well, although only on a single-issue basis. For example, in Stanley's case (p. 68), once the Independent Mental Capacity Advocate (IMCA) had completed the work regarding his feeding, there was a continued apparent lack of co-ordination of his care in relation to his multiple co-morbidities, postural management, follow-up regarding his gastrostomy tube and end-of-life care planning. Families and paid care workers attempts to fulfil an advocacy role are oftentimes thwarted. Families struggle to be heard. Care workers report feeling intimidated at times by medical professionals, as though they had little expertise, confidence or authority to take on this role (p. 67). As is noted to be truly effective professional advocates with statutory responsibilities and the authority to be able to access information, question professionals and challenge views where necessary are vitally important, especially for adults with enduring lack of mental capacity to direct their own care. However, the lack of ongoing advocacy generally places such individuals at continued risk. The CIPOLD report included a number of recommendations, including,

> the routine collection of data that provides intelligence about the reasons why people with learning disabilities die. There is a need to link data about cause of deaths with appropriate registers of adults and children with learning disabilities, so that we can monitor, at a national level, a reduction of premature deaths and the pattern of underlying and immediate causes of death of people with learning disabilities. Given the extent of the disparities between people with learning disabilities and those without learning disabilities regarding deaths amenable to good-quality healthcare, we recommend that the Department of Health sets clear targets for the reduction of amenable mortality, monitors this on an annual basis and provides a public reporting mechanism
>
> (p. 120)

This recommendation has been implemented in the form of the Learning Disabilities Mortality Review Programme (LeDR). This is located within the Department of Health and Social Care and produces an annual report (2018) including an animated video clip (see Resource list for YouTube link). The report itemised nine recommendations. Fullerton (2018) notes these are not new. He queries how we can ensure they improve the lives of people with PIMD specifically. For example, Annual Health Checks (AHC) are important but will be more effective if carried out by a GP who knows the individual well. The results of AHC's need to feed into Health Action Plans (HAP) and these need to be appropriately updated and adhered to as well. The recommendation for everyone with ID who has two or more long-term physical or mental health conditions to have a named 'health care facilitator' is most welcome. Especially for those people who do not have family or a long-term advocate who knows them well. This will most likely be the Learning Disability nurse attached to the local Specialist Health Team for people with ID. Additional funding would surely need to be available to boost the numbers as Gates (2011), Glover and Emerson (2012) and Mckew (2018) have clearly demonstrated. Numbers have fallen drastically by 40% over the last ten years. The newly published NHS Long term Plan (2019) makes no specific reference to 'learning disability nurses' although they are aiming to publish a 'workforce development plan' later in 2019. There is also a promise to,

> ... do more to ensure that all people with a learning disability, autism, or both can live happier, healthier, longer lives.

(p. 41)

The current plan looks at geographical areas of health inequalities, such as poorer towns in the North of England. Regrettably it does not also refer to specific populations (i.e. those with PIMD) who experience greater and multiple health inequalities. A flagging system, which alerts hospitals of the need for Reasonable Adjustments, either for appointments or during in-hospital admittance is now possible. Since most people with PIMD experience a range of health issues, often having to use different specialist hospitals, this flagging system should enable much easier access to someone's medical history. The recommendation for mandatory training in learning disability awareness is welcome. Hopefully it will be non-generic training, which acknowledges the heterogeneous nature of people with ID and PIMD.

> In a world where learning disabilities are just one issue among many competing for attention, it is very easy in the generic care area to talk about people with learning disabilities as if everyone involved had low support needs.

(Mansell and Beadle-Brown, 2004)

Advocacy advocacy advocacy

> I worry about the ones who don't live at home. I spoke about this to social services, about who watches out for them when their parents are dead. As parents we fight tooth and nail but what happens to those without a parent?

(NN:O)

An unpublished mapping exercise conducted across London's twenty six borough's demonstrated many people were not benefitting from the *Valuing People* promise of advocacy for all (Lyle, 2008). This had been promoted within *Valuing People* (DH, 2001) as one of the routes to people with ID's enhanced choice and control in their lives. The strategy had specifically promoted citizen advocacy, yet three years after publication the DH's commissioned survey of 'Adults with Learning Difficulties' (Emerson and Durvasula, 2005) made no mention of citizen, only self-advocacy. Lawton (2009) outlines the various approaches to 'supported self-advocacy' for adults with High Support Needs (HSN). These approaches are helpful when working on finding creative ways to include people in devising their own Communication plans, for example (see Lawton, 2009, p. 31). However, the kind of advocacy envisioned by the CIPOLD report, whereby an independent person has ongoing oversight of an individual's social and healthcare, is now supposedly covered by 'Care Act advocacy.' The Care Act (2014) stipulated that people who would have substantial difficulty being involved and where there was no appropriate individual, i.e. family member or friend

> ... then the local authority must arrange for an independent advocate to support and represent the person.
>
> (7.8)

The Act recognises such a person would also qualify for advocacy under the Mental Capacity Act (2005). It stipulates the same person can provide advocacy support under both Acts, in order to provide seamless advocacy (7.9). This would have been helpful for Stanley (Heslop, et al., p. 68), but what about 'Paul?' Whilst writing this chapter a family carer asked if I had heard about 'Paul.' I tried to discover more and was struck by how little I could find. There was the original article[10] (Burford, 2018), another in the online magazine *Unite*[11] (Campbell, 2019) and the Safeguarding Review (Pearson, 2017). This man died after spending almost two months in intensive care, experiencing much pain and distress. Prior to finally being admitted to hospital twenty-seven health professionals had been involved with him and were aware of his gangrenous infection, yet none of them took appropriate action. Those providing supposedly 24-hour care in his living arrangement even acknowledged that

> at least on one occasion a carer did not show up for a shift.
>
> (9.14)

Where was the outrage? Where was the campaign? Why did his death not prompt greater enquiry? After all this is the post 'Winterbourne View' world. Post the 'Care Act,' (2014). Post *'Transforming Care'* (2012). Post 'Raising Our Sights' (2010). Post *'Six Lives'* (2009). Post the establishing of the Care Quality Commission in 2008. Post *'Putting People First'* (DH, 2007). Post 'Death by *Indifference*' (2007). Post *'Valuing People Now'* (2009)' and post *'Valuing People'* (2001). It is clear 'Paul' was an extremely vulnerable man who was very badly let down by the medical profession in the shorter term and by those overseeing his care and support for a much longer period of time. The review of his case acknowledges it poses more questions than it answers. For example, why was no advocate present at his Care Review in 2014, or when his surgery was being planned in 2015?

> An advocate should have been involved at this point to bring an independent perspective on whether Paul's Best Interests were being met by the treatment and its lack of effect
>
> (9.11)

> there was no family member, assertive support worker or advocate who argued that things were not improving for him, which in turn raises questions about the wider safeguarding system in Newham and what might currently be missing from it
>
> (9.12)

The report mentions that the advocacy service was instructed to work with 'Paul' six times. It is not stated if the advocacy service had sought out his Person-centred Profile, Person-centred Care-Plan, Communication Plan, Positive Behaviour Support Plan (PBS) or Health Action Plan for background information. There is only mention in the report of this last plan, which was kept by the GP practice and not shared with his home. All of these documents ought to have been in place and been adhered to by everyone involved in 'Paul's' care. The review notes the strategic points at which a Best Interests meeting ought to have been called. There may have been a misperception that 'Paul's' sister was more involved, but later statements advise the reason the review took so long was because it had taken three years to locate her. The provider managing his care would have known how involved or not she was and in any case still ought to have responded to this man escalating behavioural problems much earlier, never mind the later gangrenous infection. Why were care-staff not working closely with the behaviour therapist (who attended his care Review in 2014) to devise, enact and refine his Positive Behaviour Support plan? No documents were available from the care provider apart from the minutes of a care review carried out in 2014, which was incomplete in the sense it was only attended by three people from the provider organisation (7.1) and no one from the health service. Even though he was jointly funded by health and social care?

Throughout 'Paul's' Safeguarding Adults Review, it is noticeable how reactive his support was. He was '*said to have autism*' (7.1). This suggests he had not been assessed or did not have a formal diagnosis. Why not?

> He had a strong dislike for wearing clothes this meant careful planning and strategies were needed if carers were to take him outside the flat.
>
> (7.3)

Apart from a suggestion this could have been linked to a past traumatic event, there is no reference to any work being done to analyse this behaviour, which had gone on for years. Sensory integration issues are a feature of autistic spectrum disorder (ASD). Added to which, there is reference to building works occurring nearby that were thought to disturb 'Paul.' Apart from the fact that people with ASD may experience hyperacusis (Tatum, 2012, pp. 256–257) the unexplained noises may well have been extremely frightening for him. This was a fifty-six-year-old man, living in the UK in 2015, funded by a joint amount from social and health sources. Where was his ongoing health support? Reading about the deeply troubling lack of co-ordination and oversight in this man's care over many years, one has the sense he was simply ignored and overlooked. As the report points out,

> … there was no family member, assertive support worker or advocate who argued that things were not improving for him.
>
> (9.12)

Core and essential service standards: raising the bar

> Commissioners and policy makers were not sufficiently addressing the needs of people with learning disabilities who had more complex needs, including profound and multiple learning disabilities.
>
> (Mansell, 2010)

Ideas of advocacy are currently evolving and the availability of long-term uninstructed advocacy for people with PIMD is variable across the UK. How then do we ensure a good life for our 'Pauls'? Those individuals for whom life presents major challenges to the provision of their health and social care needs. How do we ensure that those with no family directly involved do not end up overlooked and neglected? One way to encourage 'collaboration, communication and information sharing' (Dept. Health & Social Care, 2018) between Commissioners of education, health and social care and service providers is through the adoption of the recently launched Core and Essential Service Standards, 'Supporting people with profound and multiple learning disabilities,' (Doukas et al., 2017). It is envisaged that when adopted Commissioners and providers can share the expectation that people with PIMD will receive the same standard of service delivery wherever they live geographically. It is anticipated that Commissioners will use the Standards when developing service specifications and in collaborative engagement with service providers and families in order to enhance future service provision. The Standards are also an extremely useful audit tool for managers of services, including those families who are using Personal Budgets and who may also incorporate Circles of Support (see for e.g. Lyle, 2018). Local authorities could flag up on their systems, those individuals with PIMD by way of adherence to the Standards. Regulatory bodies such as the CQC could also instruct their inspectors to seek evidence of uptake within their Key Lines of Enquiry. The expectation behind this initiative is a whole-system approach (Elliot, 2017). In this way it responds to many recent calls and recommendations, with practical clear guidance. The Standards are set out in two parts. The first set of seven Standards aims to provide guidance and support to organisations. Each Standard is set out with a number of explanatory bullet points. These are supported by a number of descriptive items explaining how to evidence the aforementioned standards. Hence the first standard for Organisations is 'Leadership.' There follow six paragraphs describing the evidence we should be looking for. The remaining Standards cover Quality, Staff Development, Physical Environment, Communication, Health and Well-being and Social, Community and Family Life. The second section is for Individuals. The Standards for individuals include, Communication, Health and Well-being, Meaningful/Quality Relationships, Social and Community Life, Meaningful Time and Transitions. The Standards were devised after a group of advocates and allies (parents, academics and professionals) came together to identify a means of ensuring a voice for people with PIMD at a national level. They wanted to ensure this group of people have explicit reference in future policy and initiatives. They were concerned the lack of representation meant their specific and specialist needs are often overlooked. It is envisaged these Standards will provide focus and networking opportunities for anyone, professional or family involved in providing care and support to this group of people. They are available online and can be downloaded from a number of websites (see Resource list for details). In order to launch the Standards nationally, the 'Raising the Bar' (2017, 2018) conferences took place. This was the first national conference (followed up a year later) with a focus exclusively on profound intellectual and multiple disabilities. The fact that both conferences were hugely successful, so oversubscribed people were sitting on the stairs in the main room shows there is a hungry audience for this. Speaking as a parent, I have attended many conferences over the years. I usually arrive full of hopeful anticipation and leave more often than not, feeling somewhat dejected. Feeling rather like the parent who said to me, 'but they're not like ours. It's not the same.' How exciting instead to attend an event, where I wished I could clone myself, because there were too many sessions I wanted to join. How exciting to hear a range of speakers from parents to practitioners to academics, all with a common focus. The conference was a unique opportunity for networking, information sharing and great discussion with fellow delegates. We certainly all came away feeling extremely hopeful for the future.

Conclusion

In this last chapter, I have explored recent responses to various abuse scandals. Too often there have been cases where people's lives have simply not been valued. There has been a clear call for advocacy, reasonable adjustments and the need for coordinated services. Collaboration, communication and information sharing are seen as key. Certainly there is evidence that this in possible and has been in place in certain areas for some time. The challenge now is for disparate areas of good practice to become universal. Adopting the 'Essential and Core Standards for Supporting People' would seem a good place to start.

This book came about through a desire to focus entirely on trying to understand what happens after school, after all those early years of diagnosis and assessment for an individual with PIMD. What happens to our daughters and sons? I wanted a go-to volume that anyone inquisitive might access. Anyone that is who wanted to understand more about living life as an adult with PIMD. They could be a parent, student, care-worker, advocate, manager, commissioner or even a government minister. Or they may simply be an interested individual. We have seen some shocking events, such as recent abuse and death scandals. We have also seen the determination amongst many prominent people, including the former health minister Norman Lamb MP, to strive for better lives for people with complex needs. But have we moved on from Tredgold and his concern that society needs protection from *'the burden of their non-productiveness'* (cited in Concannon, 2005). If we include 'people with PMLD' (DH, 2009, p. 38) yet still insist on the caveat, 'people's needs are not fixed,' do we really understand who these people are? Surely an overriding general need for full support in all aspects of one's life is a fixed need for individuals with PIMD? Further if policy insists that the goal for these people is *'living independently and having paid work'* (p. 31) what about those people for whom this is an unattainable goal? In a society focussed on work as a moral responsibility for all, the feckless scrounger[12] discourse is then applied to everyone described as long-term unemployed, including those with disabilities (Garthwaite, 2011). A recent discussion with a head of 'learning disability services' confirmed this to me. He argued that whether or not an individual is cognitively aware of taking part in employment is not the issue. He maintained that in order for an individual to have any value in society they must be seen to contribute. This line of thinking clearly harks back to Tredgold. Surely if we are able to find ways of working creatively to enable people with PIMD to have meaningful encounters in their lives, we can also move beyond normative commitments? What is wrong with an all-encompassing, breadth of human experience approach? What is wrong with acknowledging difference, including intellectual difference? I feel a deep sadness that Odyssey, today, in the second decade of the 21st century, living in the fifth richest nation in the world, is still framed within a discourse of 'burdensome' by having a negative impact on her local authority's budget.

Happily there is a burgeoning literature in disabilities studies that has rapidly increased over the last decade. I am including a list of books I have found invaluable and would recommend anything from the indomitable Phoebe Caldwell or Eva Kittay. Phoebe Caldwell's books are highly illuminating and provide much insight into the world of those people who cannot report to us first hand. Eva Kittay has written extensively on care giving as well as providing a moral philosophical perspective on life with and for her daughter Sesha. Other writers include, P. Lacey, J. Mansell, M. Nind and T. Shakespeare. This list is of course far from exhaustive. I highly recommend the journal PMLD Link, which has been sharing ideas and information from and for professionals, parents and practitioners for thirty years now.

Finally, with this book I wanted to show that through a deeper understanding we can all move beyond ignorance and fear.

Notes

1 www.newhamrecorder.co.uk/news/newham-council-slammed-after-man-dies-from-gangrene-1-5819276
2 www.bbc.co.uk/news/uk-13700532
3 www.bbc.co.uk/news/uk-england-bristol-20078999
4 www.bbc.co.uk/news/uk-england-bristol-20028814; www.bbc.co.uk/news/uk-13700532; www.bbc.co.uk/news/uk-england-bristol-20078999; www.bbc.co.uk/news/uk-england-bristol-20028814; www.theguardian.com/society/2014/may/25/winter bourne-view-transfer-plan-branded-abject-failure-by-minister; www.theguardian.com/society/2015/dec/09/southern-health-nhs-trust-failed-investigate-patient-deaths-inquiry; www.ndti.org.uk/our-work/our-projects/peoples-health/improving-health-and-lives-ihal
5 www.theguardian.com/society/2014/may/25/winterbourne-view-transfer-plan-branded-abject-failure-by-minister
6 www.theguardian.com/society/2015/dec/09/southern-health-nhs-trust-failed-investi gate-patient-deaths-inquiry
7 www.ndti.org.uk/our-work/our-projects/peoples-health/improving-health-and-lives-ihal
8 www.theguardian.com/uk-news/2018/feb/08/gross-failure-in-mans-care-led-to-death-from-constipation
9 www.theguardian.com/society/2009/mar/24/neglect-nhs-learning-disabilities
10 www.newhamrecorder.co.uk/news/newham-council-slammed-after-man-dies-from-gangrene-1-5819276
11 https://unitemagazine.co.uk/man-with-downs-syndrome-dies-due-to-healthcare-fail ures-says-report/
12 www.theguardian.com/politics/2013/jan/08/strivers-shirkers-language-welfare

Resources

Caldwell, P. (1996). *Getting in Touch Ways of Working with People with Severe Learning Disabilities and Extensive Support Needs.* Joseph Rowntree Trust/Pavilion Publishing, Brighton, UK.

Caldwell, P. and Horwood, J. (2007). *From Isolation to Intimacy Making Friends without Words.* Jessica Kingsley Publishers, London, UK and Philadelphia, USA.

Gray, B. and Jackson, R. (2002). *Advocacy and Learning Disability.* Jessica Kingsley Publishers, London, UK and Philadelphia, USA.

Hughs, R. (2011). 'Friendship matters?.' *PMLD Link*, Volume 23 No 1 (68). PMLD Link, UK.

Kittay, E. (1999). *Love's Labour Essays on Women, Equality and Dependency.* Routledge, New York, USA and London, UK.

Kittay, E. and Carlson, L. (2010). *Cognitive Disability and Its Challenge to Moral Philosophy.* Wiley-Blackwell, West Sussex, UK.

Kittay, E. and Feder, E. (eds) (2002). *The Subject of CARE Feminist Perspectives on Dependency.* Rowman & Littlefield Publishers Inc, London, Boulder, New York, USA and Oxford, UK.

Lacey, P. (2011). 'Listening to challenging behaviour.' *PMLD Link*, Volume 23 No 1 (68), pp. 7–9. PMLD Link, UK.

LeDr Annual report, animated version. (online) Available from https://youtu.be/-fXylKY-jQs

Miles, B. and Riggio, M. (1999). *Remarkable Conversations a Guide to Developing Meaningful Communication with Children and Young Adults Who Are Deafblind.* Perkins School for the Blind, Watertown, Massachusetts, USA.

Nussbaum, M. (2006). *Frontiers of Justice Disability Nationality Species Membership.* The Belknap Press, Cambridge, MA, London, UK.

PAMIS: Promoting a More Inclusive Society. (online) Available from http://pamis.org.uk

Parity for People with Multiple Disabilities. (online) Available from www.parity.org.uk

'PMLD link journal.' (online) Available from www.pmldlink.org.uk

Bibliography

Allan. (2007). *Death by Indifference, Following up the Treat me Right Report.* Mencap P1. Mencap, London, UK. (online) Available from www.mencap.org.uk/sites/default/files/2016-06/DBIreport.pdf

Association of Directors of Adult Social Services (ADASS), Care Quality Commission (CQC), Department of Health, Health Education England (HEE), Local Government Association (LGA), and NHS England. (2015). *Transforming Care for People with Learning disabilities – Next Steps.* NHS, England, UK.

Bubb, S. (2014). *Winterbourne View – Time for Change Transforming the commissioning of Services for People with Learning Disabilities and/or AutismTransforming Care and Commissioning Steering Group.* NHS England, London, UK.

Bunning, K. (2009). 'Making sense of communication.' in Pawlyn, J. and Carnaby, S. (eds) *Profound Intellectual and Multiple Disabilities Nursing Complex Needs.* pp. 46–61. Wiley-Blackwell, West Sussex, UK.

Burford, R. (2018). 'Down's syndrome man in 24-hour care died after staff in Newham failed to treat gangrene.' Newham Recorder (online) Available from www.newhamrecorder.co.uk/news/newham-council-slammed-after-man-dies-from-gangrene-1-5819276

Campbell, K. (2019). 'Man with Downs syndrome dies due to healthcare failures says report.' Unite (online) Available from www.unitemagazine.co.uk/man-with-downs-syndrome-dies-due-to-healthcare-failures-says-report/

Carvel, J. (2009). 'Man with Down's syndrome dies after starving for 26 days in hospital.' The Guardian (online) Available from www.theguardian.com/society/2009/mar/24/neglect-nhs-learning-disabilities

Concannon, L. (2005). *Planning for Life Involving Adults with Learning Disabilities in Service Planning.* Routledge, London, UK and New York, USA.

Cook, D. (2016). 'Southern Derbyshire service for people with profound and multiple learning disability.' *PMLD Link*, Volume 28 No 3 (85), pp. 34–35. PMLD Link Northampton, UK. (online) Available from www.pmldlink.org.uk

Department of Health. (2001). *Valuing People: A New Strategy for Learning Disability for the 21st Century.* HMSO. London, UK.

Department of Health. (2005). *Valuing People; The Story so Far.* HMSO, London, UK.

Department of Health. (2007). *Putting People First: A Shared Vision and Commitment to the Transformation of Adult Social Care.* Crown Copyrights.

Department of Health. (2009). *Valuing People Now.* HMSO, London, UK.

Department of Health. (2012). *Transforming Care: A National Response to Winterbourne View Hospital: Department of Health Review Final Report.* HMSO, London, UK.

Department of Health. (2015). *Government Response to 'No Voice Unheard, No Right Ignored' – A Consultation for People with Learning Disabilities, Autism and Mental Health Conditions.* Crown copyrights. HMSO, London, UK.

Department of Health & Social Care. (2018). *Care and Support Statutory Guidance.* (Online) Available from www.gov.uk/government/publications/care-act-statutory-guidance/care-and-support-statutory-guidance

Doukas, T., Fergusson, A., Fullerton, M., and Grace, J. (2017). *Supporting People with Profound and Multiple Learning Disabilities. Core and Essential Service Standards.* 1st edition. Published by CMG, PMLD Link, The Sensory Projects, Choice Support, London, UK.

Elliot, K. (2017). *Supporting People with Profound and Multiple Learning Disabilities. Core and Essential Service Standards.* 1st edition. p. 9. Published by CMG, PMLD Link, The Sensory Projects, Choice Support, London, UK.

Emerson, E. and Durvasula, S. (2005). 'Editorial.' *Journal of Applied research in Intellectual Disability,* Volume 18 (2), pp. 95–96. Wiley-Backwell, UK.

Fullerton, M. (2018). 'LedeR report 2017 deaths of people with profound and multiple learning disabilities.' *PMLD Link,* Volume 30 No 3 (91), pp. 18–22. PMLD Link, Northampton, UK.

Gaffney, D. (2012). 'Dependency and disability: how to misread the evidence on social security.' In Davison, S. and Rutherford, J. (eds) *Welfare Reform the Dread of Things to Come.* Soundings Online. pp. 22–36. (Online) Available from www.lwbooks.co.uk/sites/default/files/free-book/WelfareReform.pdf

Garthwaite, K. (2011). 'The language of shirkers and scroungers? talking about illness, disability and coalition welfare reform.' *Disability & Society,* Volume 26 (3), pp. 369–372. Taylor & Francis, UK.

Gates, B. (2011). *Learning Disability Nursing: Task and Finish Group: Report for the Professional and Advisory Board for Nursing and Midwifery.* Department of Health, London, England, UK.

Glover, G. and Emerson, E. (2012). 'Patterns of decline in numbers of learning disability nurses employed by the National Health Service.' *Tizard Learning Disability Review,* Volume 17 (4), pp. 194–198. Emerald Publishing Limited, UK.

Health Ombudsman. (2009). *Six Lives: The Provision of Public Services to People with Learning Disabilities.* Parliamentary Health Ombudsman, HMSO, UK.

Heslop, P., Blair, P., Fleming, P., Hoghton, M., Marriott, A., and Russ, L. (2013). *Confidential Inquiry into Premature Deaths of People with Learning Disabilities (CIPOLD) Final Report.* Norah Fry Research, Bristol, UK.

Hughs, R. (2011). 'Friendship matters.' *PMLD Link,* Volume 23 No 1 (68), pp 6–9. PMLD Link, Northampton, UK. (online) Available from www.pmldlink.org.uk

Lawton, A. (2009). *ADULTS SERVICES REPORT 24 Personalisation and Learning Disabilities: A Review of Evidence on Advocacy and Its Practice for People with*

Learning Disabilities and High Support Needs. Social Care Institute for Excellence, London, UK.

Learning Disabilities Observatory. (2016). *People with Learning Disabilities in England 2015: Main Report.* Public Health England, London, UK.

Local Government Ombudsman and Parliamentary & Health Service Ombudsman. (2009). *Six Lives: The Provision of Public Services to People with Learning Disabilities.* House of Commons, HMSO, London, UK.

Lyle, D. (2008). *Citizen Advocacy for Adults with Learning Difficulties and additional High Support Needs: A Pan London Study* (unpublished). Middlesex University, London, UK.

Lyle, D. (2015). 'Policy to practice: a critical analysis of the valuing people policy.' (online) Available from http://eprints.mdx.ac.uk/15731/

Lyle, D. (2018). 'Developing the core & essential standards for supporting people with PMLD.' *PMLD Link*, Volume 30 No 1 (89), pp. 6–9. PMLD Link, Northampton, UK.

Mansell, J. (1993, 2007, 2011). *Services for People with Learning Disabilities and Challenging Behaviour or Mental Health Needs.* (Online) Available from www.dh.gov.uk/en/Publicationsandstatistics/Publications/PublicationsPolicyAndGuidance/DH_080129

Mansell, J. (2006). 'Deinstitutionalisation and community living: progress, problems and priorities.' *Journal of Intellectual and Developmental Disability*, Volume 31 (2), pp 65–76. Taylor & Francis, London, UK.

Mansell, J. (2008). 'Learning disability policy and practice in the UK.' *Tizard Learning Disability Review*, Volume 13 (3), pp 12–14. Emerald Publishing, Cantebury, UK.

Mansell, J. (2010). 'Raising our sights: services for adults with profound intellectual and multiple disabilities.' *Tizard Learning Disability Review*, Volume 15 (3), pp 5–12. Emerald publishing. Canterbury, UK.

Mansell, J. and Beadle-Brown, J. (2004). 'Person-centred planning or person-centred action? policy and practice in intellectual disability services.' *Journal of Applied Research in Intellectual Disabilities*, 54 (2), pp. 104–112. Wiley-Blackwell, UK.

Mazars. (2015). *Independent Review of Deaths of People with a Learning Disability or Mental Health Problem in Contact with Southern Health NHS Foundation Trust April 2011 to March 2015 Mazars LLP UK Nursing Standard.*

Mckew, M. (2018). 'Decline in learning disability nurses prompts warning.' (Online) Available from www.rcni.com

Mencap. (2007). *Death by* Indifference. Mencap, London, UK.

Mencap. (2012). *Death by* Indifference*: 74 Deaths and Counting Five Years On. A Progress Report five Years on.* Mencap, London, UK. (online) Available from www.mencap.org.uk/sites/default/files/2016-08/Death%20by%20Indifference%20%2074%20deaths%20and%20counting.pdf

Monaghan, J. (2005). *Citizen Advocacy – A Personal Perspective.* AGM paper. Liverpool Citizen Advocacy, Liverpool, UK.

NHS Digital. (Online) Available from https://files.digital.nhs.uk/pdf/b/0/health_care_learning_disabilities_2016_17_summary.pdf

NHS. (2019). (online) Available from www.nhslongtermplan.uk

Pearson, F. (2017). *Safeguarding Adults Review on "Paul".* Newham Safeguarding Adults Board, London, UK.

Public Health England. (2016). 'Making reasonable adjustments in the management of constipation for people with learning disabilities.' (online) Available from www.gov.uk/government/publications/constipation-and-people-with-learning-disabilities/constipation-making-reasonable-adjustments

Ryan, S. (2015, 2018). (online) Available from www.theguardian.com/society/2015/dec/09/southern-health-nhs-trust-failed-investigate-patient-deaths-inquiry

BBC News. '(04-04-18). Failings in learning disabilities death report finds.' (online) Available from www.bbc.co.uk/news/health-44001170

Reindal, S.M. (1999). 'Independence, dependence, interdependence: some reflections on the subject and personal autonomy.' *Disability & Society*, Volume 14 (3), pp. 353–367.

Samuel, J. and Pritchard, M. (2001). 'The ignored minority: meeting the health needs of people with profound learning disability.' *Tizard Learning Disability Review*, Volume 6 (2), pp. 34–44. Emerald Publishing Limited UK.

Tatum, D. (2012). *Autism Spectrum Disorders Through the Life Span*. Jessica Kingsley Publishers, London, UK and Philadelphia, USA.

Index

Note: Italic page numbers refer to figures.

Raising Our Sights report xiv, 17, 120, 123, 125, 131–4, 136, 145, 148, 150, 151, 168
Rapley, M. 27, 28
reasonable adjustments (RA) 112, 133, 162, 164, 165, 167, 171
Redley, M. 126
Reindal, S.M. 49
respite 54, 70, 86, 102, 108, 133, 134, 138–40
rights xiiii, 18, 60, 63, 65, 67, 69–71, 139, 160
'Rough Guide' 30
Royal College of Occupational Therapists 151
Royal Commission on Long Term Care 137
Ryan, S. 161

SALT *see* speech and language teams (SALT)
Samuel, J. 10–11, 92, 96
Schneider, A. 51
Schwandt, Denzin N. 48
SCIE *see* Social Care Institute for Excellence (SCIE)
Searle, J. 28
second-wave social model 25–7
self-advocacy xii, 2, 4, 31–4, 36, 38, 156, 168
self-directed support 128, 151
self-injurious behaviour 17, 62
sensory access 105–6
service provision 2, 4, 9, 16, 19, 25, 86, 125, 127, 162; acknowledging difference in 34–40
severe learning disability (SLD) 3–4, 158
Shakespeare, T. 22, 40, 41, 173
Sheehy, K. 71
Sherborne, V. 37
sibling carers 70, 139
The Significance of Work for the Citizenship of Disabled People (Abberley) 23–4
Sinason, Valerie 93, 123
'Six Lives' report 160, 161, 163, 164, 168
SLD *see* severe learning disability (SLD)
Smith, H. 22
Social Care Institute for Excellence (SCIE) 30
social inclusion 25, 36, 106, 138

social model 22–5; of disability 22; embodiment and 25–7; informed frameworks 40–2; post-structural 27–9
social role valorisation approach 21
social security 65
Social Services Inspectorate Report 39
South Derbyshire Community Learning Disability team 144
Sparrowhawk, Connor 161
Special Needs school 37, 109, 113
The Specific Risks of Discrimination 35
The Speculum of Ignorance (Tuana) 29
speech and language teams (SALT) 102
Stalker, K. 39

task breakdown 118–19
Taylor, S. 28
team development 116
TED talks 131
Thatcher, Margaret 64
Thomas, C. 26, 28–9
The Tizard Learning Disability Review 19
toilet facilities 35, 61, 72, 105–6, 109
Townsend, S. 150–1
training/development 116–17; *see also* workforce training, PMID adults and
'Transforming Care' (2012) 168
'Transforming Social Work Practice' 4
Trevarthen 130
Tronto, J.C. 147
trust 96–9, 111
Tuana, M. 29
Tyne, Alan 21

Union of Physically Impaired Against Segregation (UPIAS) 22–4
United Kingdom (UK): austerity agenda 59, 137, 143, 157; binary system in 3; care workforce in 137; Disability Rights Movement (DRM) 22
UPIAS *see* Union of Physically Impaired Against Segregation (UPIAS)

Valuing Employment Now 65
'*Valuing People: A New Strategy for Learning Disabilities in the 21st Century*' 48
Valuing People Now (VPN) 7, 13, 48, 51, 68, 69, 168
Valuing People (VP) x, xi, xiii, 1, 8–11, 13, 16, 18–20, 30, 50, 54, 82, 86, 90, 101, 114, 123, 127, 149, 157, 163, 168;

Printed in Great Britain
by Amazon

78874120R00115